Essential Statistics

A complete book to practice and learn the important concepts of Statistics

Essence of Statistics

A complete book to practice and learn the important concepts of Statistics

Dr Geeta Arora

Contents

Preface

This is a comprehensive statistics book designed to assist the readers in understanding the statistical concepts and their applications under various situations in the real life. This book is written in a simple and straight away. This book is an excellent resource for students pursuing sciences, management, engineering and agriculture courses.

This work is a collection of the brief details about the topic followed by the Multiple-Choice Questions (MCQs) and some unsolved problems in form of Fill in the blanks and True/False. All the important topics related to the field of statistics are covered in this book. Students will feel confident after attempting the variety of questions given after brief discussion of each topic.

The present work is a collection of the teaching practice by the author at the graduation and the post-graduation level courses of different streams. The difficulty level of the MCQ's is of mixed type. Some questions are memory-based; some need logical understanding and some need the calculation to be performed to find the right answer.

The answers to the provided problems have been verified. While efforts have been made to check the content for the typo and grammatical errors, it is possible that a few have crept in. I will be thankful to the readers if they will bring the errors into notice for their improvement.

Suggestions and comments from the readers to improve the content of the book are always appreciated. Readers are welcome to share their experience of their learning with the provided material at my mail geetadma@gmail.com.

Dr Geeta Arora

Chapter 1

Introduction to Statistics

One of the important discussions of this chapter includes the meaning of Statistics. So, let us start with the first thing to be known: What is Statistics?

Statistics can be defined as the study concerned with the analysis of data. It is a branch of mathematics that manages the data and provides the useful information. It is a tool to process and analyze the numbers. The various steps involved till the analysis includes the *collection of data, organization of data* and finally *implementation* of the statistical tools to interpret the data.

Statistics helps in reducing the uncertainty involved in decision making in the various aspects of business by the decision makers. It helps from the initial stage of presenting and describing information till drawing valid conclusions about large groups of individuals or items. Further, statistics is used in making reliable forecasts about data either concerned with health, economy, and education or any other related activity involving data. It also plays an important role in further improving the processes by giving appropriate decisions.

Thus, statistics is used for different purposes to make decisions.

For Example, statistics is used:

- For analyzing the effectiveness of the marketing strategies adopted for the promotion of the product.
- To determine the success of a newly launched drug in market for controlling blood pressure.
- To find the usefulness of the online platform in engaging the students.

1.1 Branches of Statistics

Statistics can be categorized into two types, based on the type of analysis being done on the data:

Descriptive Statistics: It involves organizing, summarizing, and displaying data. It is used to describe the important characteristics of the data with the help of tables, charts, averages, percentages etc. The measure of central tendency, the creation of graphs and the measure of dispersion are the essential part of this statistics.

Inferential Statistics: It refers to the branch of statistics in which *conclusions* are drawn about the population or *inferences* are made about a large group when only a part of it is being analyzed.

A group of entities is commonly refer as **population** and the small part of it under study is called a **sample**. The statistics thus can be defined as *interpreting the population characteristics by investigation a small sample of it.*

1.2 Raw material of Statistics

Data is the **raw material of statistics.** Data can exist in form of unarranged facts and figures that can be sorted out, arranged and classified according to the common attributes. Data which is collected from a survey for the analysis of the cause from some source to be interpreted is called as raw data.

For Example:

- The number of students getting more than 60% marks.

- The number of doctors available in the hospital with higher education.

- The number of teachers in a university.

A single observation in the data is called a **data point** and the collection of data is referred as **data set.**

A data can further be understood from the point of view it can be collected as:

- The **elements** are the entities on which data are collected.
- A **variable** is a characteristic of interest for the elements.
- The set of measurements collected for a particular element is called an **observation**.
- The total **number of data values** in a data set is the number of elements multiplied by the number of variables.

For Example: Consider the data collected for the different educational streams as Medical, Law, Sciences and Humanities for the number of students, placement held and startup initiated by the students as follows:

Educational streams	Number of students	Placement held	Startup initiated
Medical	102	45	10
Law	45	30	5
Sciences	54	27	4
Humanities	40	32	5

Here, the educational streams Medical, Law, Sciences and Humanities are the four **elements** and the three **variables** are the number of students, placement held and startup initiated under which the observations are collected. The total number of **data values** in a data set is twelve.

1.3 Classification of Data

A. Data can be classified according to the amount of information it possesses. The scale of measurement of data can be classified as:

1. **Nominal Data**- When the data can be categorized and written in form of a text it is called a nominal data. **For Example**:

   - **Gender-**Male and Female

   - **Income status-**High class and Middle class

   - **Brand of Laptop-** Dell, hp, Lenovo, Apple

A numeric code can also be used for the variables. For example: 1 can be used for male and 2 for female.

2. **Ordinal Data-**When data can be categorized and also can be arranged in some order it is called an ordinal data. Thus, the data have the properties of the nominal data and the order or rank is also meaningful.

   For Example:

   - **Quality of food-** Good, Better, Best

   - **Position in a class-** First, Second, Third

   - **Distance from the place-** Near, Far, Far away

   - **Rating of movie-** 1 for excellent, 2 for good, 3 for neutral, 4 for bad.

3. **Interval and Ratio**

Data can be further classified as **Interval** and **Ratio**.

The interval data have the properties of ordinal data and the interval between the observations can be expressed in terms of a fixed unit of measure.

For Example: Score of Ram in an exam is 120, while Kailash has a scored 109. Thus, score of Ram is 11 points more than Kailash. Further, in interval data, the difference between the values can be obtained but there exist no real zero. It means that zero has a value. **For Example**: 0 degree Celsius doesn't mean absence of temperature.

While ratio type of data refers to the counting of a data where zero means nothing. **For Example**: The number of students in the class can be 10, 20 or 0. Here zero means no student is present.

The ratio data have all the properties of interval data and the ratio of two values is meaningful. Variables such as distance, height, weight, and time use the ratio scale. Another **Example** can be considered as if the training hour of Ram is 40 and the training hour of Kailash is 20, then the training hour of Ram is twice of that of Ram.

Following is the hierarchy of the above defined data types:

B. Data is generally classified according to the type of values a variable can take. There are five different types of classifications under this category:

1. **Geographical/ Spatial classification**-Data is said to be of spatial type when the data is mentioned to discuss as per the geographical location.

   For Example:

   - Population of the different towns in a city.

   - The residential status of the students of an Institute.

   - The location of the WHO help centers located all over India.

2. **Chronological/ Temporal classifications**-Data is said to be of chronological type when it is used to mention the things that happened in a specified time. Time can be taken in any unit as years, months, week, hours, minute and seconds.

   For Example:

   - The share market ups and downs on a particular time of a day.

   - The population of hens in a poultry farm in the last three years.

   - The number of students present in the class in the last two weeks.

3. **Spatial-Temporal classifications**-Data is said to be of spatial-temporal type when the data is recorded for the time interval with respect to the geographical location as well.

   For Example:

   - Population of the different towns in a city during last ten years.

   - The residential status of the employees in a company in last one year.

   - The location of the COVID help centers created in the last two years.

4. **Qualitative classifications-** Data which can be defined on the basis of the characteristics or attributes of an entity is called as qualitative data.

   For Example:

   - The gender of the person appointed as member secretary in an election.

   - The education status of the father of the students studying at a university.

   - Record of the caste and religion of the people living in a society.

5. **Quantitative classifications-** Whenever the data is provided as a quantity of the discussed entity it is called as quantitative data. It can be numbers, values, amount or any unit that can be measured and compared.

   For Example:

   - Numbers of the active ATMs in a city.

   - The number of family members of the employees in an industry.

- Number of the patients suffering from kidney problem in an hospital.

Quantitative data can further be classified according to the values that it can take. It can be of discrete or continuous type.

i. **Discrete Data**-Data is said to be of discrete type when the data values are integers and cannot be taken in fractions.

   For Example:

   - Number of pages in a book.

   - Number of balls in a bag.

   - Number of eggs lays by a bird.

ii. **Continuous Data**-Data is said to be of continuous type when it can take any value between a range.

   For Example:

   - Height of a graduate student can be any value between 4-6 feet normally.

   - Weight of a young man can lie anywhere between 30-70 kg.

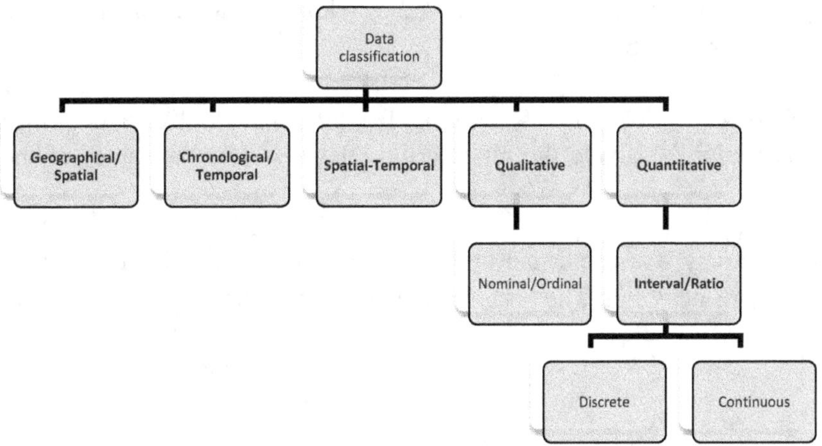

Figure 1: Classification of data

1.4 Managing Data

After obtaining the data from a reliable source the next step is to find out the type of data and to manage it. Managing of data refers to sorting and presentation of data in a tabulated form. The common term used for the data management is **frequency distribution** that involves following steps:

- Arrange data in ascending or descending order.

- Arrange data in tabular form.

The data can further be classified in a grouped frequency form known as **grouped frequency distribution**.

1.4.1 Frequency Distribution

Frequency refers to how often something occurs.

For Example:

- The number of times meal is served in a day.

- Number of students getting late for the class.

- Number of airbuses taking flight per day.

Frequency Distribution table can be created by counting the number of times a value is repeated. Rewriting the data in the class interval form gives the grouped frequency table.

1.4.2 Definitions related to the grouped frequency distribution

The class interval: It refers to the class in which the values lie between. It has two values refers as lower-class limit and upper-class limit.

Lower-class limit: These are the smallest numbers that can actually belong to different classes.

Upper-class limit: These are the largest numbers that can actually belong to different classes.

Mid-points: The mid points can be found by adding the lower-class limit to the upper-class limit and dividing the sum by two.

Class-width: It is the difference between two consecutive lower-class limits. To determine the width of a class interval, divide the range (Highest value–Lowest value) of the data by the number of classes.

For Example: A survey was conducted by a researcher to find the number of people of different ages that are active in the sports activities. The results can be written in the frequency distribution table as follows:

Age	Number of people
20-30	14
30-40	23
40-50	11
50-60	8

Here, the numbers of people aged between 20-30 years is 14. For this class intervals the lower limit is 20, the upper limit is 30 and the class width is 10 with the mid-point of class interval as 25.

In general, a frequency distribution should have at least 5 but not more than 15 classes.

1.5 Methods of Data Classification

There are two ways in which the observations of a data set can be classified on the basis of the class intervals as exclusive method and inclusive method.

Exclusive Method: In exclusive method the data is presented in a way such that the upper limit of a class interval is the lower limit of the succeeding class interval.

For Example: Consider the data of scores obtained out of thirty by 20 students as follows:

0	12	13	14	17	19	18	10	25	13
18	16	24	27	25	27	26	20	14	7

To arrange the data into class interval the data can first be arranged in either ascending or descending order and then the data can be classified in class interval using exclusive approach. Following is the data in ascending form:

1	7	10	12	13	13	14	14	16	17
18	18	19	20	24	25	25	26	27	27

Data arranged by exclusive method with class width 10 can be written as:

Class Interval	Class Interval	Frequencies
0-10	0 but less than 10	2
10-20	10 but less than 20	11
20-30	20 but less than 30	7

Inclusive Method: In Inclusive method, the data is classified in a way such that both the lower and upper limits of a class interval are included in the interval itself.

For Example: The number of students falling under the classification of the percentage can be presented as:

Class Interval	Class Interval	Frequencies
1-10	Ranging from 1 to 10	3
11-20	Ranging from 11 to 20	11
21-30	Ranging from 21 to 30	6

NOTE: An exclusive method is used to work with continuous data and an inclusive method is used to work with discrete data.

1.6 Types of Frequency Distributions

A) Cumulative Frequency Distribution:

A cumulative frequency distribution is of two types:

(i) more than type- In this type of cumulative frequency distribution, the frequency of each class interval is added successively from bottom to top and represent the cumulative number of observations greater than or equal to the lower limit of class intervals.

(ii) less than type- In this type of cumulative frequency distribution, the frequency of each class interval is added successively from top to bottom to give the number of observations less than or equal to the upper limit of class intervals.

Salary (In Lakhs)	Number of Employees (Frequency)	Lower limit	Cumulative frequency (More than)	Upper limit	Cumulative freq (Less than)
1-2	5	More than 1	30	Less than 2	5
2-3	11	More than 2	25	Less than 3	16
3-4	14	More than 3	14	Less than 4	30

B) Relative Frequency Distribution:

Relative frequency distribution is used to show the percentage of observations that fall within each class of a distribution. For calculating the relative frequency distribution, divide each class frequency by the total number of observations in the entire distribution.

Salary (In Lakhs)	Number of Employees (Frequency)	Relative Frequency	Percentage Frequency
1-2	5	$\frac{5}{30} = 0.1667$	16.67
2-3	11	$\frac{11}{30} = 0.3667$	36.67
3-4	14	$\frac{14}{30} = 0.4667$	46.67
Total	30	1	100

Chapter based Quiz

A) MCQs

1. Collecting the data for the choice of the flavor of ice cream, falls in the category of____data.
   a) Nominal
   b) Ordinal

c) Interval

d) Ratio

2. Rating of the movie by the reviewers as Excellent, Best, Good, Boar can be taken in the __________data type.

a) Interval

b) Ratio

c) Discrete

d) Ordinal

3. The number of clothes needed to be purchased for a ceremony is of _________data type.

a) Discrete

b) Continuous

c) Irrational

d) None of the above

4. The weight of the parcel to be delivered at the post office is of _________data type.

a) Discrete

b) Continuous

c) Irrational

d) None of the above

5. Data of the quality of the food from the customers feedback (Good, Better, Best) is an example of_____data.

a) Nominal

b) Ordinal

c) Interval

d) Ratio

6. In a cricket match, a player got 5 times six runs, 4 times 2 runs and 10 times 1 run. The frequency of the player to hit 2 runs is

a) 19

b) 5

c) 2

d) 4

7. Arranging the data as per the number of times it occurs (frequency) is known as

a) Frequency distribution

b) Distribution

c) Arranging data

d) Grouping data

8. The number of employees present in a meeting is a data of which type?

a) Ordinal

b) Interval

c) Ratio

d) Nominal

9. The list of the winners of a debate competition is a_______data.
a) Nominal
b) Ordinal
c) Interval
d) Ratio

10. The amount of rainfall held in the month of July is _______type of data.
a) Discrete
b) Continuous
c) Qualitative
d) Geographical

11. Population of a town in the last four months is a ____type of data.
a) Spatial temporal
b) Qualitative
c) Chronological
d) Continuous

12. Number of employees belonging to different parts of a country can be categorize as
a) Qualitative
b) Discrete
c) Continuous
d) Spatial data

13. For the given data what are the total number of data values?

Items	A	B	C	D	E
Numbers	10	13	15	10	12

a) 10
b) 40
c) 50
d) 60

14. Priscar is organizing, summarizing, and displaying data of the recent games held in India. He is applying the concept of
a) Descriptive statistics
b) Inferential Statistics
c) Time Series Analysis
d) Indexing

15. John wants to find the average height of a graduate student in India. For this he has collected a sample of 500 graduate students from different parts of the country. He is using _____.
a) Descriptive statistics
b) Inferential Statistics

c) Time Series Analysis

d) Indexing

16. Consider this data to answer the related questions:

Number of persons in a house	1-3	3-5	5-8	8-11	11-14
Number of Families	10	14	8	9	7

I. What is the class width of given data?

a) 1

b) 2

c) 3

d) 4

II. What is the total number of families taken for collection of data?

a) 10

b) 20

c) 48

d) 54

III. How many families have the number of persons more than 5?

a) 10

b) 48

c) 24

d) 20

IV. What is the lower limit of the class interval with frequency as 8?

a) 10

b) 14

c) 8

d) 5

V. Which class interval has the lowest frequency?

a) 1-3

b) 3-5

c) 5-8

d) 11-14

VI. How many families have the number of persons less than 3?

a) 10

b) 20

c) 48

d) 54

VII. How many families have the number of persons less than 8?

a) 10
b) 24
c) 32
d) 41

VIII.   What is the relative percentage frequency of the number of persons lying in the range of 5- 8?
a) 16.67
b) 32.54
c) 52.65
d) 40.34

17. The clothes needed to be purchased for a dress in meters is of _________data type
a) Discrete
b) Continuous
c) Irrational
d) None of the above

18. Population of 3 different towns in last two year is a _____type of data.
a) Spatial temporal
b) Qualitative
c) Chronological
d) Continuous

19. Which of the following variable is of continuous data type?
a) Number of employees in a company.
b) Number of medals won by the sportsman in Olympic Games.
c) Measurement of cloth for making seat cover.
d) Number of pages in a book.

20. The speed of the car is an example of
a) Continuous variable
b) Discrete variable
c) Absolute variable
d) None of these

Answers:

1-a	2-d	3-a	4-b	5-b	6-d	7-a	8-c	9-a	10-b
11-c	12-d	13-d	14-a	15-b	16(I)-b	16(II)-c	16(III)-c	16(IV)-d	16(V)-d
16(VI)-a	16(VII)-c	16(VIII)-a	17-b	18-a	19-c	20-a			

B) True or False

1. Working with hypothesis testing of a claim is a part of descriptive statistics.

2. To analyse the data, the first step is to arrange the data in either ascending or descending order.
3. Data related to the gender of the patients admitted in a hospital suffering from blood pressure is a nominal type of data.
4. The quality of the camera as reviewed by the customers falls into different rating category; this is an example of ratio data.
5. Amount of the consumption of rice at a food stall is an example of quantitative data.
6. Relative frequency distribution is used to show the percentage of observations within each class of a distribution.
7. In more than cumulative frequency distribution, the frequency of each class interval is added successively from top to bottom.
8. An exclusive method of frequency distribution is used to work with continuous data.
9. Qualitative data can be classified according to the values and is either discrete or continuous.
10. A nominal data can be an ordinal data.

Answers:

1-F   2-T   3-T   4-F   5-T   6-T   7-F   8-T   9-F   10-T

C) Fill in the blanks

1. Data in an unorganized form is called __________ data.
2. In the class interval 35- 45, the lower-class limit is __________.
3. In the class interval 25 – 35, 35 is known as __________.
4. The difference between the upper and lower limit of a class interval is called the __________ of the class interval.
5. The mid-point of the class interval 10-15 is__________.
6. The class size/width of the interval 70 – 75 is __________.
7. In the class intervals 10 –20, 20 –30, etc., respectively, 20 lies in the class __________.
8. The location of the universities offering doctorate in agriculture is__________type of data.
9. The highest qualification of a person appearing in a job interview is a ______________data.
10. A _______ data is a data whose values can take any value within a given range of values.
11. The value lying half way between the upper limit and lower limit of the class is called as______.
12. The number of observations in a particular class is called____
13. If the class mid points in a frequency distribution for age of a group of persons are 25, 32, 39, 46, 53 and 60. The size of class interval is____.
14. In a frequency distribution with classes 0 –10, 10 –20 etc., the size of the class intervals is 10. The lower limit of fourth class is____

Answers:

1-raw	2-35	3-upper limit	4-class width	5-12.5
6-5	7-20-30	8-spatial	9-nominal/qualitative	10-continuous
11-mid point	12-frequency	13-7	14-30	

NOTES:

Chapter 2

Measure of Central Tendency

Measure of central tendency is a measure which indicates the middle of the data. It is a numerical value around which most of the data values show a tendency to cluster or group. The three most commonly used measures of central tendency are: the mean, median and mode.

The two categories of central tendency measures are:

(i) Mathematical Averages- It involves the arithmetic mean called as average along with the special averages geometric and harmonic mean.

(ii) Averages of Position- It involves the measures that contribute towards the position of the data values, dividing the data in certain parts. It includes median, quartiles, deciles, percentiles and mode.

2.1 Mathematical Averages:

The methods for calculating the mathematical averages of a data can be classified in accordance of the nature of data. There are three well known mathematical averages: mean (arithmetic mean), geometric mean and harmonic mean.

2.1.1 Arithmetic Mean

The mean is the average of the data values. It requires scores that are numbers. The method of calculating the arithmetic mean can be learnt for the raw data, ungrouped data and grouped data.

A) Calculating mean for raw data

The mean for raw data is obtained by computing the sum for the entire set of values and dividing the sum by the number of scores.

For data with n values given as: $x_1, x_2, x_3, ..., x_n$. The mean is given by formula,

$$\bar{x} = \frac{\displaystyle\sum_{i=1}^{n} x_i}{n}$$

Example: Calculate the mean of 12, 10, 13, 16, 15, and 18.

Solution: Here the number of data values, $n = 6$.

The sum of data values, $\displaystyle\sum_{i=1}^{n} x_i = 84$.

Hence the mean can be calculated as:

$$\bar{x} = \frac{\displaystyle\sum_{i=1}^{n} x_i}{n} = \frac{84}{6} = 14$$

B) Calculating mean for frequency data–

When the data is provided for x along with the frequency f. The mean can be calculated using the formula,

$$\bar{x} = \frac{\displaystyle\sum_{i=1}^{n} f_i x_i}{N}$$

Where, $N = \displaystyle\sum_{i=1}^{n} f_i$

Example: Find the mean score of the data given below for the score of a cricketer along with the frequency.

Score	1	2	4	6
Frequency	4	3	5	2

Solution: Rewriting the data in column form and hence calculating the column fx will result in the summation of fx and hence dividing the value by N (sum of frequency) will result in the mean of the data as follows:

Score(x)	Frequency(f)	fx
1	4	4
2	3	6
4	5	20

| 6 | 2 | 12 |
| **Total** | 14 | 42 |

Here, the average is calculated as:

$$\bar{x} = \frac{\sum_{i=1}^{n} f_i x_i}{N} = \frac{42}{14} = 3$$

C) Calculating mean for grouped data

When the data is provided for class interval of equal width along with the frequency, the mean of the grouped data is calculated using the formula,

$$\bar{x} = \frac{\sum_i f_i m_i}{N}; \quad \sum_i f_i = N \quad .$$

Here m_i is the mid value of the ith class interval.

Example: Find the average sales of the product per day for the given data of sales of product.

Sales of products	0-10	10-20	20-30	30-40
Number of days (Frequency)	6	2	5	2

Solution: The calculation of the arithmetic mean for the given grouped data can be summarized as follows:

Sales of product(x)	Mid value (m_i)	Number of days (f)	$f_i m_i$
0-10	5	6	30
10-20	15	2	30
20-30	25	5	125
30-40	35	2	70
Total		15	255

The average sales of the product can be calculated as:

$$\overline{x} = \frac{\sum_i f_i m_i}{N} = \frac{255}{15} = 17$$

D) Combined mean

The arithmetic mean of two data sets of same nature can be combined to find the combined mean. If are the arithmetic mean of two data sets with the data size then their combined mean can be calculated as:

$$\overline{x} = \frac{n_1 \overline{x}_1 + n_2 \overline{x}_2}{n_1 + n_2}$$

Example: The mean of 20 items under study is 34 and the mean of 10 other items are 25. Find the combined mean of the 30 items together.

Solution: Here,

$$\overline{x}_1 = 34, n_1 = 20; \overline{x}_2 = 25, n_2 = 10;$$

The combined mean of the 30 items together can be calculated as:

$$\overline{x} = \frac{34 \times 20 + 25 \times 10}{30}$$

$$= \frac{680 + 250}{30}$$

$$= \frac{930}{30} = 31$$

2.1.2 Geometric Mean and Harmonic Mean

The geometric mean (G.M.) and the harmonic mean (H.M.) tell about the central value of the data about which all the set of values of data lies. For the data sets which are fluctuating or the data is added or removed regularly, calculating the average value or the central value is a difficult task. In such type of data, the geometric and harmonic means can be used efficiently to find the central value.

A) Geometric Mean:

A geometric mean is a mean or average which shows the central tendency of a set of numbers by using the product of their values.

For a set of n observations, a geometric mean is the nth root of their product. The geometric mean G.M., for a set of numbers $x_1, x_2, x_3, ..., x_n$ is given as:

$$\text{G.M.} = (x_1 . x_2 \ ... \ x_n)^{1/n}$$

On simplifying,

$$\text{G. M.} = \sqrt[n]{(x_1, x_2, \ldots, x_n)}$$

Using the formula, the geometric mean of two numbers, say x, and y is the square root of the product xy.

Similarly, for three numbers, the geometric mean is the cube root of the product of three numbers i.e., $(x\ y\ z)^{1/3}$.

In order to make the calculation easy and less time consuming the concept of logarithms is used in the calculation the geometric means.

From the formula $\text{G.M.} = (x_1. x_2 \ldots x_n)^{1/n}$

Taking log on both sides, and simplifying

$$\log \text{G.M.} = 1/n\ (\log ((x_1. x_2 \ldots x_n))$$

$$\log \text{G.M.} = 1/n\ (\log x_1 + \log x_2 + \ldots + \log x_n)$$

$$\log \text{G.M.} = (1/n) \sum \log x_i$$

$$\text{G.M.} = \text{Antilog} ((1/n) (\sum \log x_i)).$$

Example: Rate of increase of population in a town during last 3 months is 6%, 8% and 12%. The average growth rate for this period can be calculated using geometric mean as:

$$\text{G.M.} = \sqrt[3]{6 \times 8 \times 12}$$
$$= \sqrt[3]{576} = 8.320$$

The G.M. can also be calculated considering the growth rate as 106, 108,112

Geometric Mean of Frequency Distribution:

For a grouped frequency distribution, the geometric mean G.M. is

$$\text{G.M.} = (x_1^{f_1}. x_2^{f_2} \ldots x_n^{f_n})^{1/N}$$

where $N = \sum f_i$

Taking logarithms on both sides, we get

$$\log \text{G.M.} = (1/N)\ (f_1 \log x_1 + f_2 \log x_2 + \ldots + f_n \log x_n) = (1/N)\ (\sum f_i \log x_i).$$

Example: Find the geometric mean for the price of commodity increase in different years as given below:

Years	Increase rate

1993-1994	8
1994-1995	12
1995-1996	76

Solution:

The average increase can be calculated as:

$$\text{G.M.} = \sqrt[3]{8 \times 12 \times 76}$$
$$= \sqrt[3]{7296} = 19.395$$

Example: The interest in a bank deposit scheme has been given with the frequency in the last 9 months. Find the average increase rate.

x	f	x^f
2	3	8
3	2	9
4	1	4
5	3	125

Solution: Here the G.M. is the product of the last column values with the ninth root as the sum of frequencies is 9.

$$\text{G.M.} = \sqrt[9]{8 \times 9 \times 4 \times 125}$$
$$= \sqrt[9]{36000} = 3.208$$

NOTE: If any of the observations is zero, the geometric mean becomes zero. If any of the observation is negative, the geometric mean becomes imaginary

B) Harmonic Mean:

A harmonic mean is used in averaging of ratios. For a given data it is the reciprocal of the arithmetic mean of the reciprocals of the observations. In the calculation of the harmonic mean is that none of the observations should be zero. The most common examples of ratios of speed and time, cost and unit of material, work and time etc.

The harmonic mean (H.M.) of n observations is given as:

$$\text{H.M.} = n / \sum (1/x_i)$$

In the case of frequency distribution, a harmonic mean is given by

$$\text{H.M.} = N / \left(\sum (f_i / x_i) \right), \text{ where } N = \sum f_i$$

Example: Find the H.M. for 2, 3, 4

Solution: Using formula, the H.M. can be calculated as

$$\text{H.M.} = \frac{3}{\dfrac{1}{2} + \dfrac{1}{3} + \dfrac{1}{4}}$$

$$= \frac{3}{\left(\dfrac{13}{12}\right)} = \frac{36}{13} = 2.77$$

Note: The harmonic mean has the least value when compared to the geometric mean and the arithmetic mean. In both of the geometric and harmonic mean, more weight is given to small items and the fluctuations of the observations do not affect the values harmonic mean.

Example: Find the H.M. for the data given below

x	f	f/x
2	6	3
3	6	2
4	8	2
5	10	2
Total	30	9

Solution: Using the values of the summation f the frequencies and the frequency divided by the values from the table, the H.M. can be calculated as follows:

$$\text{H.M.} = \frac{\sum f_i}{\sum \dfrac{f_i}{x_i}}$$

$$= \frac{30}{9} = 3.333$$

2.1.3 Relation between arithmetic mean, geometric mean and harmonic mean

For a given data the relation between the arithmetic mean (A.M.), geometric mean (G.M.) and harmonic mean (H.M.) is given as

A.M. > G.M. > H.M.

Example: For data 1, 2, 8, and 16 verify that A.M > G.M > H.M

Solution:

$$\text{A.M.} = \frac{1+2+8+16}{4} \qquad\qquad \text{G.M.} = \sqrt[4]{1 \times 2 \times 8 \times 16} \qquad\qquad \text{H.M.} = \frac{4}{1 + \dfrac{1}{2} + \dfrac{1}{8} + \dfrac{1}{16}}$$

$$= \frac{27}{4} = 6.75 \qquad\qquad\qquad = 4 \qquad\qquad\qquad\qquad = \frac{3}{\left(\dfrac{27}{16}\right)} = \frac{48}{27} = 2.37$$

Hence A.M. > G.M. > H.M.

2.2 Averages of Position

Mean is the easy to calculate but sometimes it will not work. For instance, mean cannot be calculate for data of nominal type,

Also, when a data contains a few extreme values (very high or very low values as compared to the other values), the mean value can be pulled toward these extreme values. In this case, the mean is not a good measure of central tendency. In such cases there are alternative procedures available as follows:

2.2.1 Median

Median is defined as the midpoint of the data which is arranged in either the increasing or decreasing order. It is a value that divides the data into two halves such that half of the values are above median and half of the values are below median. One major advantage of the median over mean is that it is unaffected by the extreme scores because for calculating median arranging the data results in shifting of the extreme values at the corner.

A) Calculating median for ungrouped data:

Steps for calculating median of the ungrouped data are as follows:

1. With an **odd number** of data values, the median is the middle score in the arranged list.

    Example: 1, 4, 3, 6, 12, 8, 20

    The given values can be arranged as 1, 3, 4, 6, 8, 12, and 20. For these 7 data values, median is the middle (fourth) value of the data. Hence, median=6.

    Median for n odd arranged data values is the (n+1)/2th value of the data series.

2. With an **even number of** data values, the median is the mean of two middle score in the arranged list.

Example: 12, 23, 32, 11, 24, 18

The given values in order can be written as 11, 12, 18, 23, 24, and 32. Here the number of data values are 6. Hence median is the mean of middle terms (third and fourth value) of the data. Thus, median=(18+23)/2=20.5.

Median for n even arranged data values *(n)*the median is given by the formula:

$$Median = \frac{\left(\frac{n}{2}\right)^{th} value + \left(\frac{n}{2}+1\right)^{th} value}{2}$$

B) Calculating median for grouped data

- For the discrete frequency data, median is the value in front of the median class. Here, the median class is the class interval with the value of cumulative frequency more than $N/2$ where N is the sum of frequency.

- For the continuous frequency data, the median is given by the formula

$$Median = l + h \times \left(\frac{N/2 - c}{f}\right)$$

here,
l is the lower-limit of the median class, f is the frequency of the median class, h is the class-width, c is the cumulative frequency of the class preceding the median class and $N = \sum f$

To obtain the cumulative frequency, the frequency of current class should be added to the next class frequency. In the example given below, the first entry of the $c.f$ column is same as frequency that is 6. The next value in this column is the sum of 6 and the next frequency 4 and the $c.f$ value become 10. Again, the third frequency value 5 is added to obtained $c.f$ value 10 and the next $c.f$ entry become 15 and so on.

Example: Find median of the number of workers as per the duty hours for the data given below:

Duty hours	2	4	6	8	10
Number of workers (f)	6	4	5	3	7

Solution: For calculating the median of the given data for the number of workers as per the duty hours, the cumulative frequency ($c.f$) column is calculated as follows:

Duty hours (x)	Number of workers (f)	c.f
2	6	6
4	4	10
6	5	15
8	3	18
10	7	25

Since, the total number of workers $N = 25$. Hence, median is the value corresponding to the value of c.f more than $N/2=12.5$. The c.f. value more than 12.5 is 15. Thus, the median is the value of x corresponding to this c.f. Hence, median=6.

Example: Find the median for the continuous frequency data:

Duty hours	0-2	2-4	4-6	6-8	8-10
Number of workers (f)	6	4	5	3	7

Solution:

Duty hours	Number of workers (f)	c.f
0-2	6	6
2-4	4	10
4-6	5	15
6-8	3	18
8-10	7	25

Here, $N = 25$. Hence, the median class is a class with c.f. value more than $N/2$. In the last column, the value of c.f. more than 12.5 is 15. Hence the median class is obtained as 4-6. The value of the median can now be calculated using formula:

$$Median = l + h \times \left(\frac{N/2 - c}{f} \right)$$

Here for the highlighted median class, the lower limit $l = 4$, the frequency of the median class $f = 5$, $h = 2$ which is the difference of two lower or two upper limits; and $c = 10$, the value of c.f. above the median class. On substituting the values in the formula,

$$Median = 4 + \left(\frac{12.5 - 10}{5} \right) \times 2,$$

Hence, $median = 5$

2.2.2 Mode

It is the measure of central tendency that gives the most frequently occurring data value in a data set. Mode can be calculated for the data which is either the nominal, ordinal or interval data.

Example: Find the mode of the data 11,12,23,22,12,11,12

Solution: In this data 12 is repeating most frequently as compared to the other numbers. Hence, mode=12

Sometimes a set of data can have more than one mode.

Example: Find the mode of the data 2, 9, 5, 7, 8, 6, 4, 7, 5

Solution: Here 5 and 7 both are repeated twice while other numbers are appearing just once. Hence 5 and 7 both are the mode.

Data with two mode values is said to be *bimodal.*

Sometimes there is no mode in a set of data.

Example: Find the mode of the data 3, 8, 7, 6, 12, 11, 2, 1

Solution: Since, all the numbers in this set occur only once hence there is no mode in this given data set.

A) Calculating mode for ungrouped data

Example: Find the most frequently opted colour for the choice of the bikes by the customers, from the data of the number of bikes sold in the last month categorised as per the colour:

Colour	Number of bikes sold (f)
Red	25
Green	14
Black	30
Blue	27

Solution: From the given data it can be seen that black colour bike is the most frequently sold bike. Hence the mode of the data is 30.

B) Calculating mode for grouped data

For the data with the class interval along with the frequency, the mode is given by the formula

$$Mode = l + \left(\frac{f_1 - f_0}{2f_1 - f_0 - f_2} \right) \times h,$$

here,

l is the lower-limit of the modal class, f_0 is the frequency of the class preceding the modal class, f_1 is the frequency of the modal class and f_2 is the frequency of the class succeeding the modal class, h is the class-width.

Example: Find the mode of the data for the life time of the electrical appliances in an industry as given below:

Life time (hours)	0-20	20-40	40-60	60-80
Number of appliances	10	12	25	18

Solution: For calculating the mode, the first step is to find the maximum value of frequency to find the modal class. Here 25 is the maximum frequency, thus 20-30 is the modal class. Hence $f_1 = 25$, $f_0 = 12$ (the value of frequency above modal class) and $f_2 = 18$ (the value of frequency below the modal class).

Life time (x)	Number of appliances (f)
0-20	10
20-40	12
40-60	25
60-80	18

On substituting the values of f_0, f_1 and f_2 with class width $h = 20$ and the lower-limit of the modal class as $l = 40$, the mode can be calculated as:

$$Mode = l + \left(\frac{f_1 - f_0}{2f_1 - f_0 - f_2}\right) \times h,$$

That results in

$$Mode = 40 + \left(\frac{25 - 12}{50 - 12 - 18}\right) \times 20$$

$$= 40 + 13$$

Thus, $mode = 53$

2.2.3 An empirical relation between Mean, Median and Mode

Having the values of any two central tendency values the third value can be calculated using the empirical formula which is given as

$$Mean - Mode = 3(Mean - Median)$$

$$\text{Or, } Mode = 3\,Median - 2Mean$$

Example: If median of a given data is 16, mean is 14 what is the mode?

Solution: If median = 16, mean= 14, using empirical formula, the value of mode can be calculated as:

$Mode = 3 \times 16 - 2 \times 14 = 20$

2.2.4 Partition values

In addition to the above discussed averages, there are certain important values that divide a data or series into certain equal parts. These values are called as partition values. Following are the main three types of values:

i.   **Quartiles-**The three points which divides the data values into four equal parts are known as quartiles presented as Q_i with i from 1 to 3. Hence Q_1, Q_2, Q_3 are the three quartiles. Value of Q_2 is same as of median and lies at the mid position of data. Q_1 is the first quartile that exceeds 25% of data and Q_3 is the third quartile that exceeds 75% of the data.

ii. **Deciles-**The nine points which divides the data values into ten equal parts are called as deciles presented as D_i with i from 1 to 9. Hence $D_1, D_2, D_3,.....D_9$ are the nine deciles. Here, D_1 exceeds 10% of the data, D_2 exceeds 20% of the data, and similarly D_9 exceeds 90% of the data. Hence D_5 is similar as Q_2 and the median.

iii. **Percentiles-**The 99 points which divides the data values into 100 equal parts are called as percentiles presented as P_i with i from 1 to 99.

A) Calculating partition values for raw data

When the raw data with n data values is arranged in the ascending or descending order, the partition values can be calculated as follows:

Quartiles Q$_i$=i (n+1)/4th value in the data series, if the result is an integer.

(**Integer** is a number that is not a fraction; a whole number. Example: 1,2,3)

Similarly, for deciles $D_i = [i\,(n + 1)/10]^{th}$ value in the data series for $i = 1\ to\ 9$ and $P_i = [i(n + 1)/100]th$ value in the data series for $i = 1\ to\ 99$.

But if the resulted value in any case is a fraction (c.d), then the value can be calculated as:

$c^{th}\ value - d \times [(c + 1)^{th}\ value - c^{th}\ value]$

Example: For the given data of sales of a product in lakhs for the nine days as: 1, 14, 21, 12, 11, 10, 24, 43, 16. Find the value of the Q$_3$, D$_6$, P$_{60}$ and P$_{45}$

Solution: The value of the Q$_3$, D$_6$, P$_{60}$ and P$_{45}$ can be calculated as follows:

The first step to find partition values is to arrange the data that gives the values as:

Days	1	2	3	4	5	6	7	8	9
Sales (in Lakhs)	1	10	11	12	14	16	21	24	43

Here $n = 9$.

As, $Q_i = i(n+1)/4^{th}$ value

For Q_3 , $i = 3$. Hence $Q_3 = 3 \times (9+1)/4 = 30/4 = 7.5^{th}$ value in the series.

Since, 7.5 is not an integer, using the formula for fraction c.d (Here, c=7 and d=5) as

c^{th} value $- d \times [(c+1)^{th}$ value $-c^{th}$ value]

$Q_3 = 7^{th}$ value$+0.5 \times (8^{th}$ value-7th value)

=21+0.5 x (24-21)

=22.5

$D_6 = 6 \times (9+1)/10 = 6^{th}$ value in the series=16

$P_{60} = 60 \times (9+1)/100 = 6^{th}$ value in the series=16

$P_{46} = 46 \times (9+1)/100 = 4.6^{th}$ value in the series, Not an integer (use fraction formula with c=4 and d=6)s

=4th value+0.6 x (5th value-4th value)

=12+0.6 x (14-12)

=13.2

B) Calculating partition values for ungrouped data

The procedure for calculating the partition values for the ungrouped data is same as that for median. The first step is the calculation of the cumulative frequency (c.f.). After this, the partition value is the data value (x) in front of the $c.f.$ value more than iN/p . Here i is the ith value of the partition, N represent the number of data values and p is the number of parts by the partition value.

Thus, for quartiles, $i = 1\ to\ 3, Q_i$ is the value of x in front of $c.f.$ value more than $iN/4$.

For deciles, $i = 1\ to\ 9, D_i$ the value of x in front of $c.f.$ value more than $iN/10$.

For percentiles, $i = 1\ to\ 99, P_i$ the value of x in front of $c.f.$ value more than $iN/100$.

Example: Calculate the values of Q_1, D_6, P_{50} for scores (x) obtained out of four by 28 students in a class.

x	0	1	2	3	4
f	1	9	5	10	3

Solution:

To calculate the partition values the first step is to calculate the cumulative frequency values as follows:

x	f	Cumulative frequency $(c.f)$
0	1	1
1	9	10
2	5	15
3	10	25
4	3	28

Here $N = 28$, as $Q_i = iN/4$,

For $i = 1, N/4 = 7$, Q_1 is the value of x in front of the cumulative frequency more than 7. Thus $Q_1 = 1$.

As $D_i = iN/10$,

For $i = 6, 6N/10 = 16.8$, D_6 is the value of x in front of the cumulative frequency more than 16.8. Thus, the value of the sixth decile is 3.

As $P_i = iN/100$,

For $i = 50, 50N/100 = 14$, P_{50} is the value of x in front of the cumulative frequency more than 14. Thus, the the value of the fiftieth percentile as 2.

C) Calculating partition values for grouped data

For grouped data any of the partition value can be calculated using the common formula

$$U_i = l + h \times \left(\frac{iN/p - c}{f} \right)$$

here, l is the lower-limit of the partition class, f is the frequency of the partition class, h is the class-width, c is the cumulative frequency of the class preceding the partition class, $N = \sum f$ and p is the parts in which the data needs to be divided.

For example: To calculate the 3rd quartile $i = 3$ with $p = 4$. Other values can be fetched from the partition class.

Example: Calculate the values of Q_1, D_5, P_{80} for the number of people (f) in a specific age group (x).

x	0-4	4-8	8-12	12-16	16-20	20-24
f	9	13	8	5	3	2

Solution:

To obtain the partition values the cumulative frequency values are calculated as follows:

x	Frequency (f)	Cumulative frequency ($c.f$)
0-4	9	9
4-8	13	22
8-12	8	30
12-16	5	35
16-20	3	38
20-24	2	40

Here, $N = 40$. Hence the partition class is a class with c.f. value more than iN/p.

Calculating Q_1: Here $N/4 = 10$. The quartile class is the 4-8 class with $c.f.$ more than 10. Here $l = 4, f = 13, h = 4 \ and \ c = 9$ (value preceding $c.f.$)

Hence,

$$Q_1 = 4 + 4 \times \left(\frac{10 - 9}{13}\right) = 4 + \frac{4}{13} = 4.30$$

Calculating D_5: Here $5N/10 = 20$. The decile class is the 4-8 class with $c.f.$ more than 20. Here $l = 4, f = 13, h = 4 , c = 9$ (value preceding $c.f.$)

Hence,

$$D_5 = 4 + 4 \times \left(\frac{20 - 9}{13}\right) = 4 + \frac{44}{13} = 7.384$$

Calculating P_{80}

Here $80N/100 = 32$. The percentile class is the 12-16 class with c.f. more than 32. Here $l = 16, f = 3, h = 4 \ and \ c = 30$ (value preceding $c.f.$). Hence,

$$P_{80} = 16 + 4 \times \left(\frac{32 - 30}{3}\right) = 16 + \frac{8}{3} = 18.667$$

Chapter based Quiz

A) MCQs

1. The end of month unit sale for a mutual fund are: 52,45,47,58,89,46,27. The values shown are:
   a) Frequency distribution
   b) Raw data
   c) Grouped data
   d) Arranged data

2. Mean of the data 12, 1, 16, 10, 9, 12, 10 is
a) 10
b) 9
c) 7
d) 6

3. Sales of the four products pen, pencil, books and notebooks in a day at a mall shop are 82, 43, 57, and 64 respectively. Which is the most popular product?
a) Pen
b) Pencil
c) Books
d) Notebooks

4. The marks of a student in 10 subjects are 25, 30, 39, 44, 16, 40, 11, 32, 14, and 29. The median is____.
a) 29.5
b) 27.0
c) 31.5
d) 42.4

5. Median of the given data 8, 12, 21, 14, 15, 6, 9 is
a) 13.0
b) 17.5
c) 12.0
d) 14.5

6. Given the following grouped frequency table, answer the follow questions:

Class Interval	0-9	10-19	20-29	30-39	40-49
frequency	2	4	10	12	8

A) In which interval does the median fall?

a) 0-9
b) 10-19
c) 20-29
d) 30-39

B) In which interval does the Q_1 fall?

a) 0-9
b) 10-19
c) 20-29
d) 30-39

C) In which interval does the D_3 fall?

a) 0-9
b) 10-19
c) 20-29
d) 30-39

D) In which interval does the P_{10} fall?

a) 0-9
b) 10-19
c) 20-29
d) 30-39

7. How many total observations are included in the above given distribution?
a) 36
b) 28
c) 14
d) 10

8. Which measure of central tendency is obtained by calculating the sum of values and dividing this by the number of values in the data set?
a) Mean
b) Median
c) Mode
d) Harmonic Mean

9. For the given data, answer the follow questions:

x	1	2	3	4
$frequency$	5	4	10	2

A) What is the mean of the data?
a) 1.2
b) 3.1
c) 2.2
d) 2.4

B) What is the mode of the data?
a) 1
b) 2
c) 3
d) 4

C) What is the median of the data?
a) 3
b) 4
c) 5
d) 6

D) What is the Q3 of the data?
a) 5
b) 3
c) 2
d) 7

E) What is the D4 of the data?
a) 1
b) 2
c) 3
d) 4

10. Which of the following is not equal to median?
a) Q2
b) P50
c) D5
d) Q1

11. If mean=2, median=4, using the empirical formula what is the mode of the data?
a) 10
b) 8
c) 6
d) 4

12. In a data series with 14 values, the fifth decile is which value of the arranged data?
a) 1.5
b) 5.5
c) 7.5
d) 4.5

13. What is the empirical relation between mean, median and mode of a data?
a) mode=3 median-2 mean
b) mode=3 mean-2 median
c) mode=3 median +2 mean
d) mode=4 median-2 mean

14. Which of the following is not a correct relation if Q is for quartile, D is for decile and P is for percentile?
a) $D_1=P_{10}$
b) Q_2=Median
c) $P_{50}=Q_2$
d) $D_5=P_{25}$

15. Which decile value is similar to P_{60}?
a) D_1

b) D_5
c) D_6
d) D_8

16. Which of the following is not a measure of central tendency?
a) Mean
b) Median
c) Range
d) Mode

17. The mean of the first n integers is____________.
a) n
b) n+1
c) (n+1)/2
d) 2n

18. What is the geometric mean for 2, 8, and 32?
a) 2
b) 4
c) 6
d) 8

19. What is the harmonic mean for 1, 5, and 10?
a) 2.0
b) 2.5
c) 3.0
d) 3.5

20. Mean marks of 30 students in a class are 40. The mean of first 10 students was found to be 50. What is the mean mark of the remaining 20 students?
a) 20
b) 35
c) 40
d) 45

21. What is the harmonic mean for 1, 2, 4 and 8?
a) 2.0
b) 1.5
c) 4.0
d) 2.1

22. Mean cannot be calculated for which type of data?
a) Nominal
b) Discrete
c) Continuous
d) Ratio

23. What is the geometric mean of 3, 4, 9 and 12?
a) 2
b) 4
c) 6
d) 8

24. Which measure of central tendency is most affected by the presence of extreme values?
a) Mean
b) Mode
c) Quartile
d) Median

Answers:

1-b	2-a	3-a	4-a	5-c	6(A)-d	6(B)-c
6(C)-c	6(D)-b	7-a	8-a	9(A)-d	9(B)-c	9(C)-a
9(D)-b	9(E)-b	10-d	11-b	12-c	13-a	14-d
15-c	16-c	17-c	18-d	19-b	20-b	21-d
22-a	23-c	24-a				

B) True or False

1. For the data: 2, 3, 9, 16, 9, 3, 9. Since 16 is the highest value in the observations, is it correct to say that it is the mode of the data?
2. Mode can be calculated for the nominal data.
3. There can be more than one mode value for a given data.
4. The value of the median is same as that of the second quartile.
5. There are 90 percentile that divides the data into 100 equal parts.
6. The first percentile exceeds one percent of the data values in the series
7. A data with mean=12, mode=15 has median=13 using the empirical formula.
8. The geometric mean of 4, 8 and 2 is 2.
9. The median of 5, 8, 1, 4, 3, and 9 is 4.
10. For a given set of data values the arithmetic mean is more than the geometric mean.

Answers: –

1-F	2-T	3-T	4-T	5-F
6-T	7-T	8-F, (4)	9-F, (4.5)	10-T

C) Fill in the blanks

1. Decile divides the data in_____ equal parts.
2. The cumulative frequency column is useful in determining the_______, which is a measure of central tendency.

3. The width of each of five continuous classes in a frequency distribution is 10 and the lower limit of the lowest class is 10. The upper limit of the highest class is_____.

4. Let m be the mid-point and u be the upper class limit of a class in a continuous frequency distribution. The lower-class limit of the class is _____.

5. The mean of five numbers is 10. If one number is excluded, their mean becomes 8. The excluded number is _____.

6. If the mean of the observations: x, x + 2, x + 4, x + 6, x + 8 is 7, the mean of the first three observations is_________.

7. If each observation of the data is increased by 15, then their mean will _______by 15.

8. The mean of 10 observations is 50. If 80 replace one of the observations that were 50, the resulting mean will now be _____.

9. The mean of 6 observations is 36. Out of these observations if the mean of first 3 observations is 32 and that of the last 2 observation is 30, the fourth observation is_____.

10. The________decile exceeds 80% of the data values.

11. 75% of the observations of the data values are more than ___quartile.

12. Ten observations 6, 10, 14, 16, 2x, 2x+8, 32, 35, 40, 43 are written in an ascending order. The median of the data is 24. The value of x is____.

13. The_______ percentile value is equal to the sixth decile.

14. The geometric mean of two numbers is 12. One of the numbers is 4, the other number is___.

15. The harmonic mean of two numbers is 2.4. One of the numbers is 2, the other number is___.

16. If any of the observations is zero, the geometric mean becomes _______.

17. One of the criteria to calculate the harmonic mean is that the values should not be _____.

18. Two important conditions to calculate the geometric mean is that the values should not be _____ and _________value.

19. _____ decile value is equal to P_{80}.

20. A measure of central tendency, above which half of the values fall and below which half of the values fall is called the _______________.

Answers:

1-ten	2-median	3-60	4-(2m-u)	5-18	6-5	7-increase	8-53	9-60	10-eighth
11-first	12-10	13-60th	14-36	15-3	16-zero	17-zero	18-zero and negative	19-8th	20-median

NOTES:

Chapter 3

Measure of Dispersion

So far in the last chapter, the measure of central tendency has been discussed that talks about the concentration of the data at the central part of the distribution. But sometimes knowing the central tendency is not providing the complete information about the data values. **For Example**, consider the two data series having 5 values each

i) 9, 10,12,14,15
ii) 8, 9,13,14,16

The given two data sets have the same mean value 12 while the data values are different. Hence, there is a need of some another important characteristic of quantitative data that shows how much the data varies, or spread out. These measures of dispersion tell us about the data variability.

Statistical techniques that measure dispersion are of two types:

A measure of dispersion-It includes the statistical techniques to measure deviation of data value from a measure of central tendency.
Measures of shape- It includes the statistical techniques to describe the shape of the distribution.

There are two types of measures of dispersions:

1. **Absolute measures of dispersion:** Absolute measures of dispersion are presented in the same unit as the unit of distribution. These are useful in comparing two distributions with the same unit.
2. **Relative measures of dispersion:** Relative measures of dispersion are useful in comparing two sets of data which have different units of measurement. These are expressed as the percentage or the coefficient of the absolute measure of dispersion.

3.1 Methods of measuring dispersion

The two most common method of measuring spread are: Range; Quartile deviation; Mean deviation; Standard deviation and Variance.

3.2 Range

The difference between the maximum and minimum data entries in the data set is known as range of the data. For calculating the range, the data must be quantitative. The formula for the range can be given as:

Range = (Max. data entry) – (Min. data entry)

Example: The wait time to withdraw money at the bank teller is given for the two banks A and B. Following are the wait time in minutes. Find the mean and range for each bank.

Bank A: 6.2   7.2   8.5   5.4   10.2

Bank B: 5.4   5.8   7.8   11   7.5

Solution: For both banks A and B, the mean time is 7.5 but the range can be calculated as 10.2-5.4=4.8 for bank A, while for bank B it is 11-5.4=5.6.

As compared to the central tendency measures, the range is easy to compute, but the only disadvantage is that it only uses 2 values.

To see why range is not a popular measure of dispersion consider the given two different sets and find, if the following two data sets vary in a similar way?

Set A: 1, 2, 3, 4, 5, 6, 7, 8, 9, 10

Set B: 1, 10, 10, 10, 10, 10, 10, 10, 10, 10

The answer is obviously not, the sets are different. The element in the first set has a minimum of 1 and the maximum value is 10 while the second set B has only a single element with value 1 and all others are 10. In this given pair of data sets, the range of both the sets is 10-1=9. Hence range is not a good measure as it can mislead about the data.

Range is an *absolute measure of dispersion*. The relative measure of dispersion for range is called the **coefficient of range** and is given by the formula:

$$\text{Coefficient of range} = \frac{(\text{Max. data entry - Min. data entry})}{(\text{Max. data entry +Min. data entry})}$$

3.2.1 Calculating Range

In the above example the procedure of calculating range is presented for the individual series. Let us learn the calculation procedure for the range for the frequency data in discrete and continuous form.

Example: Calculate range and its coefficient from the following data

x	f
1	3
2	5
4	12
6	3

Solution:
For a discrete frequency distribution, range is the difference in the lowest value and the highest value of the series. Hence range =6-1=5.

$$\text{The coefficient of range} = \frac{6-1}{6+1} = \frac{5}{7} = 0.71$$

Example: Calculate range and its coefficient from the following data:

x	f
10-15	7
15-20	6
20-25	9

Solution:
Range of a continuous frequency distribution is the difference of the lower limit of the lowest class interval and the upper limit of the highest-class interval. The upper limit of the highest-class interval is 25 and the lower limit of the lowest class interval is 10.

Hence $range = 25 - 10 = 15$.

$$\text{The coefficient of range} = \frac{25-10}{25+10} = \frac{15}{35} = 0.43$$

3.3 Interquartile Range and Quartile deviation

Range does not cover all the values of the data distribution. This drawback of range can be overcome by using interquartile range. Interquartile range is the difference between the third quartile and the first quartile.

$$Interquartile\ range = Q_3 - Q_1$$

Where Q_1= first quartile or lower quartile, and Q_3= third quartile or upper quartile

Interquartile range also provides the quartile deviation or semi-interquartile range, which is obtained by dividing the interquartile range by 2, that is,

$$Quartile\ deviation\ or\ semi-interquartile\ range\ = \frac{Q_3 - Q_1}{2}$$

Quartile deviation is an absolute measure of dispersion. The relative measure is called the coefficient of quartile deviation. Coefficient of quartile deviation can be used to measure the degree of variation in two different distributions when both have different units of measurement. It is given as

$$Coefficient\ of\ quartile\ deviation = \frac{Q_3 - Q_1}{Q_3 + Q_1}$$

Example: Find the interquartile range, semi-interquartile range, and coefficient of quartile deviation if $Q_1 = 21$ and $Q_3 = 52$

Solution:

$$Interquartile\ range\ = Q_3 - Q_1 = 52 - 21 = 31$$

$$Quartile\ deviation\ or\ semi-interquartile\ range\ = \frac{31}{2} = 15.2$$

$$Coefficient\ of\ quartile\ deviation = \frac{31}{73} == 0.42$$

3.4 Mean Absolute Deviation (or Average Absolute Deviation)

A tool of measurement which considers deviation from central point or deviation from the average is called mean absolute deviation. The formula for mean absolute deviation is given as

$$Mean\ absolute\ deviation\ = \frac{\sum_{i=1}^{n} |(x - \bar{x})|}{n}$$

Here n is the number of the data values in a data set.

Mean absolute deviation is an absolute measure of dispersion. A relative measure of mean absolute deviation, also known as coefficient of mean absolute deviation, is obtained by the following formula:

$$Coefficient\ of\ mean\ absolute\ deviation\ = \frac{Mean\ absolute\ deviation}{Mean}$$

Mean absolute deviation can be determined for all types of data distribution such as individual series, discrete frequency distribution, and continuous frequency distribution.

A) For raw data

Example: Find the mean absolute deviation and coefficient of mean absolute deviation for the given data:

$$6 \qquad 12 \qquad 15 \qquad 8 \qquad 10$$

Solution:

The mean of the given data is 10.2.

Finding the difference of mean from each value of the data and ignoring the sign for the modulus provides the following values:

4.2   1.8   4.8   2.2   0.2

which on adding gives 13.2 and hence dividing by $n = 5$, gives the mean deviation.

Hence the mean deviation$= \dfrac{13.2}{5} = 2.64$

$$Coefficient\ of\ mean\ absolute\ deviation\ = \dfrac{Mean\ absolute\ deviation}{Mean}$$

$$= \dfrac{2.64}{10.2} = 0.258$$

B) For a discrete and continuous frequency data

The mean absolute deviation for a discrete frequency distribution is computed using the formula:

$$Mean\ absolute\ deviation\ = \dfrac{\displaystyle\sum_{i=1}^{n} f_i \left|(x_i - \bar{x})\right|}{\displaystyle\sum_{i=1}^{n} f_i}$$

For a continuous frequency distribution also, the mean absolute deviation and coefficient of mean absolute deviation can be obtained using the same formula. Here, class midpoints are used for the values of $x_i's$.

Example: Find the mean absolute deviation and coefficient of mean absolute deviation for the given frequency data:

Rate of a magazine (x)	Frequency
50	10
60	5
40	8
80	5

Solution:

For the calculation of the mean absolute deviation the first step is the mean and then the deviation needs to be calculated for each value of mean.

Rate of a magazine (x)	Frequency (f)	fx	$\lvert x_i - \bar{x} \rvert$	$f_i \lvert x_i - \bar{x} \rvert$
50	10	500	3.92	39.2
60	5	300	6.08	30.4
42	6	252	11.92	71.52
74	4	296	20.08	80.32
Total	**25**	**1348**	**42**	**221.44**

As the mean for the discrete frequency distribution is given by:

$$Mean(\bar{x}) = \frac{\sum\limits_{i=1}^{n} f_i x_i}{\sum\limits_{i=1}^{n} f_i} = \frac{1348}{25} = 53.92$$

And hence

$$Mean\ absolute\ deviation = \frac{\sum\limits_{i=1}^{n} f_i \lvert (x_i - \bar{x}) \rvert}{\sum\limits_{i=1}^{n} f_i} = \frac{8.8576}{25} = 0.1642$$

3.5 Variance

Variance is a measure of how data points differ from the mean. To get the insight how it works consider the two sets A and B and calculate the mean and median for the data.

Data Set A: 3, 5, 7, 10, 10
Data Set B: 7, 7, 7, 7, 7

On calculation one can observe that for the given set A and B both the mean = 7, median = 7. But it is obvious that the two data sets are not identical! Hence variance is a measure of dispersion that clarify how the data set are different.

Variance is the sum of squared deviations of the data values from their arithmetic mean divided by the sample size minus one given as

$$s^2 = \frac{\sum (x_i - \bar{x})^2}{n - 1}$$

The formula used for calculation of population variance is given as:

$$\sigma^2 = \frac{\sum (x_i - \mu)^2}{N}$$

where μ is the population arithmetic mean, x_i is the ith value of the variable x, and $N = \Sigma f$.

3.6 Standard deviation

Standard deviation is a measure of dispersion which is the square root of the variance. It can also be defined as a measure with the same unit as that of the data values. It defines how much the values differ from the mean.

The formula for the standard deviation is hence given by

$$s = \sqrt{\frac{\sum (x_i - \bar{x})^2}{n - 1}}$$

3.6.1 Steps for calculating variance and standard deviation for raw data

a) Find the mean of the given data.
b) Calculate the difference of each data item from the mean called as **deviation**.
c) Find the sum of square of the deviation values.
d) Divide the obtained sum by the number of data values minus one, (n-1) to get the variance.
e) Take the square root of the variance to find the standard deviation.

Example: Find variance and standard deviation of the given data 4, 8, 14, 10

	x	$x - \bar{x}$	$(x - \bar{x})^2$
	4	-5	25
	8	-1	1
	14	5	25
	10	1	1
Total	36	0	$\sum (x_i - \bar{x})^2 = 52$

Solution: To find the variance and hence the standard deviation, find the mean of the data.

Here, mean=36/4=9.

On subtracting the mean from each data value generates the second column of deviation and the third column is the square of the deviation values. Hence the sum of the square of deviations is calculated as 52.

The variance can thus be calculated as:

$$\sigma^2 = \frac{\sum (x_i - \bar{x})^2}{n-1}$$

$$\sigma^2 = \frac{52}{3} = 17.33$$

Taking the square root of variance gives the standard deviation as:

$$\sigma = \sqrt{17.33}$$
$$\sigma = 4.163$$

3.6.2 Standard deviation and variance for discrete and continuous frequency distributions

The formula for the sample standard deviation and sample variance for a discrete frequency distribution is given as follows:

$$\textit{Sample variance } \ s^2 = \frac{\sum_{i=1}^{n} f_i(x_i - \bar{x})^2}{N-1}$$

$$\textit{Sample standard deviation } s = \sqrt{\frac{\sum_{i=1}^{n} f_i(x_i - \bar{x})^2}{N-1}}$$

$$\textit{where, } N = \sum_{i=1}^{n} f_i$$

Standard deviation and variance for a continuous frequency distribution can also be computed by applying the same procedure as for a discrete frequency distribution.

For a continuous frequency distribution, class midpoints need to be used for the values of $x_i's$.

Example: Find variance and standard deviation of the given data

x	frequency (f)	$f\,x$	$(x_i - \bar{x})$	$(x_i - \bar{x})^2$	$f_i(x_i - \bar{x})^2$
5	5	25	-0.75	0.5625	2.8125
6	3	18	0.25	0.0625	0.1875
4	4	16	-1.75	3.0625	12.25
7	8	56	1.25	1.5625	12.5
Total	*20*	*115*			*27.75*

Solution:
The mean for the data is given by

$$Mean(\bar{x}) = \frac{\sum_{i=1}^{n} f_i x_i}{\sum_{i=1}^{n} f_i} = \frac{115}{20} = 5.75$$

And hence from the table

$$s^2 = \frac{\sum_{i=1}^{n} f_i(x_i - \bar{x})^2}{N - 1} = \frac{27.75}{19} = 1.46$$

where, N = 20

$$s = \sqrt{variance} = \sqrt{1.46} = 1.208$$

3.6.3 Properties of Standard Deviation:

Standard deviation is independent of change of origin. It remains unchanged if each data value is increased or decreased by some constant value.

If the values of a data series are multiplied (or divided) by a constant, then the standard deviation of the new data series can be obtained by multiplying (or dividing) the original standard deviation by the same constant.

3.7 Coefficient of variation

Standard deviation is an absolute measure of dispersion. Coefficient of variation is a relative measure of dispersion. Coefficient of variation is equal to standard deviation divided by the arithmetic mean and multiplied by 100. The coefficient of variation is generally denoted by C.V and is given by

$$C.V = \left(\frac{\sigma}{\bar{x}}\right)100$$

The series for which the C.V. is greater is said to be more variable

Example: In a group of adults, the mean weight was 65 kg with S.D as 8. In the same group of adults, the mean height was 160 cm with S.D as 6. Find which character shows greater variation.

Solution:

$$\text{C.V of weight} = \left(\frac{\sigma}{\bar{x}}\right)100 = \frac{8}{65} \times 100 = 12.30\% \qquad \text{C.V of height} = \left(\frac{\sigma}{\bar{x}}\right)100 = \frac{6}{160} \times 100 = 5.625\%$$

Since, the coefficient of variation of the weight is more as compared to the coefficient of variation of height. Hence weight is more variable as compared to the height in the adults.

3.8 Empirical relationship between measures of dispersion

In the case of a symmetrical distribution, the empirical relationship between the various measures of dispersion is given by:

$$Quartile\ deviation\ = \frac{2}{3}\ Standard\ deviation$$

$$Mean\ absolute\ deviation\ = \frac{4}{5}\ Standard\ deviation$$

$$Quartile\ deviation\ = \frac{5}{6}\ Mean\ absolute\ deviation$$

$$Range = 6\ Standard\ deviation$$

3.9 Measures of shape

Measures of shape are the tools used for describing the shape of a distribution of the data. There are two measures of shape: skewness and kurtosis.

3.9.1 Skewness

The distribution of data may or may not be symmetrical. A distribution where the right half of the curve is the mirror image of the left half curve, it is said to be a ***symmetrical distribution.***
For a symmetrical distribution **mean=median=mode.**
The graph of the symmetrical distribution is a bell-shaped curve called as a normal curve.
In a symmetric distribution, mean, median, and mode fall at the centre of the distribution with no skewness.

If the distribution is not symmetrical, it is said to be ***asymmetrical or skewed.***
If **mean>median>mode** then the distribution is called **positively skewed**. For a positively skewed distribution there exists a long tail on the right side of the curve.
If **mean<median<mode** then the distribution is called **negatively skewed**. For a negatively skewed distribution there exists a long tail on the left side of the curve.

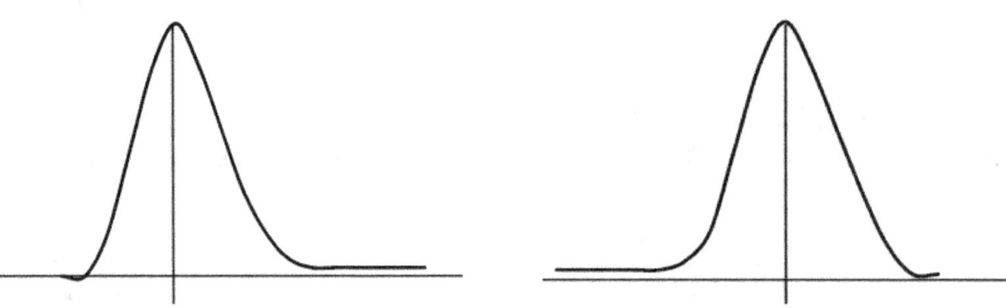

Figure 2:A positively skewed curve   **Figure 3: A negatively skewed curve**

A method for measuring skewness, referred to as the Pearsonian coefficient of skewness is given as:

$$Coeff.\ of\ skewness = \frac{Mean - Mode}{Standard\ deviation}$$

Note that for a symmetrical distribution the Pearsonian coefficient of skewness is computed as zero. For a positively skewed distribution, the coefficient of skewness will have a plus sign and for a distribution that is negatively skewed, the coefficient of skewness will have a minus sign. The actual degree of skewness can be obtained from the numerical value of the coefficient of skewness.

Greater the coefficient of skewness, the more skewed is the distribution. A distribution can have a single mode or multiple modes. Hence the coefficient of skewness can be defined with median using the empirical formula between mean, median and mode. Thus

$$Coeff.\ of\ skewness = \frac{3(Mean - Median)}{Standard\ deviation}$$

Example: A distribution has mean 25, mode 16, and standard deviation 10. Then the coefficient of skewness can be computed as

$$Coeff.\ of\ skewness = \frac{Mean - Mode}{Standard\ deviation} = \frac{25 - 16}{10} = 0.9$$

3.9.2 Kurtosis

Two distributions with same mean, variance, and skewness can be significantly different in shape. Kurtosis measures the amount of peakedness of a distribution.

A flatter distribution than normal distribution is called **platykurtic.**

A more peaked distribution than the normal distribution is referred to as **leptokurtic.**

Between these two types of distribution, there is a distribution which is flat in shape is referred as a **mesokurtic distribution**.

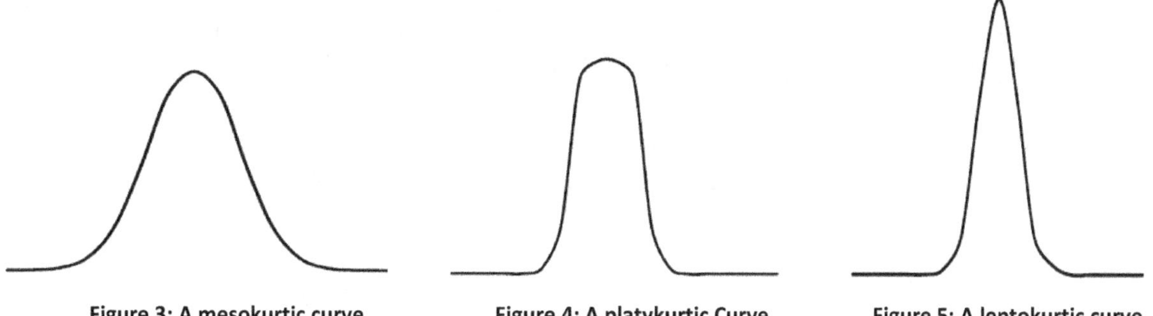

Figure 3: A mesokurtic curve	Figure 4: A platykurtic Curve	Figure 5: A leptokurtic curve

Chapter based Quiz

A) MCQs

1. Calculating the difference between the largest and smallest data value gives
a) Range
b) Interquartile range
c) Quartile deviation
d) Median

2. Calculating the difference between the first and third quartile data value gives
a) Range
b) Interquartile range
c) Quartile deviation
d) Median

3. Range of the data: 12   18   6   10   26   32   35   42
a) 29
b) 44
c) 38
d) 36

4. Which measure of central tendency provides the value that occurs with the highest frequency?
a) Mean
b) Median
c) Mode
d) Standard deviation

5. Which of the following statistics is not a measure of dispersion?
a) Standard deviation
b) Range
c) Quartile deviation
d) Median

6. For a data set, the semi-interquartile range is:
a) The difference between the minimum and maximum values.
b) The standard deviation.
c) The difference between the first and third quartiles.
d) Half of the difference between the first and third quartiles.

7. For a symmetric data, the value of $Q_1=3$, $Q_3=10$, the interquartile range is:
a) 13
b) 10
c) 7
d) 3.5

8. For a given data if the semi-interquartile range is 10, the value of first quartile is 4, the value of the third quartile is:
a) 24
b) 16
c) 14
d) 7

9. What is the variance of   5   8   11   14 ?
a) 14
b) 15
c) 10

d) 8

10. If mean is 50 and standard deviation is 5 then C.V (Coefficient of variation) is____%
a) 100
b) 10
c) 20
d) 80

11. What is the variance of   5   5   5   5 ?
a) 0
a) 1
b) 3
c) 5

12. Which of the following is a unit free quantity?
a) Standard deviation
b) Range
c) Coefficient of variation
d) Quartile deviation

13. For mean=20 and and the coefficient of variation=15, what is the standard deviation?
a) 1
b) 2
c) 3
d) 4

14. What is the coefficient of range for maximum data value 20 and the minimum data value 4?
a) 2/3
b) 3/2
c) 1/5
d) 5

15. What is the coefficient of mean absolute deviation for mean absolute deviation 2 and mean 34?
a) 0.0214
b) 0.0588
c) 0.0246
d) 0.0325

16. What is the standard deviation, if variance is 0.36?
a) 0.6
b) 0.4
c) 0.2
d) 0.8

17. The variance can never be ________ .
a) Negative
b) Zero

c) Larger than the standard deviation
d) None of the above

18. What will happen to the variance of a data set if 4 is added to every value of the data set?
a) Variance of new data series will increase by 4
b) Variance of new data series will increase by 4
c) Variance of new data series will increase by 2
d) No change

19. What will happen to the variance of a data set if 6 is multiplied to every value of the data set?
a) Variance of new data series will increase by 6
b) Variance of new data series will increase by 36
c) Variance of new data series will increase by 2
d) No change

20. What is the S.D, if the distribution has mean as 11, median as 8 and the coefficient of the skewness as 2.5?
a) 1.5
b) 3.6
c) 6.4
d) 72

Answers:

1-a	2-b	3-d	4-c	5-d	6-d	7-c	8-b	9-15	10-b
11-a	12-c	13-c	14-a	15-b	16-a	17-a	18-d	19-b	20-b

B) True or False

1. The standard deviation is measured in the same unit as the observations of the data set.
2. The difference of each data item from the mean is called as deviation.
3. Standard deviation is independent of change of origin and scale.
4. In a symmetric distribution, mean, median, and mode fall at the center of the distribution with no skewness.
5. Peakedness of a distribution is measured by calculating the skewness of the data.
6. A more peaked distribution than the normal distribution is referred as mesokurtic.
7. The average of the squared deviation from the arithmetic mean is called the mean deviation.
8. Half of the difference between the first and third quartiles is called the quartile deviation.
9. A distribution has mean=3, median=4 and S.D =1. The coefficient of the skewness is negative.
10. A distribution with mean as 8, mode as 6.5 and the coefficient of the skewness as 3 has S.D 0.5.
11. If mean<median<mode then the distribution is called positively skewed.
12. The graph of the symmetrical distribution is a bell-shaped curve called as a normal curve.
13. Kurtosis refers to the lack of symmetry in a distribution.

14. The numerical value of a standard deviation can never be negative.
15. Range is a measure of dispersion that can attain a negative value.

Answers:

1-T	**2**-T	**3**-F	**4**-T	**5**-F
6-F	**7**-F	**8**-T	**9**-T	**10**-T
11-F	**12**-T	**13**-F	**14**-T	**15**-T

C) Fill in the blanks

1. Variance of a data is to measure the spread of data values about ______.
2. The ratio of the standard deviation to the mean expressed as a percentage is called______________.
3. The variance of a data with non-zero data values is zero only if all observations are______.
4. The measure of dispersion which uses only two data values is called______.
5. The measure of dispersion which is expressed in the same units as the units of observation is ____________.
6. Range of a continuous frequency distribution is the difference of the ______limit of the lowest class interval and the ________limit of the highest-class interval.
7. Variance is the sum of squared deviations of the data values from their ______divided by the sample size minus one.
8. The standard deviation is the measure of dispersion which is the square root of the____________.
9. A distribution where the right half is the mirror image of the left half is said to be _________.
10. For a symmetrical distribution the Pearsonian coefficient of skewness is computed as ______.
11. For a __________skewed distribution, the coefficient of skewness will have a plus sign.
12. Kurtosis measures the amount of __________of a distribution.
13. A flatter distribution than normal distribution is called ________.
14. A distribution______ peaked distribution than the normal distribution is referred to as leptokurtic.
15. If S.D of a data series is 1.2 and the data is updated by multiplying all data values by 4 then the S.D of the updated data is____.
16. If mean>median>mode then the distribution is called ______skewed.
17. For a negatively skewed distribution there exists a long tail on the ______ side of the curve.
18. If the dispersion is small, the standard deviation is____________

Answers:

1-mean	**2**- Coefficient of variation	**3**-same	**4**-range	**5**- standard deviation	**6**- lower, upper
7- arithmetic mean	**8**- variance	**9**- symmetrical	**10**-zero	**11**- positively	**12**- peakedness
13- platykurtic	**14**-more	**15**-4.8	**16**-positively	**17**-left	**18**-small

Chapter 4

Graphical Representation of Data

Categorical data can be summarized in form of tables and graphs. A **summary table** is the tabulated way to present the frequency, amount, or percentage of items in a category that enable presenter to compare and differentiate between the categories.

For Example: A summary table for the choice of vehicle to commute to the work place regularly:

Vehicle Preference	Percentage of people
Car	16%
Bike	26%
Bus	17%
Bicycle	41%

A picture is said to be more effective than words for describing a data.

A graphic representation of data is said to be the geometrical image of a data that enables us to think about a statistical problem in visual terms. It is an effective way for the presentation, understanding and interpretation of the data to be analysed and presented. **Graphs** are used to make the data understandable to a layman. Data presented in form of a graph can be memorised for a long time and can be used to compare different types of analysis performed on the data.

In statistical terms, it can be said that graphs play an important role to present data through charts and diagrams when the data is quantitative. It is useful in comparison of data and presenting the relative positions of the components in comparison to each other.

Types of Graphical Representation

Graphs can be framed as per the data is either grouped or ungrouped.

Different types of graphs that can be drawn for the ungrouped data includes: Line graph, Bar graph and Pie diagram.

For the grouped data the most common graphs include the Histogram, Frequency Polygon, Frequency curve and Ogive.

4.1 Line Graph:

Line graphs are the simple and the most common graphs that can be easily drawn on the graph paper. In line graph the independent variable is taken horizontally on x-axis with respect to dependent variable vertically on y-axis.

A line graph displays a data that changes continuously over periods of time. To draw a line graph, the intersecting point (x, y) of the x and y axis is located and a straight line is drawn joining these points.

Example: Draw a line graph for the number of enquiries coming at the police station on a day at different time.

Time	10	11	12	1	2	3	4	5	6
No. of People	2	5	4	12	4	9	7	7	12

Solution: The line graph for the given data is obtained by marking the points for the number of people on y axis with respect to the time taken as independent variable on x-axis.

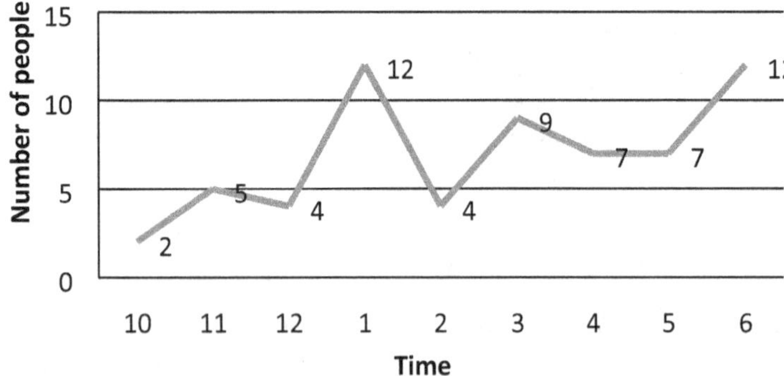

4.2 Bar diagram

Bar charts are often used for categorical data. In bar diagram, data is represented by bars. The bars can be made in any direction i.e., vertical or horizontal. The bars are taken of equal weight and start from a common horizontal or vertical line and their length indicates the corresponding values of statistical data. Length of bar shows the frequency or percentage for each category. A bar chart can be used to present a data as frequency, relative frequency, or percentage frequency.

The types of bar diagrams are as follows: simple, multiple, component and percentage bar diagram.

To draw the bar diagram, the class intervals or the values are specified on the x-axis of the graph. The frequencies are specified on the y-axis of the graph. Following is an example to demonstrate the procedure of constructing a bar chart.

Example: draw a bar diagram for an air conditioner manufacture company to analyse the sales of various stores located in various cities in India in the summer season.

Cities	A	B	C	D	E	F
Sales in thousands	12	4	8	16	24	11

Solution: To draw the bar diagram the bars are taken for the values of the sales on y-axis taking the cities on the x-axis.

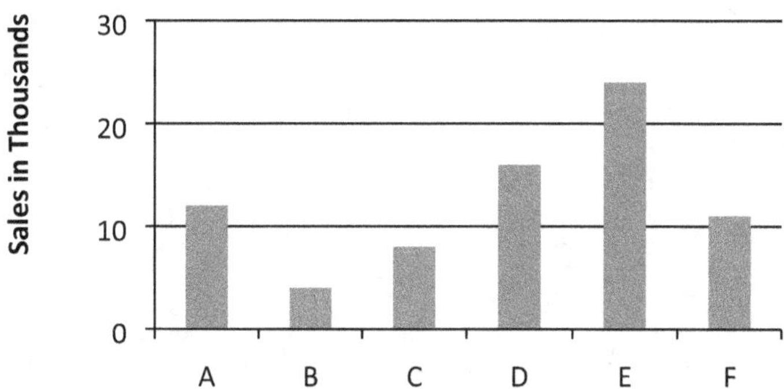

4.2.1 Multiple bar diagram

In a multiple bar diagram two or more sets of inter-related data are represented using different bars using different shades, colours, or dots to distinguish between different entities.

Example: Draw a multiple bar diagram for the following data to analyse the sales and profit of a company in past 8 years.

Year	1980	1985	1990	1995	2000	2005	2010	2015	2020
Sales	80	84	74	74	50	60	52	58	66
Profit	30	40	50	22	45	50	35	45	27

Solution: To draw the multiple bar diagram, two different bars are drawn for the sales and profit in each year, taking the years as independent variable on the x-axis.

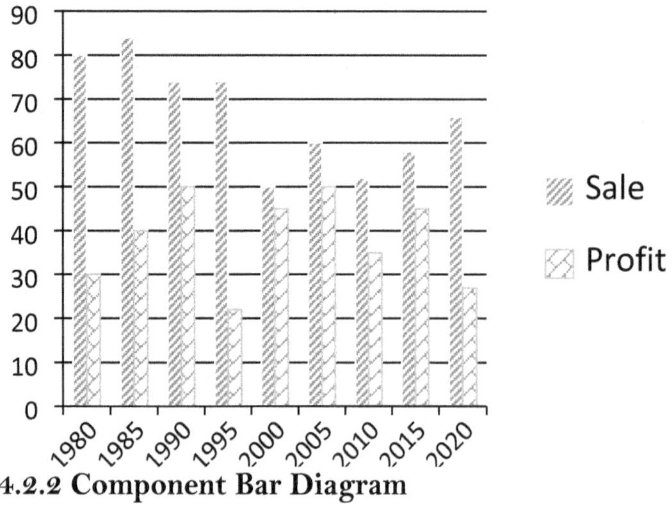

4.2.2 Component Bar Diagram

A sub-divided or component bar diagram is used to represent data in which the total magnitude is divided into different components, also called as *stacked chart*.

To draw this diagram, make simple bars for each class taking the total magnitude in that class and then divide these simple bars into parts in the ratio of various components. This type of diagram shows the variation in different components within each class as well as between different classes.

Example: Draw a component bar diagram for the share of different mobile companies in rural and urban areas.

Year	A	B	C	D	E	F
Rural	40	20	30	50	40	46
Urban	30	47	49	57	48	64

Solution: To draw the component or stacked bar diagram the different bars are drawn with the total length of bar for each year as the sum of values of the share in rural and urban areas. The values are then marked on the same bar taking one above another.

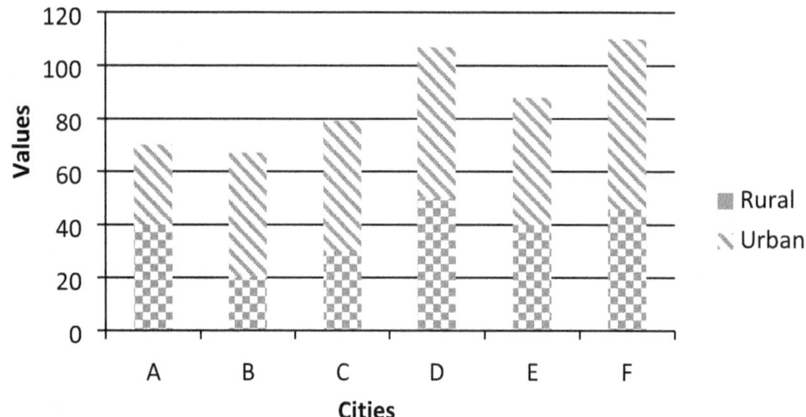

4.2.3 Percentage Component Bar Diagram

A percentage component bar diagram is drawn on the percentage basis. To draw it, express each component as the percentage of its respective total. In drawing a percentage bar diagram, bars equal of length (=100) is drawn for each class and sub-divided into the proportion of the percentage of their component. The diagram so obtained is called a percentage component bar chart or percentage stacked bar diagram. This type of diagram is useful in comparing components of the total in percentage.

Example: Draw a percentage component bar diagram for the yield of wheat and rice in the five states.

States	V	W	X	Y	Z
Wheat	45	60	70	70	50
Rice	55	80	70	60	70
Total	100	140	140	130	120

Solution: To draw a percentage component bar diagram, the total and the percentage of the yields calculated from 100.

States	V	W	X	Y	Z
Wheat	45	42.85714	50	53.84615	41.66667
Rice	55	57.14286	50	46.15385	58.33333
Total	100	100	100	100	100

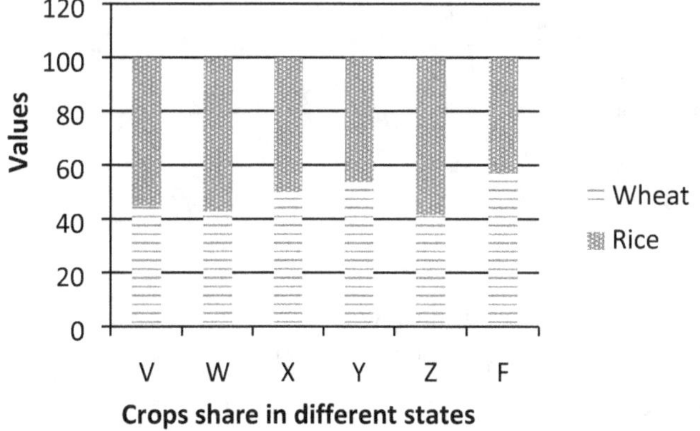

4.3 Pie diagram

The pie chart is a circle broken up into sector representing different categories. The size of each sector of the pie varies according to the percentage in each category. A pie-graph is used to compare parts to the whole. A set of sectorial areas are presented in the proportion to the values of the items. To draw a pie diagram, first the value of each category is expressed as a percentage of the total and then the angle 360^0 is divided. The requirement to draw a pie diagram is that the data should be in in percentage of the total.

Example: Draw a pie diagram for the data of students getting first, second, third division and failure in a class

Division	First	Second	Third	Failure
Number of students	15	32	11	4

Solution: To draw the pie diagram, the percentage is calculated for the number of students getting these division out of the total number of students as (number of student/ Total students) *100.

Now the percentage is calculated as a fraction of 360 degrees to find the degrees of each sector in the last column as shown below:

Division	Number of students	Percent	Percent of 360
First	15	(=15/62) *100 24.19	(=24.19/360) *100 87.096
Second	32	(=32/62) *100 51.61	185.806
Third	11	(=11/62) *100 17.74	63.870
Failure	4	= (4/62) *100 6.45	23.225
Total	62	100	360

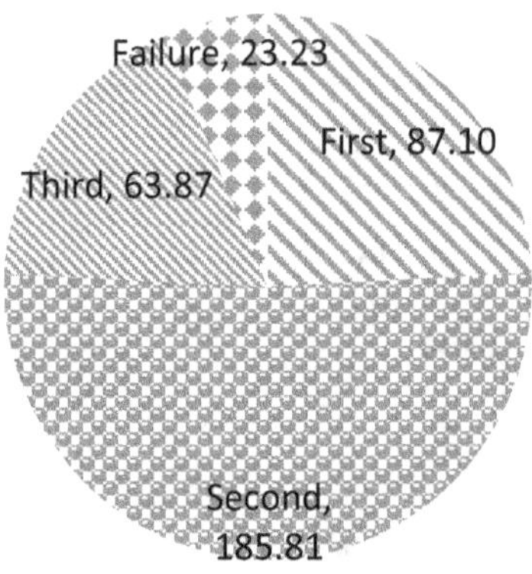

4.4 Histogram

A histogram is a form of the bar diagram for a frequency distribution data with no gaps between adjacent bars. It can be constructed for equal as well as unequal class intervals. Histogram has adjacent rectangles with class intervals as width and frequency of corresponding class interval as its height. The area of any rectangle of a histogram is proportional to the frequency of that class.

Histogram is used when the data is given in the form of frequencies and when there is a need to display the class interval by a diagram. ***Histogram also provides the mode of a distribution graphically.***

Example: Draw the histogram for the given data

Class interval	0-10	10-20	20-30	30-40	40-50
Number of students	5	10	15	12	8

Solution: The given data can be presented as a histogram taking the class intervals on x axis and the corresponding number of students on y axis. While plotting a histogram there shouldn't be any gaps between the bars that occur in a bar diagram.

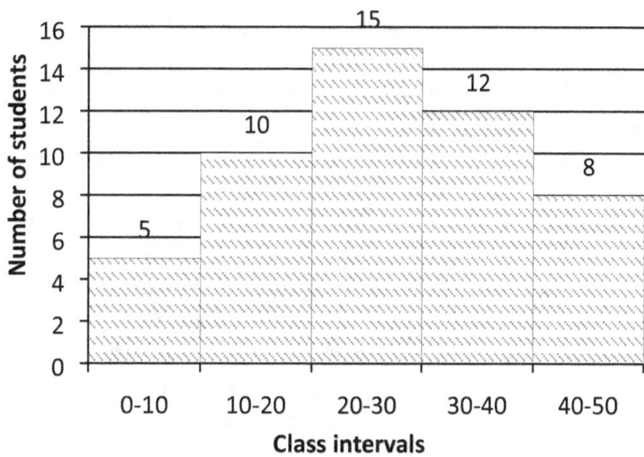

Histogram needs to be drawn carefully based on the type of data for which it is drawn. Following are the two cases that frequently need to be taken care of:

A) When the class interval is exclusive-

When the class intervals are exclusive (not continuous) the data must be converted to inclusive (continuous) form by modifying the class intervals.

To modify the class intervals if h is the difference between lower-limit of second-class interval and the upper-limit of the first-class interval, the limits can be recalculated as follows:

$$lower\ limit = lower\ limit - h/2$$

$$upper\ limit = upper\ limit + h/2$$

Example: Draw the histogram for the given data

Class interval	10-14	15-19	20-24	25-29	30-34
frequency	2	6	8	4	5

Solution: In the given data, $h = 15 - 14 = 1$.

Hence, rewriting the class intervals by subtracting $h/2$ from the lower limits and adding $h/2$ to the upper limits provides the following:

Class interval	9.5-14.5	14.5-19.5	19.5-24.5	24.5-29.5	29.5-34.5
frequency	2	6	8	4	5

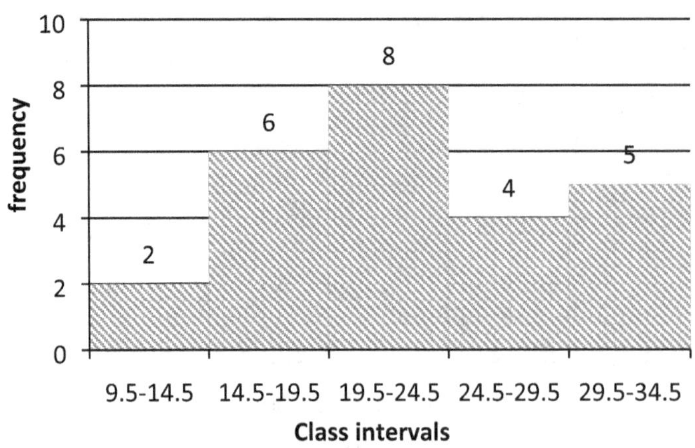

B) When the class intervals are not of equal width

When the class intervals are of different width the histogram should be drawn on the basis of frequency density.

$$Frequency\ density = \frac{Frequency}{class\ width}$$

Example: Draw the histogram for the given data

Class interval	0-5	5-10	10-16	16-22	22-30
frequency	30	80	36	96	64

Solution: To draw the histogram, the frequency density needs to be plotted against each class interval that can be calculated by dividing the frequency by class width.

Class interval	0-5	5-10	10-16	16-22	22-30
Frequency density	6 (=30/5)	16 (=80/5)	6 (=36/6)	6 (=96/6)	8 (=64/8)

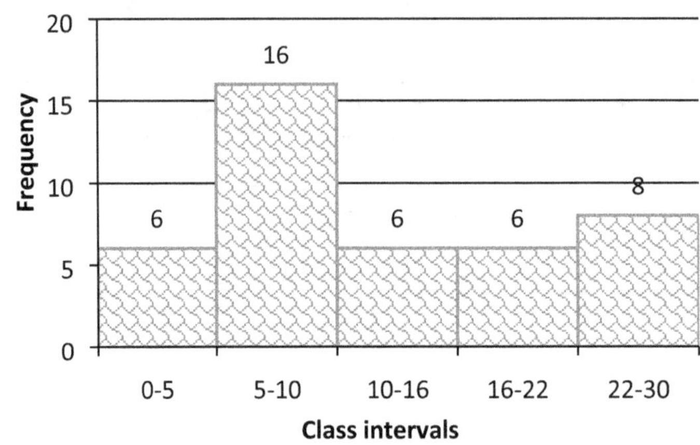

4.5 Frequency Polygon

A frequency polygon is a line graph for the class interval data. It can be drawn from a histogram, connecting the mid points of the upper bases of the rectangles by straight lines. It is not essential to plot a histogram to draw a polygon. It can be constructed directly from a given frequency distribution. It is useful when there are two or more groups to compare.

It is called a polygon as it has number of lines resembling a polygon.

4.6 Frequency Curve

A frequency-curve is a smooth curve for which the total area is taken to be unity. It is a limiting form of a histogram or frequency polygon. The frequency-curve for a distribution can be obtained by drawing a smooth free hand curve joining the mid-points of the upper sides of the rectangles forming the histogram. It is used when the numbers of class intervals are very large while the width of the class intervals is very small.

Example: Draw the frequency polygon and frequency curve for the following data

Class interval	20 - 25	25 - 30	30 - 35	35 - 40	40 - 45
Frequency	110	170	80	45	40

Solution: To draw the frequency polygon and frequency curve, the mid points need to be calculated with the extra points to be added at the top and the bottom. Also, the first and the last row are added with value of frequency as zero. The graph is shown for the frequency polygon shown by solid line and the frequency curve as the dashed lines

Class	Frequency	Mid points
15-20	0	17.5
20 - 25	110	22.5
25 - 30	170	27.5
30 - 35	80	32.5
35 - 40	45	37.5
40 - 45	40	42.5
45 - 50	35	47.5
50-55	0	52.5

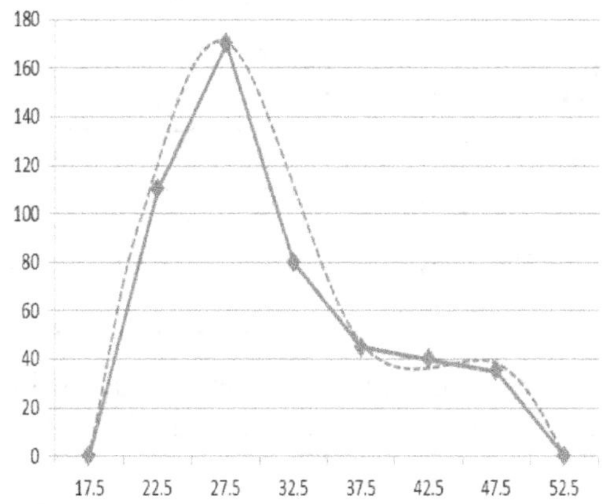

4.7 Ogive

Ogive is graph used to estimate number of data values that lie below or above a particular value in the data. Ogive or the cumulative frequency graphs are used to *find the median* of the given set of data. Ogives are also used in computing the *partition values*.

There are two types of ogives: less than and more than ogive. If both, less than and greater than ogives are drawn together, the point at which both the curve intersects gives the *median value*.

4.7.1 Less than ogive:

To draw a less than ogive, the frequencies of all preceding classes are added to the frequency of a class. This series is called a **less than cumulative series**. It is calculated by adding the first-class frequency to the second-class frequency and then to the third-class frequency and so on.

4.7.2 More than ogive:

To draw a more than ogive, the frequencies of the classes are obtained by subtracting the class frequencies from the total frequency. This series is called the **more than cumulative series**.

To draw the *less than ogive, the upper limits of the class intervals* are taken on the horizontal axis (x-axis) and their corresponding cumulative frequencies are marked on the vertical axis (y-axis). The free hand smooth graph joining these points is a less than ogive. *The line obtained in the less than Ogive is going upward*.

Similarly, to draw *the more than ogive the lower limits of the class intervals* are taken on the horizontal axis (x-axis) and their corresponding cumulative frequencies are marked on the vertical axis (y-axis). The free hand smooth graph joining these points is a more than ogive. *The line obtained in the less than Ogive is going downward.*

For drawing ogives, it should be ensured that the class intervals are continuous. Also, the class preceding the first class is assumed to exist with zero frequency in the less than ogive while the class succeeding the last class is assumed to exist with zero frequency in the more than ogive.

Example: Draw both the less than and more than ogive for the given data of the daily income of 50 workers of a factory.

Daily Income	200 - 250	250 - 300	300 - 350	350 - 400	400 - 450
Wages	10	12	8	14	6

Solution: To draw the ogive the less than and more than frequency are calculated as follows:

Daily Income	Wages	upper limit	less than frequency	lower limit	more than frequency
200 - 250	10	250	10	200	50
250 - 300	12	300	22	250	40

300 - 350	8	350	30	300	28
350 - 400	14	400	44	350	20
400 - 450	6	450	50	400	6

To draw the less than ogive, taking the upper limits of the class intervals with respect to the corresponding cumulative less than frequencies and to draw the more than ogive the lower limits of the class intervals are taken with respect to the corresponding cumulative more than frequencies.

Less than Ogive

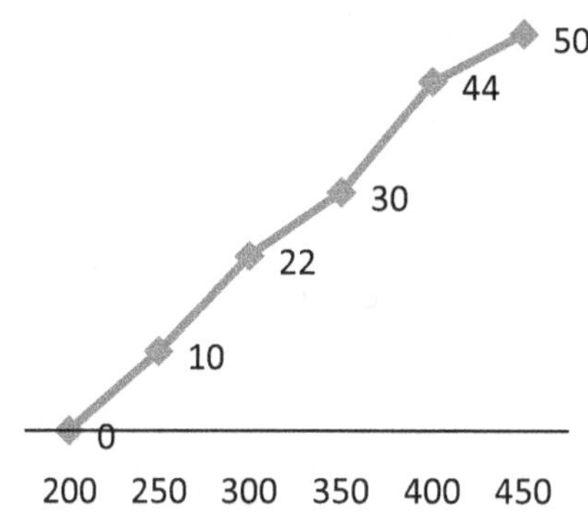

More than Ogive

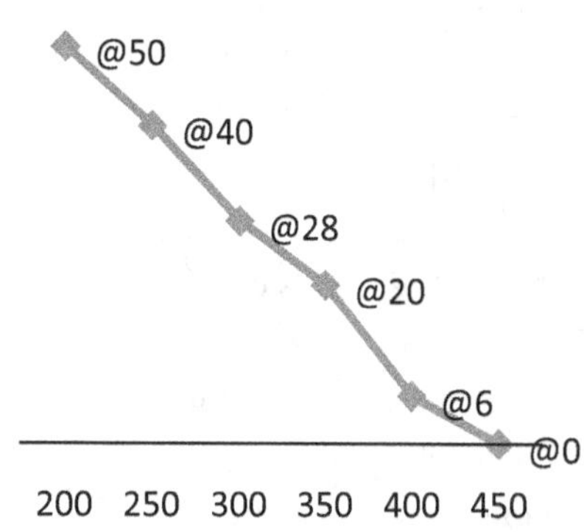

Chapter based Quiz

A) MCQs

1. Which diagram represents the various quantities as a sector of the circle?
a) Histogram
b) Pie diagram
c) Bar graph
d) Line graph

2. While creating the graphs, the dependent variable must be taken on _____ axis and the independent variable must be taken on _____ axis.
a) X, Y
b) Y, X
c) X, X
d) None of the above

3. A graph of the cumulative frequency distribution is called a
a) Histogram
b) Pie diagram
c) Ogive
d) Line graph

4. In a pie diagram the angles of the sector are calculated using the formula
a) (Component x Total)/360

b) (Component /Total) x360
c) (Component x Total)/100
d) (Component /Total) x 100

5. A frequency polygon is constructed by plotting frequency of the class interval with respect to the
a) upper limit of the class
b) lower limit of the class
c) mid-point of the class
d) class size of the class

6. A histogram is constructed using the ________
a) adjacent rectangles
b) non-adjacent rectangles
c) adjacent squares
d) non-adjacent squares

7. A bar diagram is constructed using the ________
a) adjacent rectangles
b) non-adjacent rectangles
c) adjacent squares
d) non-adjacent squares

8. The mode of a frequency distribution can be determined graphically by
a) Histogram
b) Frequency curve
c) Frequency polygon
d) Ogive

9. The median of a frequency distribution is found graphically with the help of
a) Histogram
b) Frequency curve
c) Frequency polygon
d) Ogive

10. Out of 50 persons in a company, 20 are vaccinated with one dose, 10 are vaccinated with 2 dose and
    20 are unvaccinated. The angle to present the unvaccinated people in the pie diagram is
a) 72
b) 90
c) 144
d) 185

11. Following are the cost of construction of a house, that was presented by pie diagram

Items	Expenditure
Cement	25%
Bricks	10%
Iron Rods	5%
Woods	10%

What is the degree of the sector for the cement?

a) 90

b) 180

c) 120

d) 270

12. From the data of Q_{11}, what is the degree of the sector for the iron rods?

a) 90

b) 18

c) 120

d) 270

13. Which of the following graph provides the partition value of a given data series?

a) Histogram

b) Frequency curve

c) Frequency polygon

d) Ogive

14. The height of a rectangle in a histogram shows the

a) width of the class

b) upper limit of the class

c) lower limit of the class

d) frequency of the class

15. In a pie chart, the total angle at the center of the circle is

a) $90°$

b) $180°$

c) $270°$

d) $360°$

16. If the cumulative frequency is plotted at the upper limit of the class interval, the curve is called

a) Histogram

b) Frequency curve

c) Less than Ogive

d) More than Ogive

17. Construction of a cumulative frequency table is useful in determining the

a) mean

b) median

c) mode

d) all the above three measures

18. The cumulative frequencies for the given data

Sections	A	B	C	D

| **No. of students** | 12 | 4 | 8 | 10 |

a) 12,16,24,34
b) 12,18,36,46
c) 10,18,22,34
d) None of the above

19. In the given pie diagram for the expenditure on the different items in the budget. Which item has the maximum share as compared to others?
a) Food
b) Miscellaneous
c) Clothing
d) Education

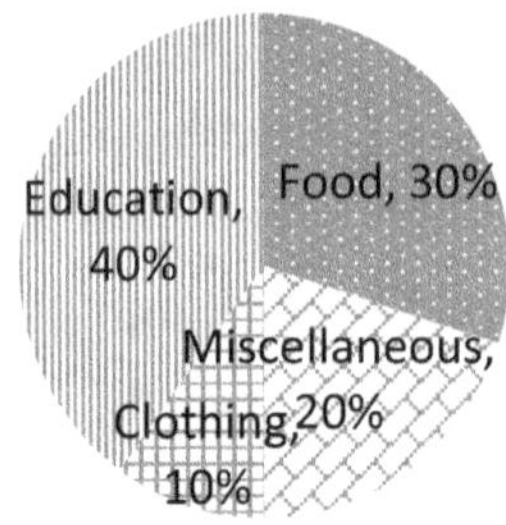

20. A pie chart is divided into 4 parts with the angles measuring as $x, x, 2x$ and $2x$ respectively. What is the value of x?
a) 60
b) 90
c) 80
d) 70

Answers:

1-b	2-b	3-c	4-b	5-c	6-a	7-b	8-a	9-d	10-c
11-a	12-b	13-d	14-d	15-d	16-c	17-b	18-a	19-d	20-a

B) True or False

1. The end points of the frequency curve are joined to the base line at the end of the frequency distribution taking the extra frequency interval with zero frequency.
2. Multiple bar diagram is drawn for related data values with common categories.
3. The bar diagram can only be drawn with bars in vertical directions.
4. Multiple bar graphs are also called as stacked bar graph.
5. In component bar graph the height of bar is always 100.
6. In percentage component bar graph the height of bars are always 100 with the percentage of different components shown differently.
7. If a component has 75% contribution to the total, the angle of the sector in the pie diagram is 180 degrees.
8. Area under the frequency curve is approximately same as the frequency polygon.

9. The class preceding the first class is assumed to exist with zero frequency in the less than ogive.
10. A pizza is divided among 4 friends. Three of the friends taken out the share with central angle as 65^0, 75^0, and 120^0. The angle measure of the remaining friend is 100.

Answers:

1-T   2-T   3-F   4-F   5-F   6-T   7-F   8-T   9-T   10-T

C) Fill in the blanks

1. The line graph of the frequency distribution is also called ________________.
2. The mid points of the top sides of the rectangles are joined in ______to give a frequency polygon.
3. ______________ is obtained by drawing a smooth curve from the frequency polygon.
4. Curve drawn from the cumulative frequency values is called _______.
5. An ogive is used to find the __________values.
6. For drawing graphs, the _________variable is taken on x-axis and ______variable is taken on y-axis.
7. If the angle of a pie diagram for a component is 90 degrees, the percentage value of the component is __________.
8. While plotting less than ogive, the cumulative frequencies are plotted at the ______limit of the class interval.
9. If data with class intervals for a distribution are 10-14, 15-19, 20-24 then the intervals can be converted to continuous form by subtracting ________ from the lower limits and adding _______ to the upper limits.
10. The class succeeding the last class is assumed to exist with zero frequency in the ________than ogive.

Answers:

1-frequency polygon   2-histogram   3-frequency curve   4-ogive   5-partition

6-independent, dependent   7-25   8-lower   9-0.5, 0.5   10- more

NOTES:

Chapter 5

Probability

5.1 Probability

The study of probability provides a basis for inferential statistics. It is a measure of how likely an event can occur.

For example:

Today there is 30% chance of snowfall in Shimla.

It is 99% sure that this book is useful in practicing the concepts of statistics.

By making these statements, probability of the event happening or not happening can be discussed. Hence, probability is the likelihood or chance that a particular event will occur or will not occur. Probabilities of an event can be written in fractions from 0 to 1, in decimals from 0 to 1 or in percentage from 0% to 100%.

- If an event is certain to happen, then the probability of the event is 1 or 100%.
- If an event will NEVER happen, then the probability of the event is 0 or 0%.
- If an event is just as likely to happen as not to happen, then the probability of the event is ½, 0.5 or 50%.

For example: If there is 98% probability of success of a new product in the market. It means that there is 2% chance that the product is not successful in the market. If the probability of success is 50%, then it indicates that the product is just as likely to be successful as it is not.

5.2 Fundamental concepts of probability

5.2.1 Union of sets

The union of two sets X and Y is denoted by X U Y, which is a set containing all the elements that either belongs to X or Y or both of them. An element is the member of X U Y if it belongs to either X or Y or both.

For example:
If X = {1, 2, 4} and Y = {6, 8}

X U Y = {1, 2, 4, 5, 6, 8}

5.2.2 Intersection of sets

Intersection is denoted by the symbol ∩. If there are two sets X and Y, the intersection of these two sets is denoted by X∩Y. The intersection of two sets X and Y, X∩ Y is a set containing all the elements that belongs to both X and Y.

For example:
If X = {1,4, 7} and Y = {4, 6,8}
X ∩Y = {4}

5.2.3 Disjoint Sets

Two sets are said to be disjoint if the intersection of the two sets is an empty set. Hence, there is no common element in both of the sets. When the two sets X and Y are disjoint, X ∩ Y= ϕ

For example:
If X = {1, 5, 7, 9} and Y = {6, 8, 10}
X ∩ Y= ϕ

5.2.4 Random Experiment

A process whose outcome is known but cannot be predicted in advance is called a random experiment.

For example:
- Tossing a coin can produce either a head or a tail.
- Rolling a dice can have any one of the six possible outcomes as {1, 2, 3, 4, 5, 6} on the upper face of the dice

A possible result of a random experiment is called its ***outcome***.

For example: In the experiment of tossing a coin twice, the possible outcomes are HH, HT, TH, TT.

5.2.5 Event

An event is the outcome that is observed on a single repetition of the experiment. Events are generally denoted by italics, uppercase letters (e.g., A and E_1, E_2, E_3, …).

For example:
- In the experiment to roll a dice, an event is obtaining a 2 on the upper face of the dice.
- In the experiment is to toss a fair coin, an event can be obtaining a head on the throw of a coin.

If an event has a single possible outcome, it is called a simple event.

5.2.6 Compound Event

The joint occurrence of two or more simple events is known as a compound event.

For example:

Tossing of two coins that give one head and one tail is a compound event.

5.2.7 Sample space

A set of all simple events of an experiment is called a sample space denoted as S.
For example:
- On throwing a coin, the outcome can be either a Head (H) or a Tail (T). Hence, Samples space $S = \{H, T\}$
- On rolling of a dice, the outcome is the number that appears on its upper face. Samples space $S = \{1,2,3,4,5,6\}$
- A pack of cards has 52 cards with 13 cards of each suit namely spades, clubs, hearts and diamonds. Cards of spades and clubs are black cards while the cards of hearts and diamonds are red cards. There are 4 honors of each unit as kings, queens and jacks called as face cards. Set of all 52 cards makes a sample space.
- On throwing two coins samples space $S = \{HH, HT, TH, TT\}$.

5.2.8 Independent Events

Two events are called as independent if happening of one event is independent of happening of another event.
For example:
On tossing a coin two times getting a tail on the first toss does not affect the possibility of getting a tail on the second toss.

5.2.9 Mutually Exclusive Events

Two or more events are said to be mutually exclusive if the occurrence of one event negates the occurrence of the other.
In other words, if one event is happening than the other event cannot happen.
For example:
- Tossing of a coin can give either a head or a tail but the two cannot occur together.
- While rolling a dice, two numbers 6 and 4 cannot occur on the upper face in one throw together at the same time.

If X and Y are two mutually exclusive events, then P (X $\cap$ Y) = 0

5.2.10 Equally Likely Outcomes

The outcomes are said to be equally likely if the chances of occurrence of the outcomes are same. In other words, one particular outcome cannot be expected in preference to other.

For example:
- In throwing of a single die, each number is equally likely to occur at the top.
- In tossing of an unbiased coin, head and tail, have an equal chance of occurrence.

5.2.11 Exhaustive Events

In a random experiment, two or more events are called as exhaustive events if the union of the events is a sample space. A set of events $(E_1, E_2, E_3, ...E_n)$ is called as exhaustive if $S = (E_1 \cup E_2 \cup E_3 ...\cup E_n)$.
For example:
If E_1 is an event of getting a black card and E_2 is another event of getting a red card from a pack of cards. Then
E_1 and E_2 are the exhaustive events whose union is the set of all cards.

5.2.12 Complementary Events

An event B is said to be the complementary event of event A, if occurrence of event A means negates the occurrence event B. The complementary event B of event A is denoted as A'.
$$\text{Hence, } P(A') = 1 - P(A)$$

For example:
- If the probability of getting success in an experiment is 0.65 then there is 0.35 probability of getting failure.
- If the probability of passing an exam is 75% then there is 25% chance of not passing in the exam.

5.3 Axioms of Probability

1. The probability of any event A, P(A), must be between 0 and 1 inclusive. That is,
$$0 < P(A) < 1.$$
2. If an event is impossible, the probability of the event is 0.
3. If an event is a certain to happen, the probability of the event is 1.
4. If $S = \{E1, E2, E3, ...En\}$, then $P(E1) + P(E2) + ... + P(En) = 1.$
5. The complement of an event A is the outcome that occurs when event A will not occur $A' = 1 - A$.

5.4 Techniques for counting experimental outcomes

There are some basic mathematical rules and techniques that are used in statistics for counting the number of experimental outcomes.

5.4.1 Combinations

The number of ways in which n items can be selected out of N, without replacement is given by the combination $^{N}C_n$ written as:
$$_nC^N = \frac{N!}{(N-n)!n!}$$
Here, $n!$ represents the factorial of n, that can be calculated as $n \times (n-1) \times (n-2) \times ...1$.
For example: $5! = 5 \times 4 \times 3 \times 2 \times 1 = 120$.

Example: In how many ways three students can be selected out of five?
Solution: The number of ways of selecting the 3 students out of 5 can be calculated as:

$$^5C_3 = \frac{5!}{3!2!}$$

$$= \frac{5 \times 4 \times 3 \times 2 \times 1}{(3 \times 2 \times 1)(2 \times 1)} = \frac{20}{2} = 10$$

Hence there are 10 ways to select 3 students out of 5.

Some Quick formulas:

Following are some formulas of factorial and combinations that are helpful in doing the calculation:

$$a) 0! = 1$$

$$b)\,^nC_r = \,^nC_{n-r}$$

$$c) n! = n \times (n-1)$$

$$d)\,^nC_0 = 1 \quad e)\,^nC_n = 1$$

$$f)\,^nC_1 = n$$

$$g)\,^nC_2 = n \times (n-1)/2!$$

$$h)\,^nC_3 = n \times (n-1) \times (n-2)/3!$$

5.4.2 Permutations

The number of ways in which n items are to be selected from a set of N items in a particular order is given by permutation. The n items selected in a different order would be considered as a different experimental outcome. The number of permutations of N items taken n at a time is given by

$$^NP_n = n! \times \,^NC_n = \frac{N!}{(N-n)!}$$

Example: In how many ways two colored pens can be ordered from a set of 5 colored pens?

Solution: Using permutations, taking N = 5 and n = 2

$$^5P_2 = \frac{5!}{3!} = 20$$

Thus, there are 20 outcomes if 2 pens are selected from a group of 5, when the order of selection is also considered. If these pens are labeled as A, B, C, D, and E, the 20 permutations are AB, BA, AC, CA, AD, DA, AE, EA, BC, CB, BD, DB, BE, EB, CD, DC, CE, EC, DE, and ED.

5.5 Calculating Probability

The probability of an event can be calculated as:

$$P(Event) = \frac{Number\ of\ ways\ event\ can\ occur}{Total\ number\ of\ possible\ outcomes}$$

Example 1: What is the probability that the spinner with three parts will stop on any of the part?

Solution: Here, the total numbers of possible outcomes are 3 and the spinner can stop on any one part. Hence the probability is 1/3.

Example 2: What is the probability to select an even number from a given set of numbers as $\{1, 2, 3, 4\}$?

Solution: Here, the total numbers of possible outcomes are 4 and the even numbers in the set are two as $\{2,4\}$. Hence the probability of selecting an even number is 2/4=1/2.

Example 3: What is the probability that a leap year has 53 Sundays?

Solution: In a leap year there are 366 days that can be written as 52 weeks and 2 days on dividing 366 by 7. The remaining 2 days can be any one of the following:

$\{SM, MT, TW, WTH, ThF, FS, SS\}$

Favorable events for Sunday are {SM, SS} which are 2 out of 7.
Hence probability is 2/7.

Example 4: What is the probability of getting a black ball from a bag having 6 white and 9 black balls?

Solution: The total numbers of balls in a bag $6 + 9 = 15$ and the number of outcomes in favor is 9. Hence probability is $9/15 = 3/5$.

Example 5: Find the probability of getting 2 heads in tossing of two coins.

Solution: The total numbers of possible outcomes in tossing of two coins are 4, $S = \{HH, HT, TH, TT\}$. Out of four, 2 heads can occur in only 1 way. Hence, probability is 1/4.

Example 6: What is the probability that if a card is drawn at random from a pack of cards, it will be a red card?

Solution: Here the total numbers of possible outcomes are 52, the total number of cards in a pack. Out of 52 there are 26 red cards. Hence, probability is 1/2.

Example 7: A bag contains 3 red and 6 blue socks. Two socks are drawn at random. Determine the probability that:
1. Both the socks are red
2. Both the socks are blue
3. One of the socks is red and the other is blue.

Solution: Total number of socks is 9.

1. The number of ways in which 2 red socks are selected out of 9 is $^9C_2 = 36$, which are the total number of possible outcomes. The number of ways in which 2 red socks are selected out of 3 red socks is $^3C_2 = 3.$

Also, the number of elements common to A and B are {3}. Hence $P(A \cap B) = 1/6$.

Using addition theorem, $P(A \cup B) = P(A) + P(B) - P(A \cap B)$

Hence,

$$P(A \cup B) = \frac{1}{6} + \frac{2}{6} - \frac{1}{6} = \frac{1}{3}$$

Hence the required probability of selecting 2 red socks is 3/36=1/12.

2. The number of ways in which 2 blue socks are selected out of 9 is
$^9C_2 = 36$ which are the total number of possible outcomes. The number of ways in which 2 blue socks are selected out of 6 blue socks is
$^6C_2 = 15.$ Hence the required probability of selecting 2 blue socks is 15/36=5/12.

3. The number of ways in which 2 socks are selected out of 9 is $^9C_2 = 36$, which are the total number of possible outcomes.

   The number of ways in which 1 red and 1 blue sock are selected out of 3 red and 6 blue socks is
   $^3C_1 \times {}^6C_1 = 18$. Hence the required probability of selecting 1 red and 1 blue sock is 18/36=1/2.

5.6 Addition Theorem

If A and B are two events in a sample space S. Then the probability of occurrence of at least one of the events A and B is given by

$$P(A \cup B) = P(A) + P(B) - P(A \cap B)$$

If A and B are the mutually exclusive events, $A \cap B = \varphi$.

$$\text{Then, } P(A \cup B) = P(A) + P(B).$$

Example 1: Given two mutually exclusive events A and B such P (A) is 0.4 and P (B)=0.2. Find P (A U B).

Solution: Using addition theorem, P (A U B) =P(A)+P(B)=0.6

Example 2: A dice is rolled. Find the probability that number 2 or 6 may appear on the top of a dice in a throw.

Solution: Event of getting number 2 or 6 on rolling a dice are the mutually exclusive events.

Let A is an event of getting number 2, $P(A) = 1/6$

Let B is an event of getting number 6, $P(B) = 1/6$.

Hence, using addition theorem, probability that number 2 or 6 may appear on the top of a dice is given as

$$P(A \cup B) = \frac{1}{6} + \frac{1}{6} = \frac{1}{3}$$

Example 3: What is the probability of getting a 3 or a number which is multiple of 3 in tossing a dice?

Solution: Event of getting number 3 and the number which is multiple of 3 in tossing a dice are not mutually exclusive events.

Let A is an event of getting number 3 on tossing a dice. Then $P(A) = 1/6$.

Let B is an event of getting a number which is multiple of 3 on tossing a dice. Here number of outcomes are 6 and the numbers of outcomes in favor are $\{3, 6\}$ hence 2.

Then $P(B) = 2/6$.

5.7 Multiplication Theorem

If A and B are two independent events, the probability of happening of both event A and B is

$P(A \cap B) = P(A) \times P(B)$

Example 1: If 3 coins are tossed, what is the probability of getting all heads?

Solution: Tossing of 3 coins is an independent event, with the probability of getting head on a single coin as 1/2. When 3 coins are tossed, the probability of getting heads on each of the 3 coins can be calculated using multiplication theorem as

$$P(A \cap B) = \left(\frac{1}{2}\right)\left(\frac{1}{2}\right)\left(\frac{1}{2}\right) = \frac{1}{8}$$

Example 2: If probability of drawing an ace from a pack of cards is $13/52 = 1/4$ and probability of drawing a queen from a pack of cards is $4/52 = 1/13$. What is the probability of getting a queen of ace?

Solution: The event of drawing an ace from a pack of cards and the event of drawing a queen from a pack of cards are independent. Hence the probability of getting a queen of aces can be calculated as:

$P(A \cap B) = (1/4)\,(1/13) = 1/52$.

5.8 Some Important deductions of Multiplication Theorem

Let A and B are the two independent events, then by multiplication theorem, the probability of happening of both event A and B is $P(A \cap B) = P(A) \times P(B)$

Extending the theorem, the probability of not happening of both event A and B is $(1\text{-}P(A)) \times (1 - P(B)) = P(A')P(B')$

The probability of happening of at least one of the event A or B is $1 - P(A')P(B')$

The probability of happening of A only is

$$P(A \cap B') = P(A) - P(A \cap B)$$
$$= P(A) - P(A)P(B)$$
$$= P(A)(1 - P(B))$$
$$= P(A)P(B')$$

The probability of happening of B only is

$$P(A' \cap B) = P(B) - P(A \cap B)$$
$$= P(B) - P(A)P(B)$$
$$= P(B)(1 - P(A))$$
$$= P(B)P(A')$$

The probability of happening of exactly one of A and B is

$$P(A' \cap B) + P(A \cap B') = P(A \cup B) - P(A \cap B)$$

Chapter based Quiz

A) MCQs

1. When a dice is thrown, the probability of getting an odd number less than 4 is
   a) 1/2
   b) 1/3
   c) 1/4
   d) 2/5

2. A card is drawn from a deck of 52 cards. The probability of getting an ace of heart is
   a) 1/52
   b) 1/13
   c) 1/14
   d) 2/15

3. The probability of getting a damaged screw in a lot of 500 is 0.05. The number of damaged screws in the lot is
   a) 12
   b) 25
   c) 36
   d) 52

4. One ticket is drawn at random from a bag containing tickets numbered 1 to 10. The probability that the selected ticket has a number which is a multiple of 5 is
   a) 1/2
   b) 2/5
   c) 1/5
   d) 2/3

5. A number is chosen from 1 to 10. The probability that the number is a prime number is

a) 1/3
b) 2/5
c) 1/4
d) 2/7

6. One card is drawn from a pack of 52 cards. What is the probability of drawing an ace?
a) 1/12
b) 1/14
c) 1/11
d) 1/13

7. One card is drawn from a pack of 52 cards. What is the probability of drawing a heart of spade?
a) 1/4
b) 1/2
c) 1/26
d) 1/52

8. A dice is thrown. What is the probability of getting a number less than 6?
a) 1/4
b) 1/3
c) 5/6
d) 1/6

9. A dice is thrown. What is the probability of getting a number which is multiple of 2?
a) 1/4
b) 1/2
c) 5/6
d) 1/6

10. If 2/11 is the probability of an event A. What is probability of not happening of A?
a) 4/11
b) 1/6
c) 9/11
d) 1/11

11. What are number of elements in the sample space of tossing a coin two times is
a) 8
b) 6
c) 4
d) 10

12. What is the probability of drawing a white ball from a bag containing 3 black balls and 4 white balls?
a) 3/7
b) 4/7
c) 5/7
d) 1/7

13. If an event is certain to happen, the probability of happening of the event is?
a) 1
b) 2
c) 0
d) ½

14. What is the sum of probability of all the events of a sample space?
a) 0
b) 1
c) 1/3
d) 1/6

15. What is the probability of getting an even number greater than 4 in toss of a dice?
a) 1/2
b) 1/6
c) 1/5
d) 2/3

16. What is the probability of getting an even number or a number greater than 4 in toss of a dice?
a) 1/2
b) 1/6
c) 1/5
d) 2/3

17. In tossing a dice, what is the probability of getting an odd number more than 4?
a) 2/3
b) 1/3
c) 3/4
d) 1/6

18. Event of getting an '8' on the die
a) is a simple event
b) is an impossible event
c) has probability 1
d) exhaustive event

19. If $S = \{E1, E2, E3\}$, $P(E1) = 1/3$, $P(E2)1/6$. What is the value of $P(E3)$?
a) 1
b) 1/2
c) 0
d) 1/6

20. Probability of selecting a coin is 1/4; Probability of selecting a dice is 1/5. Find probability that both of them selected.
a) 1/20
b) 12/35

c) 3/5
d) 9/20

21. In a bag there are 100 bulbs out of which 30 are defective. A bulb is selected at random. What is the probability of selecting a good bulb?
a) 0.5
b) 0.3
c) 1
d) 0.7

22. If a dice is tossed, what is the probability that number 3 or less will appear on the top?
a) 1/6
b) 1/3
c) 1/2
d) 5/6

23. Which of the following can be the probability of an event?
a) −0.4
b) 1.01
c) 8/2
d) 5/7

24. If the chances of occurrence of the events in a random experiment is same, then the events are called
a) Equally likely
b) Mutually Exclusive
c) Independent
d) Exhaustive events

25. Chance to get success in an experiment by using the two different approaches are 1/2 and 1/5. What is the probability that the success will be gained by any one of the approaches?
a) 2/5
b) 3/2
c) 1/2
d) 1/5

26. For given Q. 25 above. What is the probability that the success will be gained by at least one of the approaches?
a) 2/5
b) 3/5
c) 4/5
d) 1/5

27. For given Q. 25 above. What is the probability that the success will not be achieved?
a) 2/5
b) 3/5

c) 4/5
d) 1/5

28. If $P(B) = 3/5$, $P(B')$ is given as
a) 1/5
b) 2/5
c) 3/5
d) 4/5

29. *If* $P(A)$ is 2/5, $P(B)$ is 2/5, $P(A \cap B)$ is 3/5, what is the value of $P(A \cup B)$?
a) 1/5
b) 2/5
c) 3/5
d) 4/5

30. If $P(A)$ is 3/4, $P(A \cap B)$ is 1/4, $P(A \cup B)$ is 3/4. What is the value of $P(B)$?
a) 1/2
b) 1/3
c) 1/4
d) 1/5

31. Which of the following can be the probabilities of the events E_1, E_2, E_3, when $S = \{E_1, E_2, E_3\}$?
a) 1/2, 1/2,1
b) 1/2, -1,1/2
c) -1/2, 1, 1/2
d) 1/3,0, -1/3

32. If A and B are the two independent events with $P(A) = 1/2$, $P(B) = 2/5$.

    A. What is the value of $P(A \cap B)$?
    a) 1/5
    b) 2/5
    c) 3/5
    d) 4/5

    B. What is the value of $P(A \cap B')$?
    a) 1/5
    b) 3/4
    c) 3/10
    d) 4/5

    C. What is the value of $P(A' \cap B)$?
    a) 1/5
    b) 2/5
    c) 3/5
    d) 4/5

D. What is the value of $P(A' \cup B')$?
a) 1/5
b) 2/5
c) 3/5
d) 4/5

33. The number of elements in the sample space of tossing three coins together is _______________.
a) 8
b) 6
c) 4
d) 10

34. If the two dice are thrown simultaneously, what is the number of elements in the sample space?
a) 6
b) 24
c) 12
d) 36

35. If the two dice are thrown simultaneously, what is the probability of getting total of 9?
a) 1/6
b) 1/4
c) 1/7
d) 1/9

36. If the two dice are thrown simultaneously, what is the probability of getting total of 10?
a) 1/16
b) 1/14
c) 1/12
d) 1/9

37. A bag contains 3 red, 4 white and 5 blue balls. Two balls are drawn at random. What is the probability that both the balls are white?
a) 1/15
b) 1/11
c) 1/12
d) 1/14

Answers:

1-b	2-a	3-b	4-c	5-b	6-d
Here favorable outcomes are {1,3}	There is only one card which is in favor of the event.	0.05=x/500 x=25	Multiple of 5 from 1 to 10 are {5,10} Hence, prob=2/10	Prime numbers from 1 to 10 are {1, 3, 5, 7}. Hence,	There are 4 aces in a pack of cards. Hence, prob=4/52

7-d	**8-c**	**9-b**	**10-c**	prob=4/10	
				11-c	**12-b**
There is only one heart of spade in the pack of cards. Hence, prob=1/52	Numbers less than 6 are {1,2,3,4,5} Hence, prob=5/6	Number multiple of 2 are {2,4,6} Hence, prob=3/6=1/2	1-2/11=9/11	{HH, TT, HT, TH}	4/ (4+3) =4/7

13-a **14-b**

15-b There is only one even number greater than 4 {6}. Hence, prob=1/6

16-d P (even no.) =3/6 P(no.>4) =2/6 P (even no. greater than 4) =1/6. Use addition theorem to find the right ans

17-d Odd number more than 4= {5}

18-b

19-b $P(E3) = 1-P(E2)- P(E1)$

20-a Using multiplication theorem.

21-d Prob of selecting a good bulb=1- prob of selecting a defective bulb. =1-0.3

22-c Here outcomes in favor are {1,2,3}. Hence, probability=3/6= 1/2

23-d Probability cannot be negative or more than 1

24-a

25-c
$$=\left(\frac{1}{2}\right)\left(1-\frac{1}{5}\right)+\left(1-\frac{1}{2}\right)\left(\frac{1}{5}\right)$$
$$=\left(\frac{1}{2}\right)\left(\frac{4}{5}\right)+\left(\frac{1}{2}\right)\left(\frac{1}{5}\right)$$
$$=1/2$$

26-b
$$=1-\left(1-\frac{1}{2}\right)\left(1-\frac{1}{5}\right)$$
$$=1-\left(\frac{1}{2}\right)\left(\frac{4}{5}\right)$$
$$=3/5$$

27-a
$$=\left(1-\frac{1}{2}\right)\left(1-\frac{1}{5}\right)$$
$$=\left(\frac{1}{2}\right)\left(\frac{4}{5}\right)$$
$$=2/5$$

28-b
$$=\left(1-\frac{3}{5}\right)$$
$$= 2/5$$

29-a Using addition theorem
$$=\frac{2}{5}+\frac{2}{5}-\frac{3}{5}$$
$$=1/5$$

30-c Using addition theorem
$$\frac{3}{4}=\frac{3}{4}+P(B)-\frac{1}{4}$$
$$P(B) = 1/4$$

31-c Sum of probabilities of the events in a sample space should be 1

32(A)-a $P(A \cap B) = P(A)P(B)$

32(B)-c $P(A \cap B')$ $=P(A)-P(A \cap B)$

32(C)-a $P(A' \cap B)$ $=P(B)-P(A \cap B)$

32(D)-d $P(A' \cup B')$ $=1-P(A \cap B)$

33-a

34-d There are 6 elements on one dice. Hence each number on the first dice can appear with each number on the other. Hence total is 6 x 6=36.

35-d Sum of two dice can be 9 when the order pairs are {(3,6), (4,5), (5,4), (6,3)}. Hence prob=4/36=1/9.

36-c Sum of two dice can be 10 when the order pairs are {(4,6), (5,5), (6,4)}. Hence prob=3/36=1/12.

37-b 2 balls can be selected out of total 12 in ways
$$^{12}C_2 = \frac{12\times11}{2} = 66$$
selecting 2 white balls out of 4 is
$$^{4}C_2 = \frac{4\times3}{2} = 6$$
The probability is hence 6/66=1/11.

B) Fill in the blanks

1. If A and B are two independent events, then P (A ∩ B) is equal to_____________.
2. If X and Y are two mutually exclusive events, then P (X ∩Y) is equal to________.

3. Probability of getting an odd number if a dice is thrown is________.
4. The probability of getting a sum as 2 if two dice are thrown together is_____________.
5. The probability of getting two heads on tossing two coins is __________.
6. The probability of getting a sum of two dice values a prime number is _____________.
7. If the probability of winning a game is 0.35, the probability of losing is________.
8. If a number is selected at random from the first 10 natural numbers, the probability of the selected number to be a multiple of 2 and 3 is___________.
9. If a number is selected at random from the first 10 natural numbers, the probability of the selected number to be a multiple of 2 or 3 is________.
10. If A and B are two mutually exclusive events. Then P (A + B) is equal to _____________.

Answers:

1-P(A)P(B)	**2**-zero	**3**-1/2	**4**-1/18	**5**-1/2
6-15/36=5/12	**7**-0.65	**8**-1/10	**9**-7/10	**10**-P(A)+P(B).

NOTES:

____
____
____
____
____
____
____
____
____
____
____
____
____
____
____
____
____
____
____
____
____

Chapter 6

Probability Distribution

Many times, in different situations there is a need to take decision that involves uncertainty due to the different possible outcomes. This chapter will provide insight to the probabilities of various outcomes that can occur in an experiment with the concept of random variable and probability distribution.

6.1 Important concepts

6.1.1 Random variable

A numerical value which is determined by chance for each outcome of a procedure can be written in a variable. The variable that stores this value is called a random variable.

Few examples of experiments that lead to outcomes to be stored in a random variable are as follows:
a) Measuring heights of students in a sports club.
b) Maintaining a roaster of mileage for a new launched car.
c) Tossing a coin and observing the face that appears on the top.
d) Testing products in a company to be defective or acceptable before sending out for sale.
e) Measuring fog density in a winter season.

6.1.2 Broad classification of random variable

A random variable may be either discrete or continuous.
A discrete random variable can take only a finite or countably infinite number of distinct values such as 0, 1, 2, …, n.
A continuous random variable can take any numerical value in an interval or in a collection of intervals. A continuous random variable is usually the result of experimental outcomes that are based on measurement scales.
For example: The numbers of e-mails sent during a particular time period, the numbers of emergency calls to a doctor on a given day, the number of vehicles arriving at a service station, and so on, are a few examples of discrete random variables.

On the other hand, outcomes of measuring volume, time, distance, weight, and temperature can be explained by continuous random variables.

Another example:

- The number of vehicles passing on a road during a time interval of 2 minutes may vary from 0 to n. These outcome (0, 1, 2, 3, 4, … n) are the values of a **discrete random variable.**

- The weight of the students of tenth class in a school when measured on a digital scale cannot be explained by a whole number because weight can be any number as 60.2, 54.3 and so on. Thus, variable to stores outcomes of weight is a **continuous random variable.**

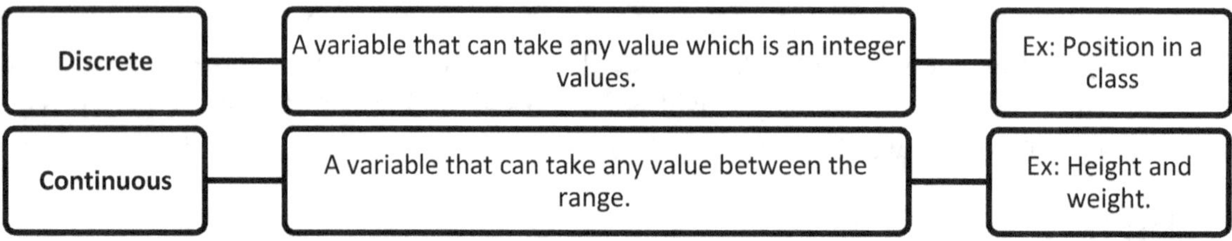

6.1.3 Probability distribution:

A description that gives the probability for each value of the random variable can be expressed in the form of a graph, table, or formula is known as the *probability distribution*.

Thus, probability distribution for a random variable specifies how probabilities are distributed. For a random variable x, the probability distribution is described by a *probability function* $f(x)$ that provides the probability for each value of the random variable.
The probability distribution can be classified according to the type of random variable as discrete or continuous and has named as *discrete probability distribution or continuous probability distribution*.

In this chapter for the discrete probability distribution, the Binomial and Poisson distribution are discussed while under the continuous distribution only the normal distribution is discussed.

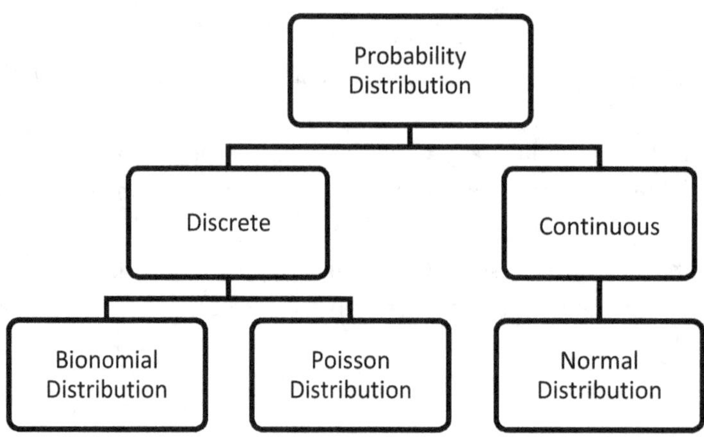

For example:

If x is a discrete random variable that denotes the number of books sold online then it can assume any value from 0, 1, 2, to n. From the analysis of sales in the past 100 days on the number of books sold, there were 25 days when zero books are sold, 45 days when one book is sold, 25 days with two books are sold, and 5 days with three books sold.

In terms of probability of outcomes, P (0) indicates the probability of zero books sold day, P (1) indicates the probability of one book sold, P (2) is the probability of two books sold in a day that can be calculated as follows:

x (Number of books sold online)	*Number of days*	*$P(x)$ (Probability)*
0	25	P (0) =0.25 (25/100)
1	45	P (1) =0.45
2	25	P (2) =0.25
3	5	P (3) =0.5
Total	**100**	**1**

Here, $P(x)$ is the probability distribution of the random variable x.

6.1.4 Probability Function

A function that gives the probability of a random variable to take a particular value is called a ***probability function***. It has been named differently for both discrete and continuous cases.

A probability mass function (pmf) is a function that gives the probability of a discrete random variable while for the continuous random variable the function is called as **probability density function (pdf).**

6.2 Discrete Probability Distribution

6.2.1 Mean and Variance

The measure of central tendency (mean) and the measure of dispersion (variance) can be calculated for the discrete probability distribution as follows:

Mean: Mean or expected value of a discrete probability distribution is given as

$$\mu = E(x) = \sum xP(x)$$

here, $E(x)$ is called the expected value which represents the mean value μ of outcome x, and can be calculated as the product of the outcome x with the probability of that outcome $P(x)$.

For example:

The expected value for the number of books sold in a day can be calculated as 1.1(approx. 1) for the example discussed above as follows:

x	$P(x)$	$x\,P(x)$
0	0.25=25/100	0
1	0.45=45/100	0.45
2	0.25=25/100	0.5
3	0.05=5/100	0.15
Total	1	1.1

Variance: Variance of a discrete probability distribution is given as

$$\sigma^2 = \sum (x - \mu)^2 P(x)$$

Here, $P(x)$ is the probability of the outcome x in a random experiment, and μ is the mean.

For example:

The variance for the number of books sold during a day can be calculated as a product of the probability with the square of the difference of data values from mean (taking $\mu = 1.1$) as follows:

x	**P(x)**	$x - \mu$	$(x - \mu)^2$	$(x - \mu)^2 P(x)$
0	0.25	-1.1	1.21	0.3025
1	0.45	-0.1	0.01	0.0045
2	0.25	0.9	0.81	0.2025
3	0.05	1.9	3.61	0.1805
Total	1	1.6	5.64	**0.69**

Hence, variance is calculated as

$$\sigma^2 = \sum (x - \mu)^2 P(x) = 0.69$$

As standard deviation is the square root of the variance, hence is given as

$$\sigma = \sqrt{0.69} = 0.83$$

6.2.2 The Binomial Distribution (B.D)

Bi" means "two" (like a bicycle has two wheels). Binomial distribution is the most commonly used distribution that deals with the random experiment with two results.

For example:
- Tossing a coin: results in either Head (H) or Tail (T)
- Passing in an exam: results in either pass or failure.
- Winning a lottery: either winning or losing.

Binomial distribution requirements

A binomial probability distribution results from an experiment that meets the following requirements:
1. The number of trials in an experiment must be fixed.
2. The trials must be independent. (The outcome of any individual trial should not affect the probabilities in the other trials.)

3. Each trial must have all outcomes classified into two categories (success and failure).
4. The probability of a success remains same in all trials.

Probability mass function of binomial distribution

The probability mass function for calculating probability of $x = r$ success in n trials in an experiment that follows binomial probability distribution is given as:

$$P(x = r) = {}^nC_r\, p^r q^{n-r}, \ r = 0 \ \text{to} \ n$$

Here, p is the probability of success of each event and q is the probability of failure such that $p + q = 1$. Thus, the probability of happening of r success out of n is given by probability mass function with n and p as the **parameters of B.D.**

Mean and Variance

For a binomial experiment with n trials, and the probability of success p for a given trial, the mean and variance are given as:

$$\text{Mean: } \mu = np$$

$$\text{Variance: } \sigma^2 = npq$$

$$\text{Standard deviation: } \sigma = \sqrt{npq}$$

If an experiment (each consisting of n trials) is repeated N times, the probability mass function is given as:

$$P(x = r) = N\,{}^nC_r\, p^r q^{n-r}, \ r = 0 \ \text{to} \ n$$

Examples of Binomial distribution

1. The probability of winning a lottery draw is 0.2. If a person participates in the draw 20 times, what is the probability that he will win 5 times?

   Solution: The probability of success in a lottery draw is p=0.2. The number of times is $n = 20$ and 5 is the number of successes out of 20. Hence, applying the formula of binomial distribution

   $$P(x = 5) = {}^{20}C_5 p^5 q^{15}, with\, p = 0.2; q = 1 - 0.2 = 0.8$$

   Hence,
   $$P(x = 5) = {}^{20}C_5 (0.2)^5 (0.8)^{20-5} = \frac{20!}{5!15!}(0.2)^5(0.8)^{15}$$

   $$P(x = 5) = 0.174$$
   Hence, the probability of the person to win 5 times out of 20 is 0.174.

2. In an Olympic event the player hits a target 70% of the time. He fires five shots at the target. What is the probability that exactly 3 shots hit the target?

   Solution: The probability of success to hit the target is $p = 70/100 = 0.7$. The number of times is $n = 5$ and 3 is the number of successes out of 5. Hence, using the formula of binomial distribution

$$P(x = 3) = {}^5C_3 p^3 q^{5-3} \text{ with } p = 0.7; q = 1 - 0.7 = 0.3$$

$$P(x = 3) = \frac{5!}{3!2!}(0.7)^3(0.3)^{5-3}$$

$$= 10(0.7)^3(0.3)^2$$

$$= 0.3087$$

Hence, the probability of player to hit 3 out of 5 shots at the target is 0.3087.

3. Discuss about the statement that says that the mean of a binomial distribution is 3 and variance is 4.

Solution: In the binomial distribution, n and p are the parameters with mean as $np = 3$ and variance $npq = 4$

On solving, the expressions for mean and variance provides the value of q=4/3,

Since, the value of either p or q can't be more than one.

Hence the given statement is incorrect.

4. The mean and variance of binomial distribution are 4 and 4/3. Find P (x=2).

Solution: Given, the value of mean is 4 and variance is 4/3.

Here, $np = 4, npq = 4/3 \Rightarrow 4q = 4/3 \text{ or}, q = 1/3$ Hence, $p = 1 - 1/3 = 2/3$ From

$np = 4, n = 4/p \Rightarrow n = 6$ Using formula, $P(x = 2) = {}^6C_2 p^2 q^4 = \frac{6!}{4!2!}\left(\frac{2}{3}\right)^2\left(\frac{1}{3}\right)^4$

$$= 15\left(\frac{4}{729}\right)$$

$$= 0.082$$

5. In a fair coin tossing experiment, what is the probability of getting 3 or fewer heads in 10 trials?

Solution: The probability of r success in n trials in a binomial experiment is given by

$P(x = r) = {}^nC_r p^r q^{n-r}, r = 0 \text{ to } n.$ here, $p = q = 1/2, n = 10, r = 3$

Probability of getting 3 or fewer heads in 10 trials can be calculated as follows using the addition rule

$$P(x \le 3) = P(x = 0) + P(x = 1) + P(x = 2) + P(x = 3)$$

$$P(x \le 3) = {}^{10}C_0 p^0 q^{10-0} + {}^{10}C_1 p^1 q^{10-1} + {}^{10}C_2 p^2 q^{10-2} + {}^{10}C_3 p^3 q^{10-3}$$

$$= q^{10} + 10 p^1 q^9 + 45 p^2 q^8 + 120 p^3 q^7$$

$$= \left(\frac{1}{2}\right)^{10} + 10\left(\frac{1}{2}\right)^1\left(\frac{1}{2}\right)^9 + 45\left(\frac{1}{2}\right)^2\left(\frac{1}{2}\right)^8 + 120\left(\frac{1}{2}\right)^3\left(\frac{1}{2}\right)^7$$

Using formula,

$$= 0.1718$$

6.2.3 The Poisson Distribution (P.D.)

The Poisson distribution is another discrete probability distribution which is often used for describing the behaviour of rare events (with small probabilities). The binomial distribution describes distribution of two possible outcomes of an event: either success or failure. The Poisson distribution focuses on the number of discrete occurrences of an event over an interval.

For example:

- The number of accident arrivals at an automobile service station in last 10 hours.
- The number of patients arriving at a health centre diagnosed with a rare disease every day.
- The number of defects per unit length in a cloth manufactured by a company during a month.
- The number of typo errors per page in a book.

Poisson distribution requirements

A Poisson probability distribution results from an experiment that meets the following requirements:
- The random variable x is the number of occurrences of an event over some interval.
- The occurrences must be random.
- The occurrences must be independent of each other.
- The occurrences must be uniformly distributed over the used interval.

Probability mass function of Poisson distribution

The probability of x occurrences in an interval can be calculated with the following formula of probability mass function of Poisson distribution:

$$P(X = x) = \frac{e^{-\lambda}\lambda^x}{x!}$$

Where $P(x)$ is the probability of x occurrences in an interval, λ is the expected value or mean number of occurrences in an interval, and $e = 2.7183$ (base of natural logarithm system)

Poisson distribution as an approximation to binomial distribution

The Poisson distribution is sometimes used to approximate the binomial distribution when n is large and p is small. Thus, when the number of trials is large but the probability of success is small, binomial distribution can be approximated by the Poisson distribution.
Hence the mean of the binomial distribution is used to approximate the mean of the Poisson distribution. Thus,

$$P(X = x) = \frac{e^{-\lambda}\lambda^x}{x!}; \lambda = np$$

Mean and Variance

For an event satisfying the Poisson distribution with n trials, and the probability of occurrence as p, the mean and variance are given as

$$Mean = \lambda = np;$$
$$Variance = \lambda$$
$$\text{Standard deviation} = \sqrt{\lambda}$$

Examples of Poisson distribution

1. On investigating the number of patients suffering from a rare disease visiting hospitals revealed that on an average 8 patients are reporting in the hospital per month. If the number of cases follows Poisson distribution. What is the probability of exactly 4 cases reported in a month?

   Solution: Here, $\lambda = 8, x = 4$

   Using probability formula for Poisson distribution gives:

   $$P(X = 4) = \frac{e^{-\lambda}\lambda^4}{4!}$$

   $$= \frac{e^{-8}(8)^4}{4!}$$

   $$= 0.05725$$

2. A printing company has 25 printing machines. The probability that any one of them will not function during a day is 0.02. What is the probability that exactly two machines will be out of order on the same day?

   Solution: Here, $n = 25, p = 0.02, x = 2$.

   Therefore $\lambda = np = 25 \times 0.02 = 0.5$

   Putting all these values in the probability formula for Poisson distribution gives:

   $$P(X = 2) = \frac{e^{-\lambda}\lambda^2}{2!}$$

   $$= \frac{e^{-0.5}(0.5)^2}{2!}$$

   $$= 0.07581$$

3. 2% products of a company are defective. Find the probability of getting no defective product in a sample of 100 articles using Poisson distribution.

   Solution: Here, $n = 100, p = 2/100 = 0.02, x = 0$.

   Therefore $\lambda = np = 100 \times 0.02 = 2$

   Putting all these values in the probability formula for Poisson distribution gives:

   $$P(X = 0) = \frac{e^{-\lambda}\lambda^0}{0!}$$

   $$= e^{-2}(0! = 1, \lambda^0 = 1)$$

   $$= 0.1353$$

4. In a book for proof reading, author found that there are 25 typo errors in a book with total pages 500. If the errors are randomly distributed through the book, what is the probability that a randomly selected 20 pages are free from error?

   Solution: Here, the probability of 25 errors randomly distributed over 500 pages is p =25/500=0.05, For finding the probability that randomly selected 20 pages are free from error, x = 0, and n=20. Therefore,

   $$\lambda = np = 20 \times \frac{25}{500} = 1$$

   Using the values of λ and n in the probability formula for Poisson distribution gives:

$$P(X = 0) = \frac{e^{-\lambda}\lambda^0}{0!}$$

$$= e^{-1}(0! = 1, \lambda^0 = 1)$$

$$= 0.36787$$

5. If a random variable follows Poisson distribution has $P(X = 1) = P(X = 2)$. Find $P(X = 4)$

Solution: As, $P(X = 1) = P(X = 2)$

Using formula,

$$\frac{e^{-\lambda}\lambda^1}{1!} = \frac{e^{-\lambda}\lambda^2}{2!}$$

On solving, $\lambda = 2$. Hence,

$$P(X = 4) = \frac{e^{-2}2^4}{4!}$$

$$= 0.09022$$

6.3 Continuous Probability Distribution

There are various types of continuous probability distributions in statistics. One of the most important continuous probability distributions is normal distribution. As for discrete random variables, the probability mass function provides the probability for each value of the random variable. Similarly for continuous probability distributions, probability density function provides the area under the curve for $f(x)$ which is the probability that the continuous random variable x assumes a value in the interval; with the property that the area under the whole curve is unity.

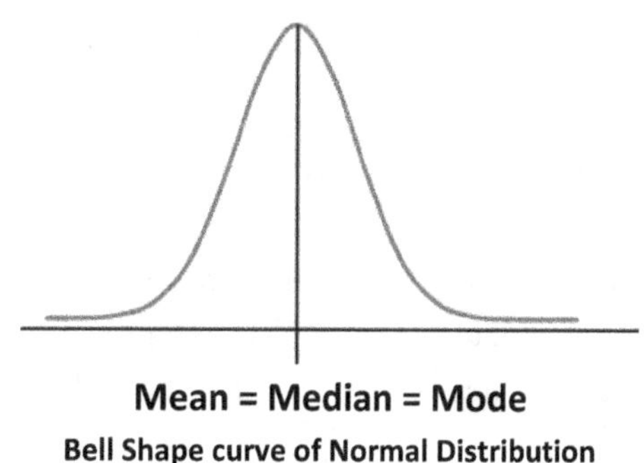

Bell Shape curve of Normal Distribution

6.3.1 Normal Probability Distribution

The normal probability distribution possesses some important properties defined as follows:
1. Normal probability distribution has a bell-shaped curve.
2. The bell shape curve in normal probability distribution is symmetrical about mean.
3. In a normal distribution, mean, median, and mode are same.
4. Two tails of the normal curve (left-tail and right-tail) extend indefinitely in both the direction but never touch the horizontal axis.
5. The shape and location of the normal curve changes with change in mean and standard deviation.
6. The standard deviation determines the scatteredness of the normal curve. Large the value of standard deviation more is the variability in the data.

7. Area under the normal curve specifies the probabilities for the normal random variable.
    i. Approximately 68% of the values of a random variable lie with in ±1 standard deviation from the mean.
    ii. Approximately 95.5% of the values of a random variable lie with in ±2 standard deviation from the mean.
    iii. Approximately 99.7% of the values of a random variable lie within ±3 standard deviation from the mean.

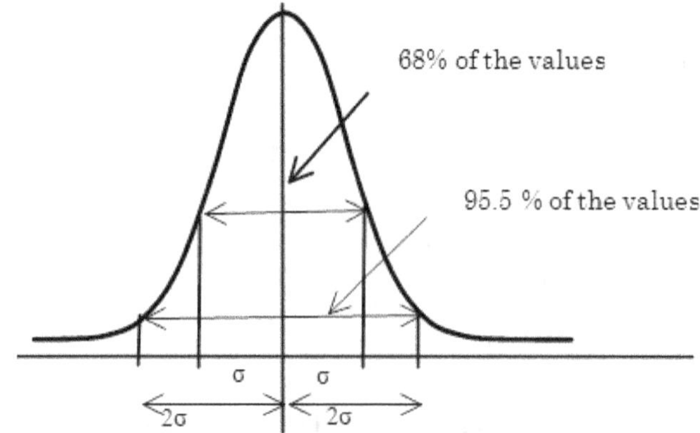

6.3.2 Probability Density Function of a Normal Distribution

The probability density function of the normal probability distribution with two parameters mean and standard deviation is given as follows:

$$f(x) = \frac{1}{\sigma\sqrt{2\pi}} e^{-\frac{1}{2}\left(\frac{x-\mu}{\sigma}\right)^2} \quad for \; -\infty < x < \infty$$

$$e = 2.7183 \quad \pi = 3.1416$$

where

,μ and σ are the population mean and standard deviation respectively.

6.3.3 Standard Normal Probability Distribution

To find the probability of the continuous random variable in an interval, P (a <x <b), the area under the appropriate normal curve needs to be calculated. To simplify the tabulation of these areas, each value of x is standardized by expressing it as a z-score. The standard formula for calculating the z-score is:

$$z = \frac{x - \mu}{\sigma}$$

The z-score can be defined as the number of standard deviations for which value x is above or below the mean of the distribution. If the value of x is less than the mean, the z-score is negative, if the value of x is more than the mean, the z-score is positive and if the value of x is equal to the mean, the z score is zero.

Properties for standard normal distribution:

1. For a standard normal distribution, mean is 0 and standard deviation is 1.
2. The curve for standard normal distribution is symmetric about $z = 0$.

3. In the curve, the values of z to the left of center are negative and the values of z to the right of center are positive.
4. Total area under the curve is 1.

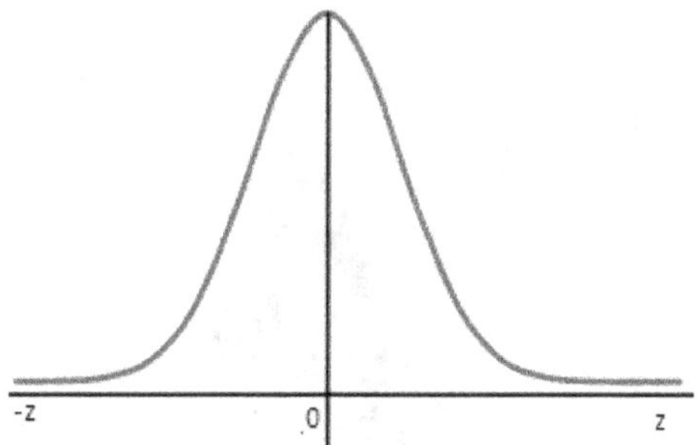

Bell Shape curve of standard normal distribution with mean 0 and standard deviation 1

Examples of Normal distribution

To work with the normal distributions, the value of the probability needs to be calculated using the z-score. The $P\ (a \leq x \leq b)$ = area under the curve between a and b.

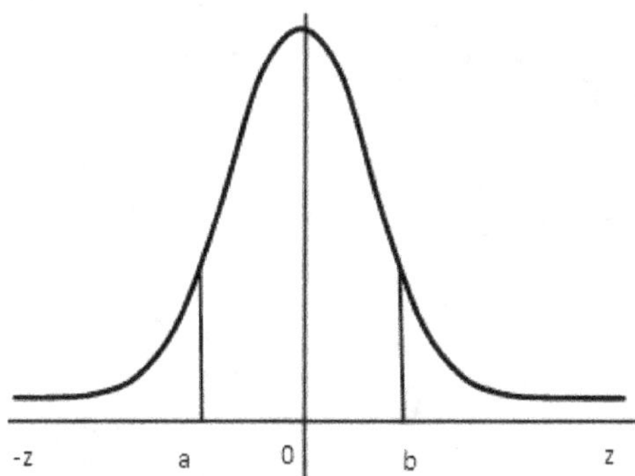

To understand the concept of calculating probability from the area under the curve, following are the examples. Use the table given in the appendix for the value of the probability that z lies between $0\ and\ a$:

1. Find the probability of P $(0 \leq z \leq 1.86)$.

   Solution: From the z-table, locating the value of 1.8 on the left side of the table and then moving across to the 0.06 column, P $(0 \leq z \leq 1.86) = 0.4686$.

2. Find the probability of P $(-2.5 \leq z \leq 2.5)$.

Solution: Since the normal probability curve is symmetric on both the sides,

P (-2.5 ≤z≤0) = P (0 ≤z≤2.5).

Hence,

P (-2.5 ≤z≤2.5) = P (-2.5 ≤z≤0) + P (0 ≤z≤2.5).

$$= 0.4938 + 0.4938 = 0.9876$$

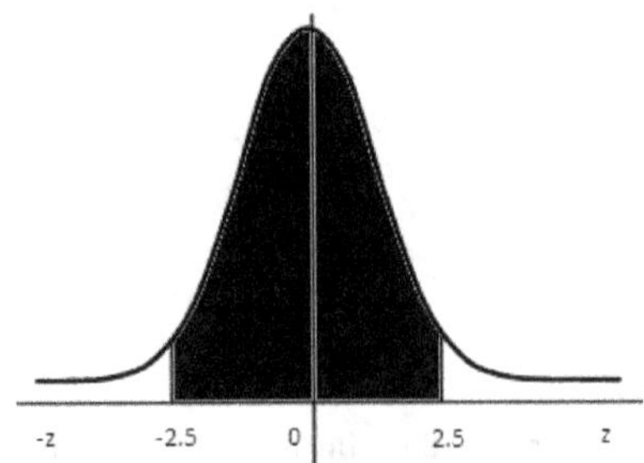

3. Find the probability of P (z >1.5).

Solution: To find the value of P (z >1.5), the value of z at 1.5 need to be taken from the z-table. From the z-table, locating the value of 1.5 on the left side of the table P(0≤z≤1.5) = 0.4332. As the total area under the curve is one and hence on side of the curve its 0.5.

Hence, P (z >1.5) = 0.5- P (0≤ z ≤1.5)

$$= 0.5\text{-}0.4332 = 0.0668$$

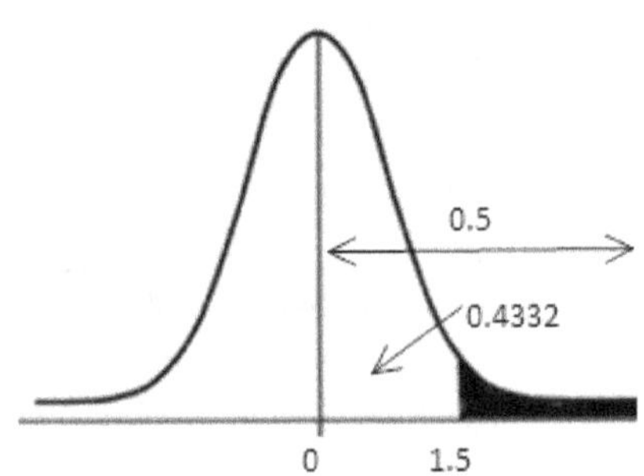

4. Find the probability of P (-1.2 ≤ z ≤ 0).

Solution: Since the normal probability curve is symmetric on both the sides,

P (-1.2≤ z ≤0) = P (0 ≤ z ≤1.2).

Hence,

P (-1.2 ≤z ≤0) =0.3849

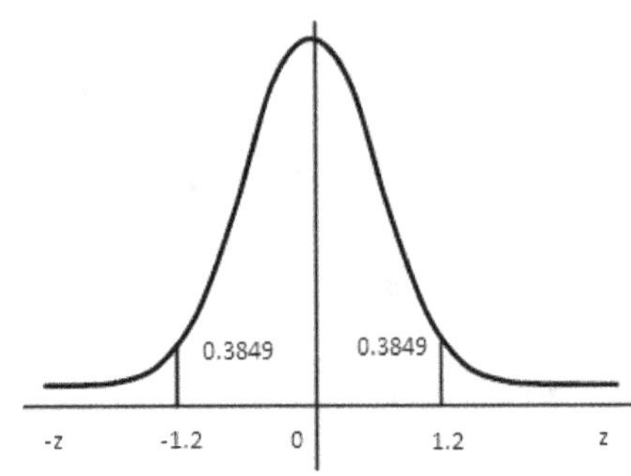

5. Find the probability of P $(1.2 \leq z \leq 1.56)$.

Solution: Since both the values lies on the same side of curve. Hence, the area for probability can be calculated as the difference between the probability values.

P $(1.2 \leq z \leq 1.56) = $ P $(0 \leq z \leq 1.56)$-P $(0 \leq z \leq 1.2)$

$$= 0.4406 - 0.3849$$
$$= 0.0557$$

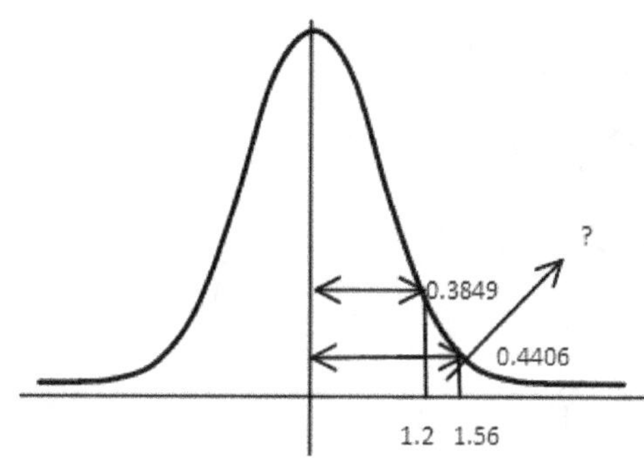

6. The weights of the sacks of wheat are normally distributed with mean 10 kg and standard deviation 0.20. What is the probability that a randomly selected sack weighs between 9.5 and 10.1 kg?

Solution: Here it is given that $\mu = 10, \sigma = 0.20$

To find P $(9.5 \leq x \leq 9.9)$, the first step is to convert x to z.

$$P \ (9.5 \leq x \leq 10.1) = P \left(\frac{9.5 - \mu}{\sigma} \leq \frac{x - \mu}{\sigma} \leq \frac{10.1 - \mu}{\sigma} \right)$$

On putting $\mu = 10, \sigma = 0.20$

$$P \ (9.5 \leq x \leq 10.1) = P \left(\frac{9.5 - 10}{0.20} \leq \frac{x - \mu}{\sigma} \leq \frac{10.1 - 10}{0.20} \right)$$

$$= P \left(\frac{9.5 - 10}{0.20} \leq \frac{x - \mu}{\sigma} \leq \frac{10.1 - 10}{0.20} \right)$$

$$= P \left(\frac{9.5 - 10}{0.20} \leq z \leq \frac{10.1 - 10}{0.20} \right)$$

$$= P \ (- 2.5 \leq z \leq 0.5)$$
$$= P \ (- 2.5 \leq z \leq 0) + P \ (0 \leq z \leq 0.5)$$
$$= P \ (0 \leq z \leq 2.5) + P \ (0 \leq z \leq 0.5)$$
$$= 0.4938 + 0.1915 = 0.6853$$

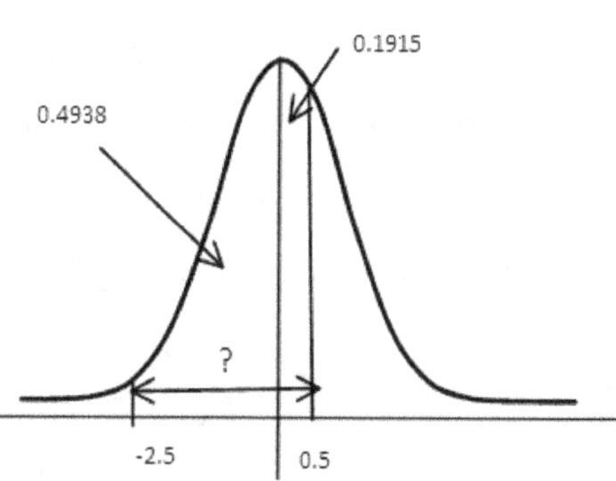

7. A placement company has conducted a written test to recruit people. The test marks are normally distributed with mean 120 and standard deviation 50. Calculate the following:
a) Probability of randomly obtaining scores greater than 200 in the test.
b) Probability of randomly obtaining a score that is 180 or less.
c) Probability of randomly obtaining a score between 100 and 120.

Solution:
a) Probability of randomly obtaining scores greater than 200 in the test.

$$P\ (x > 200) = P\left(\frac{x - \mu}{\sigma} > \frac{200 - \mu}{\sigma}\right)$$

Here, $\mu = 120, \sigma = 50$

$$P\ (x > 200) = P\left(\frac{x - \mu}{\sigma} > \frac{200 - 120}{50}\right)$$

$$= P\ (z > 1.6)$$
$$= 0.5 - P\ (0 < z < 1.6))$$
$$= 0.5 - 0.4452$$
$$= 0.0548$$

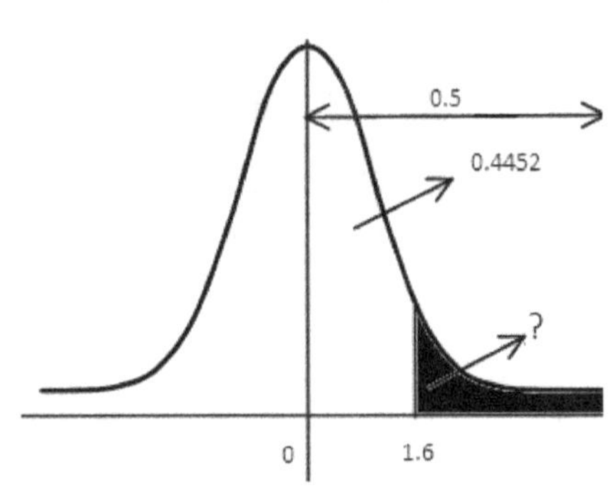

b) Probability of randomly obtaining a score that is 180 or less.

$$P\ (x \le 180) = P\left(\frac{x - \mu}{\sigma} \le \frac{180 - \mu}{\sigma}\right)$$

Here, $\mu = 120, \sigma = 50$

$$P\ (x \le 180) = P\left(\frac{x - \mu}{\sigma} \le \frac{180 - 120}{50}\right)$$

$$= P\ (z \le 1.2)$$
$$= 0.5 + P\ (0 \le z \le 1.2)$$
$$= 0.5 + 0.3849$$
$$= 0.8849$$

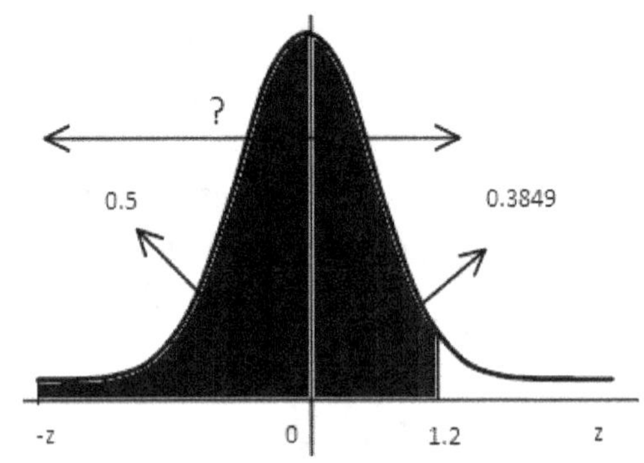

c) Probability of randomly obtaining a score between 100 and 120.

$$P\ (100 \le x \le 140) = P\left(100 \le \frac{x - \mu}{\sigma} \le 140\right)$$

$$Using, \mu = 120, \sigma = 50$$

$$P\ (100 \le x \le 140) = P\left(\frac{80 - 120}{50} \le z \le \frac{140 - 120}{50}\right)$$

$$Thus,\ P\left(\frac{80 - 120}{50} \le z \le \frac{140 - 120}{50}\right)$$

$$= P\ (-0.8 \le z \le 0.4)$$
$$= P\ (-0.8 \le z \le 0) + P\ (0 \le z \le 0.4)$$
$$= P\ (0 \le z \le 0.8) + P\ (0 \le z \le 0.4)$$
$$= 0.2881 + 0.1554$$
$$= 0.4435$$

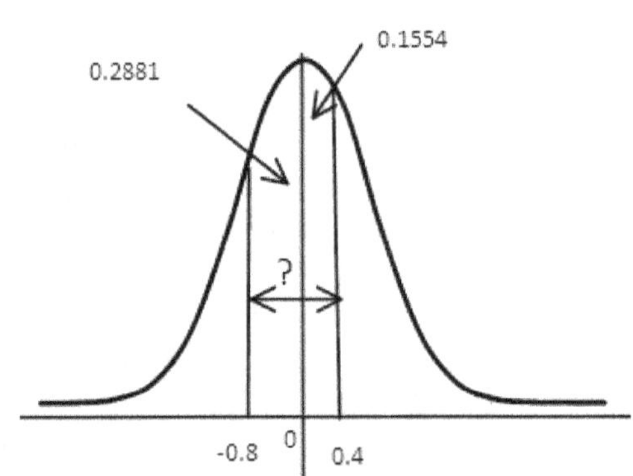

Chapter based Quiz

A) MCQs

1. Nature of the binomial random variable x is
a) Quantitative
b) Qualitative
c) Discrete
d) Continuous

2. In a binomial probability distribution, the sum of probability of failure and probability of success is always:
a) Zero
b) Less than 0.5
c) Greater than 0.5
d) One

3. In a binomial experiment, which of the following is incorrect for the successive trials?
a) Dependent
b) Independent
c) Mutually exclusive
d) Fixed

4. What are the parameters of the binomial distribution?
a) n and p
b) p and q
c) np and nq
d) np and npq

5. What is the range of binomial distribution?
a) 0 to n
b) 0 to ∞
c) -1 to +1
d) 0 to 1

6. The mean and variance of the binomial probability distribution are ______________.
a) np and npq
b) np and p
c) np and nq
d) n and p

7. In a binomial experiment with three trials, the variable can take__________ values.
a) 2
b) 3
c) 4
d) 5

8. The mean of a binomial distribution depends on______________.
a) Number of trials
b) Probability of success
c) Probability of failure
d) Number of trials and probability of success

9. Which of the following is not property of a binomial experiment?
a) Probability of success remains constant
b) n is fixed
c) Successive trials are independent
d) It has three parameters

10. In case of B.D. if mean=60, variance=30. What is the value of p?
a) 1/2
b) 1/3
c) 1/4
d) 1/6

11. In case of P.D. if variance=40, n=200. What is the value of p?
a) 1/3
b) 1/4
c) 1/6
d) 1/5

12. A variable that can assume any possible value between two points is called a_________.
a) discrete random variable
b) continuous random variable
c) discrete sample space
d) random variable

13. For a Poisson distribution, if probability of success is 0.4, n=160. What is the standard deviation?
a) 6
b) 8
c) 0.64
d) 64

14. Which of the following is correct for a binomial experiment with n trials and probability of success p?
a) Mean=np; variance $= nq$
b) Mean=nq; variance $= npq$
c) Mean=npq; variance $= nq$
d) Mean=np; variance $= npq$

15. For a binomial distribution with n trials and probability of success p. What is the relation between p and q?

a) p-q=1
b) p=1-q
c) p=1+q
d) q=1+p

16. For which condition P.D is an approximate case of B.D?
a) n+p=1
b) p is large and n is small.
c) n=p
d) n is large and p is small

17. The_____________ distribution is a continuous frequency distribution
a) Normal
b) Binomial
c) Poisson
d) Random

18. The number of deaths in a city by a rare disease is an example of ____________ distribution.
a) Normal
b) Binomial
c) Poisson
d) Random

19. The probability of Poisson distribution is given by

a) $\dfrac{e^{-\lambda}\lambda^{x}}{x!}; \lambda = np$

b) $\dfrac{e^{-\lambda}\lambda^{x}}{x!}; \lambda = nq$

c) $\dfrac{e^{\lambda}\lambda^{x}}{x!}; \lambda = np$

d) $\dfrac{e^{\lambda}\lambda^{x}}{x!}; \lambda = nq$

20. In case of P.D. if standard deviation=8, the value of p=0.5, then the value of n is________,
a) 128
b) 160
c) 40
d) 80

21. Which of the following requires a discrete random variable?
a) The time it takes by the mechanic to assemble a device.
b) The weight of athletes participating in an event.
c) The number of laptops sold during a mega online sale.
d) The marks obtained by a student in a multiple-choice test with negative marking of 0.25.

22. A standard normal distribution has
a) the mean equal to the variance.

b) mean equal 0 and standard deviation equal 1.
c) mean equal 1 and variance equal 0.
d) mean equal 0 and standard deviation equal 0.

23. For which distribution mean and variance are equal?
a) Normal
b) Binomial
c) Poisson
d) Random

24. In a standard normal distribution, the area under the curve is __________.
a) 0
b) 1
c) 2
d) Depend upon the limits

25. In normal distribution:
a) Mean = Median = Mode
b) Mean < Median < Mode
c) Mean> Median > Mode
d) Mean $\neq$ Median $\neq$ Mode

26. The p.d.f of the normal distribution is:

$$a)\frac{1}{\sigma\sqrt{2\pi}}e^{-\frac{1}{2}\left(\frac{x+\mu}{\sigma}\right)^2} \qquad b)\frac{1}{\sigma\sqrt{2\pi}}e^{\frac{1}{2}\left(\frac{x-\mu}{\sigma}\right)^2} \qquad c)\frac{1}{\sqrt{2\sigma\pi}}e^{-\frac{1}{2}\left(\frac{x+\mu}{\sigma}\right)^2} \qquad d)\frac{1}{\sigma\sqrt{2\pi}}e^{-\frac{1}{2}\left(\frac{x-\mu}{\sigma}\right)^2}$$

27. If the area from 0 to z=1.24 on a standard normal curve is 0.3925. What is the area to the right of 1.24?
a) 0.1075
b) 0.8925
c) 0.6075
d) 1.3925

28. On a standard normal curve, if the area from 0 to z=0.54 is 0.2054; the area from 0 to z=1.73 is 0.4582. The area between 0.54 and 1.73 is:
a) 0.2472
b) 0.3328
c) 0.6638
d) 0.2528

29. A normal distribution with mean μ and standard deviation σ, can be converted to a standard normal distribution by finding z-score given as

$$a)z = \frac{x-\sigma}{\mu} \qquad b)z = \frac{x+\mu}{\sigma} \qquad c)z = \frac{x-\mu}{\sqrt{\sigma}} \qquad d)z = \frac{x-\mu}{\sigma}$$

30. In flipping a fair coin 10 times. What is the probability of getting 8 heads?

$$a)\,^{10}C_8\left(\frac{1}{2}\right)^8 \quad b)\,^{10}C_8\left(\frac{1}{2}\right)^{16} \quad c)\,^{10}C_6\left(\frac{1}{2}\right)^8 \quad d)\,^{10}C_8\left(\frac{1}{2}\right)^8\left(\frac{1}{2}\right)^2$$

31. What is the probability that out of 5 shots, 3 shots will hit the target? If the probability of hitting a goal is 1/2.

$$a)\,^{5}C_3\left(\frac{1}{2}\right)^3\left(\frac{1}{2}\right)^2 \quad b)\,^{5}C_3\left(\frac{1}{2}\right)^2 \quad c)\,^{10}C_2\left(\frac{1}{2}\right)^8 \quad d)\,^{5}C_2\left(\frac{1}{2}\right)^2\left(\frac{1}{2}\right)^3$$

32. Probability that an individual suffer from a rare disease is 0.001. What is the probability that out of n persons, more than 1 will be affected?

$a)P(x \geq 1)$

$b)1 - P(0)$

$c)1 - \{P(0) + P(1)\}$

$d)P(x = 1)$

33. A company makes electric motors. The probability that an electric motor is defective is 0.01. What is the probability that a sample of 300 electric motors will contain exactly 5 defective motors? ($e^{-3}=0.05$)
a) 0.00155
b) 0.10125
c) 0.10254
d) 0.20138

34. Which one of the following requires a continuous random variable?
a) The time it takes a randomly selected student to complete an exam.
b) The number of tattoos a randomly selected person has.
c) The number of women taller than 68 inches in a random sample of 5 women.
d) The number of correct guesses on a multiple-choice test.

35. In a binomial distribution with n=10 and mean=6. What is the variance?
a) 5.0
b) 3.5
c) 2.4
d) 3.5

Answers:

1-c	2-d	3-a	4-a	5-a
6-a	7-c	8-d	9-d	10-a
11-d	12-b	13-b	14-d	15-b
16-d	17-a	18-c	19-a	20-a
21-c	22-b	23-c	24-b	25-a
26-d	27-a	28-d	29-d	30-d

B) True or False

1. If in a Poisson distribution, P (3) =P (2), the value of the mean is 3.
2. In normal distribution, approximately 99.7% of the values of a random variable lie within ±3 standard deviation from the mean.
3. If mean value in a Poisson distribution is 64 then variance is 8.
4. For a binomial distribution with n=6, p=0.5, the mean is 3.
5. In a normal distribution, if the mean value is 10.5. the median value is 12.5.
6. The expected value for the given probability distribution is 2.

1	2	3	4
0.4	0.3	0.2	0.1

7. The probability of happening of an event is -0.5. Hence there is very less chance of happening of the event.
8. A table with the values of the random variables with the corresponding probabilities is called probability mass function.
9. The normal distribution curve is asymptotic on both the ends.
10. Poisson distribution is appropriate for the events that happened randomly, rarely and independent in the due course of time.

Answers:

1-T	2-T	3-F	4-T	5-T
6-T	7-F	8-F	9-T	10-T

C) Fill in the blanks

1. In normal distribution, approximately ___________ of the values of a random variable lie within ±1 standard deviation from the mean.
2. Area under the normal curve is_______.
3. Poisson distribution approximates binomial distribution for large value of ___.
4. Number of patients arriving at hospital in a day diagnosed by heart attack is an example of ________________.
5. If the median of normal distribution is 4, then its mode is ___________.
6. The distribution of whose mean, mode and median are same is known is ________________ distribution.
7. The discrete distribution for which mean is always greater than its variance is ________________ distribution.
8. The formula to calculate the z-score when the mean and standard deviation is known: ________________.
9. The payoff (x) for a game has the following probability distribution.

x	0	1	2

| P(x) | 0.7 | 0.2 | 0.1 |

The expected value of payoff is ________.

10. The time it takes a randomly selected student to complete an exam is an example of ____________(continuous/discrete) random variable.

11. The number of men with weight more than 68 kg in a random sample of 5 men is an example of ____________(continuous/discrete) random variable.

12. Speed of cars in a race has a normal distribution with a mean equal to 60 mph and standard deviation equal to 4 mph. The z-score for a speed of 54 mph is ____.

13. Heights of adult men are approximately normally distributed with a mean of 160 inches and a standard deviation of 5 inches. The proportion of men having height more than 150 is given by the probability.

14. If $'x'$ is a discrete random variable, the function $f(x)$ is called its ________________.

15. On tossing 4 coins, the random variable with the number of heads can be ___________.

Answers:

1-68%	**2**-unity	**3**-n	**4**- Poisson distribution	**5**-4
6-normal	**7**-Poisson	**8**- $z = \dfrac{x - \mu}{\sigma}$	**9**-0.4	**10**-continuous
11-discrete	**12-b**	**13**- P (x>150)=P $(z > -2)$	**14**- Probability function	**15**-0, 1, 2, 3, 4

NOTES:

____

____

____

____

____

____

____

____

____

____

____

____

____

____

____

____

Chapter 7

Correlation and Regression

Measures of association are statistical tools for measuring the strength of a relationship between two variables. In this chapter the correlation for two numerical variables is discussed with regression analysis. Regression is a tool to find how much two things depend upon each other. In other words, correlation is used to find whether the two entities depend on each other or not and either they are positively or negatively related with how much strength and the regression provides the tool to predict one of the variables when the other is known.

7.1 Correlation

A correlation exists between two variables when one of them is related to the other in some way. Correlation analysis shows us how to determine both the nature and strength of relationship between two variables.

For example: Relationship can be studied between:

- Sales and the marketing strategy.
- Income and the expenditure.
- Quantity of fertilizer and the yield of crops.
- Frequency of consuming alcohol and chances of kidney damage.

7.1.1 Types of correlation

There are three broad categories of correlation:

1. Positive and negative
2. Linear and non-linear
3. Simple, partial, and multiple

In this chapter only the simple linear positive or negative correlation is discussed.

Positive correlation-The two related variables are positively correlated when an increase (or decrease) in one variable shows the same trend in another variable.

For example: Age and weight

Negative correlation-The two related variables are negatively correlated when an increase in one variable shows the decrease in other and vice-versa.

For example: Age of car and its maintenance.

Linear correlation- A relation between the two variables is linear when variation in one variable leads to the proportionate variation in another variable.

When the values of the linearly correlated variables are plotted on a graph paper, the line joining these points can be presented in form of a straight line.

Non-Linear correlation- If the variation in one variable is affecting another variable but the change is neither proportionate nor fixed it is called nonlinear relation.

When the values of the non-linearly correlated variables are plotted on a graph paper, the line joining these points is a curve which is not a straight line.

Simple, Partial, and Multiple Correlation

The distinction between these types of correlation is based upon the number of variables taken in the correlation analysis.

Simple correlation is the study of the relation between the two variables only.

For example: Effect of marketing on the sales of a product.

Partial correlation also involves the study of relation between two variables but the effects of other influencing variables are kept constant.

For example: Effect of marketing on the sales of a product assuming the advertising expenditure, price, competitors, distribution, and other factors as constants.

Multiple correlation is the study of the relationship between more than two variables.

For Example: Effect of marketing, advertising expenditure, price, competitors, distribution, employees, quality of the product is analyzed for the effect on the sales of a product.

If the variables are independent then there is ***no correlation*** between them.

7.1.2 Methods of Studying Correlation

The correlation between the two variables can be measured statistically as the correlation coefficient (r). It shows the degree of relation between two variables. The ***sign of correlation*** coefficient signifies the nature of ***association between the variables*** while the ***value*** of it denotes the ***strength of association***.

If the sign of correlation coefficient is positive, it means the relation between variables is a ***positive correlation*** and negative sign of correlation coefficient implies the ***negative correlation*** between the variables. The value of correlation coefficient lies between ***-1 and +1***. The value of this denotes the strength of the association as follows:

- $r = 0$ It means there is no association or correlation between the two variables.
- $0 < r < 0.25$ depicts weak correlation.
- $0.25 \leq r < 0.75$ depicts intermediate correlation.

- **0.75 ≤ r < 1** depicts strong correlation.
- **r = 1** depicts perfect correlation.

Similar is the strength for the negative values.

Methods of finding the correlation coefficient between two variables are as follows:
- **A.** Scatter diagram method
- **B.** Karl Pearson's coefficient of correlation
- **C.** Spearman's rank correlation method

A. Scatter diagram method

Scatter diagram/plot is a diagram which is plotted between the two variables to visualize the relationship between them. The pattern of data is indicative of the type of relationship between variables: positive relationship, negative relationship, no relationship.

Two linearly related variables are **positively associated** if an increase (or decrease) in one variable results in an increase (or decrease) in the other. In other words when one variable is increasing, other will also increase and when one variable is decreasing then other will also show a decreasing trend.

In positive association, the points of the scatter diagram are concentrated along the line in increasing direction going up from left to right.

The two linearly related variables are **negatively associated** if an increase in one causes a decrease in the other. *In negative association, the points of the scatter diagram are concentrated along the line in decreasing direction going down from left to right.*

If the data points are spread in a random manner that does not show any pattern, then these variables have no association between them.

Following are the scatter diagrams showing the spread of the points on the graph:

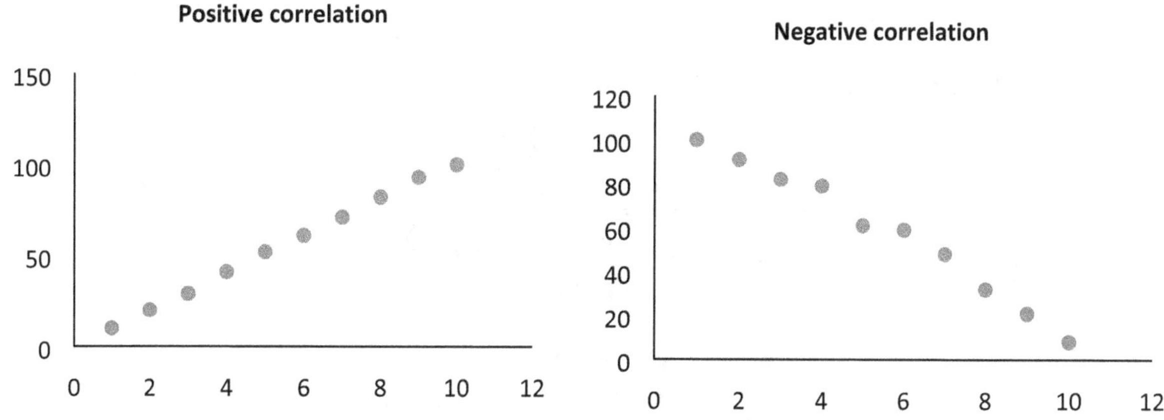

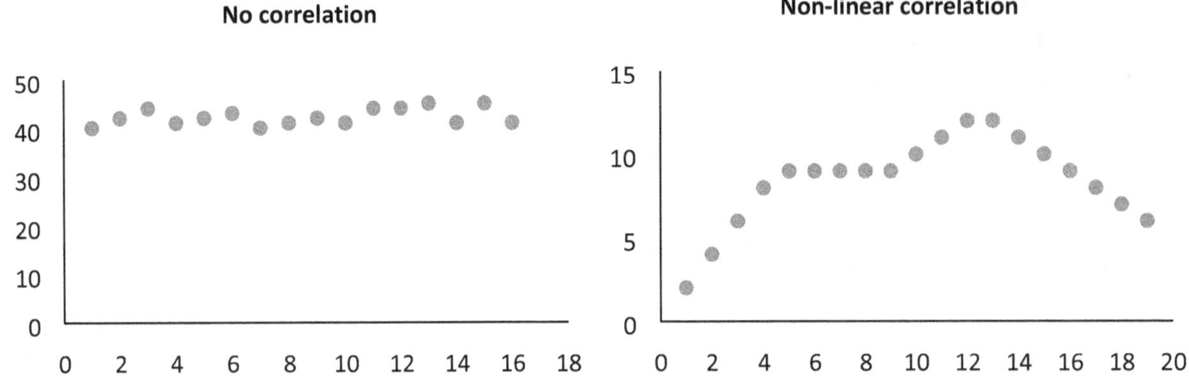

B. Karl Pearson's coefficient of correlation

Karl Pearson's coefficient of correlation is a quantitative measure of the degree of relationship between two variables which is presented by r.

The value of correlation coefficient is independent of the change of origin and scale of reference.
Hence the value of correlation coefficient remains unchanged on the addition or subtraction of a constant from whole data (**change of scale**) and on multiplying or dividing a constant from whole data (**change of origin**).
Also, the correlation coefficient is a number which is *independent of the unit of the data*.

If the two variables are x and y, then Karl Pearson's coefficient of correlation in terms of covariance and the standard deviations of x and y series is defined as:

$$r = \frac{Cov(x,y)}{\sigma_x \sigma_y} = \frac{\frac{1}{n}\sum (x_i - \bar{x})(y_i - \bar{y})}{\sqrt{\frac{(x_i - \bar{x})^2}{n}}\sqrt{\frac{(y_i - \bar{y})^2}{n}}}$$

Here, $Cov(x,y)$ is the covariance between variables x and y and σ_x and σ_y are the standard deviation of the x and y data series.

The correlation coefficient can also be defined in terms of the data values as:

$$r = \frac{\sum xy - \frac{\sum x \sum y}{n}}{\sqrt{\left(\sum x^2 - \frac{(\sum x)^2}{n}\right)\cdot\left(\sum y^2 - \frac{(\sum y)^2}{n}\right)}}$$

$$r = \frac{n\sum xy - \sum x \sum y}{\sqrt{\left(n\sum x^2 - (\sum x)^2\right)\cdot\left(n\sum y^2 - (\sum y)^2\right)}}$$

Example: Find the coefficient of correlation between demand and sales from the given data.

Demand	1	2	4	6	8	9
Sales (in thousands)	4	5	3	5	8	10

Solution: For the required values in the formula of the correlation coefficient, the values are calculated as follows:

	x	y	xy	x^2	y^2
	1	4	4	1	16
	2	5	10	4	25
	4	3	12	16	9
	6	5	30	36	25
	8	8	64	64	64
	9	10	90	81	100
Total	$\sum x=30$	$\sum y=35$	$\sum xy=210$	$\sum x^2=202$	$\sum y^2=239$

Here, $n = 6$. On substituting the values in the formula gives the correlation coefficient.

$$r = \frac{\sum xy - \frac{\sum x \sum y}{n}}{\sqrt{\left(\sum x^2 - \frac{(\sum x)^2}{n}\right)\cdot\left(\sum y^2 - \frac{(\sum y)^2}{n}\right)}}$$

$$r = \frac{210 - \frac{30 \times 35}{6}}{\sqrt{\left(202 - \frac{30^2}{6}\right)\cdot\left(239 - \frac{35^2}{6}\right)}}$$

$$r = \frac{35}{\sqrt{52 \times 34.83}} = 0.822$$

Hence the correlation between the demand and sales is positive and strong.

C. Spearman's rank correlation method

When the variables under study are not a quantitative measurement but can be arranged in a serial order (also called rank) then the Pearson's correlation coefficient cannot be used.

For example: For data related to abstract or qualitative data such as beauty, good habits, IQ, judgement etc. relation between the two variables can be studied for the rank correlation.

The Spearman's rank correlation can be calculated as:

$$R = 1 - \frac{6\sum d^2}{n(n^2 - 1)}$$

Here, R is the rank correlation coefficient, d is the difference of rank between paired items in two series and n is the total number of observations.

The value of rank correlation coefficient, *R ranges from -1 to +1.*

If **R = +1,** then there is complete agreement in the order of the ranks and *the ranks are in the same direction.*
If **R = -1,** then there is no agreement in the order of the ranks and the *ranks are in the opposite direction.*
If **R = 0,** then there is *no correlation.*
Spearman's rank correlation coefficient can be calculated for the data given without rank and also for the data whose ranks are given.

When ranks are given

When observations in the data are arranged in a particular order (rank), the differences between then ranks gives the difference (d) and hence the formula of the rank correlation can be used directly to see whether the set of data values are related or not.

Example: The ranks of 6 students in Science and English are given below. Find Spearman's rank correlation coefficient.

Science	1	2	5	4	3	6
English	1	3	4	6	2	5

Solution: Since ranks of students with respect to their performance in two subjects are given, calculations for rank correlation coefficient are as follows:

Science	English	d	d^2
1	1	0	0
2	3	-1	1
5	4	1	1
4	6	-2	4
3	2	1	1
6	5	1	1
Total			**8**

$$R = 1 - \frac{6\sum d^2}{n(n^2 - 1)}$$

$$R = 1 - \frac{6 \times 8}{6(6^2 - 1)} = 1 - \frac{8}{35} = 0.771$$

The result shows a strong degree of positive correlation between performances of students in two subjects.

When ranks are not given

When observations in the data set are not ranked, the ranks can be assigned by taking the highest value as 1 for the data values.

Example: The marks of 6 students given by the two examiners in statistics are given below. Find Spearman's rank correlation coefficient.

Examiner 1	21	32	25	34	23	36
Examiner 2	22	29	35	26	19	32

Solution: Since marks of students are given by the two examiners, assigning the rank to the data with the highest value as 1 for both the variables gives the following ranks:

S. No.	Examiner 1	Examiner 2	Rank-1	Rank-2	d	d^2
1	21	22	6	5	1	1
2	32	29	3	3	0	0
3	25	35	4	1	3	9
4	34	26	2	4	-2	4
5	23	19	5	6	-1	1
6	36	32	1	2	-1	1
Total						16

$$R = 1 - \frac{6\sum d^2}{n(n^2 - 1)}$$

$$= 1 - \frac{6 \times 16}{6(6^2 - 1)} = 1 - \frac{16}{35} = 0.5428$$

The result shows an intermediate degree of positive correlation between the marks given by the two examiners.

Special case: When ranks are equal

While assigning the ranks to the set of data values, if there occur a tie i.e., the data has same values that can be given same rank. For such values, an average of the ranks can be assigned as a rank.
For example, if two observations are equal at the fourth and fifth place, then the average rank of (4+5)/2 = 4.5, can be assigned to these two observations.
In case of tie in ranks, the Spearman rank correlation coefficient can be calculated in the same way as earlier but with a modified formula as follows:

$$R = 1 - \frac{6\left(\sum d^2 + \frac{1}{12}m_1(m_1^2 - 1) + \frac{1}{12}m_2(m_2^2 - 1) + ...\right)}{n(n^2 - 1)}$$

where m_i ($i = 1, 2, 3, \ldots$) stands for the number of times an observation is repeated in the data set for both variables.

Example: Find the rank correlation coefficient between the variables x and y from the following pairs of observed values:

x	10	12	13	14	11	10	15
y	8	10	12	8	12	8	11

Solution: Giving the rank to the data with the highest value as 1 for both the variables and taking the average of the data with tied ranks gives the following ranks:
Here in series x, tie occur at 5th and 6th position, hence m_1=2 (number of ties) with an average rank given as (5+6)/2 as 5.5.

In series y, tie occur at 3rd, 4th and 5th position, hence m_2=3 (number of ties) with an average rank given as (3+4+5)/3 as 3.

S. No.	x	y	Rank-1	Rank-2	d	d^2
1	10	8	7	7	0	0
2	12	12	4	3	1	1
3	13	12	3	3	0	0
4	14	9	2	6	-4	16
5	11	12	5.5	3	2.5	6.25
6	11	14	5.5	1	4.5	20.25
7	15	11	1	5	-4	16
Total						59.5

$$R = 1 - \frac{6\left(\sum d^2 + \frac{1}{12}m_1\left(m_1^2 - 1\right) + \frac{1}{12}m_2\left(m_2^2 - 1\right) + \ldots\right)}{n\left(n^2 - 1\right)}$$

$$R = 1 - \frac{6\left(59.5 + \frac{1}{12}2\left(2^2 - 1\right) + \frac{1}{12}3\left(3^2 - 1\right)\right)}{7\left(7^2 - 1\right)}$$

$$= 1 - \frac{6\left(59.5 + \frac{6}{12} + \frac{24}{12}\right)}{7\left(7^2 - 1\right)}$$

$$= 1 - \frac{6(59.5 + 0.5 + 2)}{7 \times 48}$$

$$= 1 - \frac{6 \times 62}{7 \times 48}$$

Hence, $R = -0.1071$

The result shows a weak negative correlation between the two variables.

7.2 Regression analysis

While correlation describes the strength of a linear relationship between two variables, regression talks about how to draw the straight line described by the correlation. Regression analysis is concerned with predicting one of the variables (the dependent variable) from the other (the independent variable). *It can be defined as the process of estimating one variable when another is known.*

In linear regression analysis one variable is considered as dependent variable and other as independent variable, while in correlation analysis both variables are considered to be independent.

7.2.1 Two lines of regression:

There are two lines of regression:

When y is to be estimated from x, the equation is called *a regression equation of y on x* and the corresponding curve is called *a regression line of y on x*.

Similarly, when x is to be estimated from y, the equation is called *a regression equation of x on y* and the corresponding curve is called *a regression line of x on y*.

The regression equations can be written as follows:

Regression line of y on x:

$$(y - \bar{y}) = b_{yx}(x - \bar{x}) \, from \, y = a + bx$$

Regression line of x on y:

$$(x - \bar{x}) = b_{xy}(y - \bar{y}) \, from \, x = a + by$$

where, b_{yx} is the regression coefficient of y on x and b_{xy} is the regression coefficient of x on y. The regression coefficients can be calculated using the mean values of the x and y data series or using the standard deviation formulas with the covariance.

A) Regression coefficients using data values

Using the data values of variables x and y, the regression coefficients can be calculated as follows:

$$b_{yx} = \frac{n \sum xy - \sum x \sum y}{n \sum x^2 - \left(\sum x\right)^2}$$

$$b_{xy} = \frac{n\sum xy - \sum x \sum y}{n\sum y^2 - \left(\sum y\right)^2}$$

It can be observed that both the regression coefficients have same numerator value and the denominator is taken in x values only when it is the regression coefficient of y on x. Similarly, the denominator is taken in y values only for regression coefficient of x on y.

B) *Regression coefficients using standard deviations of x and y*

If deviations of the data values are taken from actual mean values, then the values of regression coefficients can be calculated as follows:

$$b_{yx} = \frac{Cov(x,y)}{\sigma_x^2} = \frac{\sum(x_i - \bar{x})(y_i - \bar{y})}{\sum(x_i - \bar{x})^2} = r\frac{\sigma_y}{\sigma_x};$$

$$b_{xy} = \frac{Cov(x,y)}{\sigma_y^2} = \frac{\sum(x_i - \bar{x})(y_i - \bar{y})}{\sum(y_i - \bar{y})^2} = r\frac{\sigma_x}{\sigma_y}$$

where,
r is the coefficient of correlation,
σ_x is standard deviation of x,
σ_y is standard deviation of y.

7.2.2 Properties of regression coefficients

- Using the formula of the regression coefficient in terms of standard deviation, it can be observed that the ***correlation coefficient is the geometric mean of two regression coefficients.***
  Hence, $r^2 = b_{yx} \times b_{yx}$
- If ***one regression coefficient is greater than one, then other regression coefficient must be less than one***, because the maximum value of correlation coefficient r is one as r lie in range -1 to 1. However, both the regression coefficients may be less than one.
- Both ***regression coefficients must have the same sign*** (either positive or negative).
- The correlation coefficient will have the same sign (either positive or negative) as that of the two regression coefficients.
  For example: If b_{xy}=0.4, b_{yx}=0.9, $r^2 = 0.4 \times 0.9. \Rightarrow r = 0.6$.
  Similarly, if b_{xy}=-0.8, b_{yx}=-0.2, $r^2 = -0.8 \times -0.2 \Rightarrow r = -0.4$
- Regression coefficients are ***independent of origin but not of scale.***

7.2.3 Properties of regression lines

- The two lines of regression are ***perpendicular to each other when r=0.***
- The two lines of regression ***intersect at the point as mean of x and mean of y***, where x and y are the variables under consideration.

- The *two lines of regression coincide i.e., become identical when r= -1 or +1,* when there is a perfect negative or positive correlation between the two variables under discussion.
- When the *degree of correlation is low, the two regression lines are far apart*.
- When the *degree of correlation is high, the two regression lines come near each other* and hence finally got merge into one as its correlation coefficient becomes 1.

Example: The sales and advertisement expenses for a company are given as follows. Compute the regression line for the impact of advertisement on sales.

Advertisement (in thousand rupees)	3	4	5	7	8	9
Sales (in thousand rupees)	4	6	8	10	12	14

Solution: For the calculations of regression line, the three columns need to be calculated as follows:

	Advertisement (x)	Sales (y)	xy	x²	y²
	3	4	12	9	16
	4	6	24	16	36
	5	8	40	25	64
	7	10	70	49	100
	8	12	96	64	144
	9	14	126	81	196
Total	**36**	**54**	**368**	**244**	**556**

Here, the mean of x and y can be calculated as:

$$\bar{x} = \frac{36}{6} = 6; \qquad \bar{y} = \frac{54}{6} = 9$$

The regression coefficient of y on x is given by

$$b_{yx} = \frac{n\sum xy - \sum x \sum y}{n\sum x^2 - \left(\sum x\right)^2}$$

$$b_{yx} = \dfrac{6 \times 368 - 36 \times 54}{6 \times 244 - (36)^2}$$

$$= \dfrac{264}{168}$$

$$b_{yx} = 1.57$$

Hence, the regression line of y on x is given by:

$$(y - \bar{y}) = b_{yx}(x - \bar{x})$$
$$y - 9 = 1.57(x - 6)$$
$$y = 1.57x - 0.42$$

This line of regression indicates that for each unit increase in x (advertisement), y (sales) is predicted to increase by 1.57 units. The constant is the intercept that indicates the value of y when $x= 0$. It indicates that when there is no expenditure on advertisement, sales are predicted to decrease by 0.42 thousand rupees. The scatter diagram with the regression line can be shown as follows:

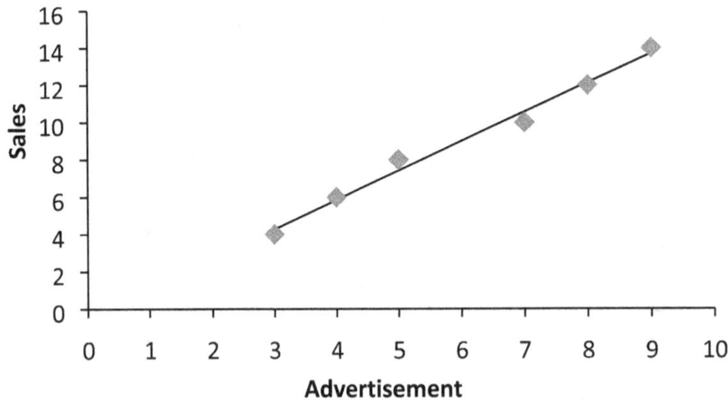

Example: For the variables x and y, the regression equations are given as $4x + 3y - 17 = 0$ and $5x - 2y - 4 = 0$. Find the arithmetic means of x and y.

Solution: By property, always the two lines of regression intersect at the mean of x and mean of y. Solving the given two regression equations, the point of intersection is (3, 2), which provides the mean of x and mean of

Example: Find the most likely price of a product in Bangalore corresponding to the price of Rs. 80 in Delhi. The average price and the standard deviation of the price of the product are provided when the correlation coefficient of the price of product in the two cities is 0.75.

	Bangalore	Delhi
Average	65	70
Standard deviation	1.2	1.5

Solution: Given are the values of r=0.75. Taking price of the product in Bangalore as x and price at Delhi as y,

$$\overline{x} = 6; \qquad \overline{y} = 7; \qquad \sigma_x = 1.2; \qquad \sigma_y = 1.5$$

The regression line of x on y is given as

$$(x - \overline{x}) = b_{xy}(y - \overline{y})$$

$$b_{xy} = r\frac{\sigma_x}{\sigma_y}$$

Here,

$$b_{xy} = r\frac{\sigma_x}{\sigma_y} = 0.75 \times \frac{1.2}{1.5} = 0.6$$

Hence the line of regression is given as:

$$(x - 65) = 0.6(y - 70)$$

$$x = 0.6y + 23$$

Thus, for the price of product at Delhi as 80 (y) the price of the product in Bangalore (x) can be calculated using the line of regression as with y as 80. That gives $x = 0.6 \times 80 + 23 = 71$

Chapter based Quiz

A) MCQs

1. If r=0, the variables are _______________.
   a) positively correlated
   b) negatively correlated
   c) dependent
   d) independent

2. If the plotted points in a scatter diagram are close. There is_________ between the two variables.
   a) high degree of correlation
   b) low degree of correlation
   c) no correlation
   d) none of the above

3. If there is no correlation between the variables then the points on the scatter plot are _____________.
   a) scattered away from line
   b) scattered near the line
   c) scattered all over the graph
   d) not appeared

4. What is the type of correlation between the amount of rainfall and the water in a sea?
   a) Negative correlation
   b) No correlation
   c) Positive correlation
   d) None of the above

5. What is the type of correlation between the sale of the woolen garments and the summer season?
   a) Positive correlation
   b) Negative correlation

c) No correlation
d) None of the above

6. Which of the following shows the negative correlation?
a) Demand and price of the goods under the normal condition
b) Age of a car and its maintenance cost.
c) Number of hours spent practicing and the performance in the sports.
d) Age of the applicant for health insurance and the premium amount.

7. The scatter diagram is not suitable when the number of the observations are ___________ .
a) small
b) large
c) not defined
d) none of the above

8. What is the type of correlation if the value of r=-0.52?
a) Positive intermediate correlation
b) Negative weak correlation
c) Negative strong correlation
d) Negative intermediate correlation

9. What is the type of correlation if the value of r=-0.75?
a) Positive intermediate correlation
b) Negative weak correlation
c) Negative strong correlation
d) Negative intermediate correlation

10. There is a positive correlation if the line of correlation runs from the______ left corner to the ________right corner.
a) lower, upper
b) upper, lower
c) lower, lower
d) upper, upper

11. A/An ____________exists between two variables when one of them is related to the other in some way.
a) Correlation
b) Regression
c) Conflict
d) Engagement

12. The _________of correlation coefficient denotes the nature of association, while the ______of correlation coefficient denotes the strength of association.
a) value, sign
b) magnitude, symbol
c) sign, magnitude
d) form, symbol

13. The relationship between variables is positive if
A. an increase in one variable is associated with an increase in the other variable
B. a decrease in one variable is associated with a decrease in the other variable.
C. an increase in one variable is associated with a decrease in the other.
a) Both A and B
b) Both A and C
c) Both B and C
d) All of the above

14. The relationship between variables is negative if
A. an increase in one variable is associated with an increase in the other variable
B. a decrease in one variable is associated with a decrease in the other variable.
C. an increase in one variable is associated with a decrease in the other.
a) A
b) B
c) C
d) All of the above

15. Match the correct pairs for correlation coefficient

A	$r=0$	i	strong correlation.
B	$0 < r < 0.25$	ii	no correlation.
C	$0.75 \leq r < 1$	iii	weak correlation.
		iv	Intermediate correlation.

a) A-ii, B-iii, C-i
b) A-ii, B-iii, C-iv
c) A-i, B-iii, C-ii
d) A-ii, B-i, C-iv

16. Which of the following is **incorrect** for correlation coefficient r?
a) r always lies between +1 and -1
b) Two independent variables are uncorrelated
c) r is independent of change in origin and scale
d) r is the A.M. of two regression coefficients

17. Regression analysis is concerned with predicting ___________.
A. x variable using variable y
B. y variable using variable x

a) Both A and B
b) A
c) B
d) None of the above

18. The strength of a linear relationship between two variables is discussed using _____while__________
signifies how to depict the straight line.

a) correlation, skewness
b) regression, correlation
c) correlation, regression
d) regression, measurement

19. Which of the following is the regression of line of x on y for $\bar{x}=8, \bar{y}=10, b_{xy}=4$?

a) $y = 2x - 8$
b) $x = 4y + 36$
c) $y = 2x + 8$
d) $x = 4y - 32$

20. What is the correlation coefficient between the variables x: 1, 2,3 with respect to the values of variable y: 10, 5,0?

a) -1
b) 0
c) 1
d) 2

21. If b_{xy}=-0.9 and b_{yx}=-0.4. What is the value of r, correlation coefficient?

a) 0.6
b) -0.6
c) 0.4
d) -0.4

22. If the correlation coefficient is 0.6, regression coefficient b_{xy}= 1.2. What will be the value of b_{yx}?

a) 0.2
b) 0.3
c) 0.4
d) 0.72

23. Which of the following is correct for regression coefficients?

a) If b_{xy} is less than 1, then the value of b_{yx} will also be less than 1
b) If b_{xy} is less than 0, then the value of b_{yx} is greater than 0
c) If b_{xy} is less than 1, then the value of b_{yx} is greater than 1
d) None of the above

24. In regression analysis, the variable that is being predicted is the____________.
a) response, or dependent variable
b) independent variable
c) intervening variable
d) is usually x

25. What is the regression line of x on y for $\bar{x}=8, \bar{y}=10, \sigma_x=4, \sigma_y=2, r=0.2$?

a) 5+0.3y
b) 0.4x+6.8
c) 0.4x+13.8

d) 4+0.4y

26. What is the regression coefficient of y on x, b_{yx} for $\bar{x}=8, \bar{y}=10, \sigma_x=1, \sigma_y=2, r=0.4$?

a)
b) 0.2
c) 0.1
d) 0.8

Answers:

1-d	**2-a**	**3-c**	**4-c**	**5-b**	**6-b**	**7-b**	**8-d**	**9-c**	**10-a**
11-a	**12-c**	**13-a**	**14-c**	**15-a**	**16-d**	**17-a**	**18-c**	**19-d**	**20-a**
21-b	**22-b**	**23-c**	**24-a**	**25-d**	**26-d**				

B) True or False

1. The coefficient of correlation is -0.25. It means that the relationship between two data is intermediate and negative.
2. In multiple regression, there is one dependent variable and more than one independent variable/s.
3. In case of perfect correlation there exists only one regression line.
4. Higher the degree of correlation between the two variables nearer the regression lines.
5. If the two regression lines are perpendicular to each other it implies strong correlation between the two variables.
6. If the regression line of x on y is given by $x = 2.5y + 8$ and regression line of y on x is $y = 2x - 4$. The value of y at $x = 3$ is 2.
7. There is a high direct association between the hours spend in preparation and the performance of student in an exam.
8. The value of regression coefficient of y on x is 3.2, if $r = 0.8$, $\sigma_x = 0.16$, variance $\sigma_y = 0.64$.
9. The correlation coefficient lies between 0 and 1.
10. The correlation is positive and perfect when the correlation coefficient r is +1.
11. The independent variable is used to explain the dependent variable in linear regression analysis.
12. If the values of two variables move in the same direction, the correlation is said to be non-linear.
13. The coefficient of correlation is independent of the change of scale and change of origin for the given data.
14. The point of intersection of two regression lines represents average value of two variables.
15. The regression coefficients are independent of the change of origin but not of scale.

Answers:

1-F	**2-T**	**3-T**	**4-T**	**5-F**
6-T	**7-T**	**8-T**	**9-F**	**10-T**
11-T	**12-F**	**13-T**	**14-T**	**15-T**

C) Fill in the blanks

1. The correlation is negative and perfect when the correlation coefficient r is________________.

2. In linear correlation there exists a ___________ correlation if the line of correlation runs from the upper left corner to the lower right corner.
3. The value of correlation coefficient is independent of change of _____________.
4. If b_{xy} is less than 1, then the value of b_{yx} is greater than ___________________
5. Correlation coefficient is measure of ____________ between two data values.
6. Regression line helps to _______________ the value of unknown variables with help of available data.
7. Correlation Coefficient values lies between______________
8. If x and y are independent of each other, the coefficient of correlation is___________.
9. The correlation coefficient (r) is ________ for data of 6 values with

$$\sum x = 10, \sum y = 12, \sum xy = 21, \sum x^2 = 42, \sum y^2 = 32$$

10. The regression line of x on y is______________for given data below:
$$\bar{x} = 10, \bar{y} = 8, b_{xy} = 1.2, b_{yx} = 3.2$$

11. In case of perfect correlation, the two regression lines ________________.
12. If the regression line of x on y is given by $x = 2.5y + 8$, the regression coefficient of x on y is

________.

13. The correlation coefficient, r is the _________mean of two regression coefficients.
14. If the correlation coefficient between x and y is 0.4, covariance between x and y is 20, variance of x is 24. The variance of y is_____.
15. The correlation coefficient between x and y is _____, if the covariance between x and y is 15, variance of x is 9. The variance of y is 10.

Answers:

1-minus 1	2-negative	3-scale and origin	4-one	5- relation
6- predict	7- -1 and 1	8-zero	9-0.070	10- x=0.4+1.2y
11-overlap each other	12-2.5	13- geometric mean	14-25/12	15-0.16

NOTES:

____

____

____

____

____

____

____

____

____

____

____

Chapter 8

Sampling Techniques

The process of selecting a portion of elements from a large group of elements under consideration is called *sampling.*

For example:

- Chairman of a university randomly selects set of students from a class for interview to analyze the satisfaction of the students in online learning. This class is a sample of all the students learning online.
- When a doctor recommends a test. A few drops of blood is taken to draw conclusions about the health status of certain cells in our body. The few drops of blood are a sample of the blood in the human body.

Hence *sampling is a process to analyze the whole set while a certain portion of the set is analyzed.*

This chapter deals with the concepts of sampling and sampling distributions with discussion on the sampling distribution of sample mean.

8.1 Related Definitions:

Population-The largest collection or group of units that are under observation is called as population.

For example:

- All women of a society.
- Patients in a hospital.

Sample- A part of population under study is called as sample.

For example:

- A group of women of a society of age between 20-35.
- 10 Patients of malaria in a hospital.

Unit- The smallest object of a sample that can be investigated for analyzing the sample characteristics is called a unit.

For example:

- A woman of a society aged between 20-35.
- A patient of malaria in a hospital.

8.2 Population Parameter and Sample Statistic

Parameter is a numerical measurement describing some characteristic of a population. ***The quantities computed from the population are called parameter*** and is usually denoted as lower-case Greek alphabets.

For example: mean of population is denoted as μ, standard deviation of population is denoted by σ and variance as σ^2.

Statistic is a numerical measurement describing some characteristic of a sample. Sample statistics are usually denoted by Roman letters such as mean of sample is denoted as $\bar{x}$, standard deviation as s, and variance as s^2.

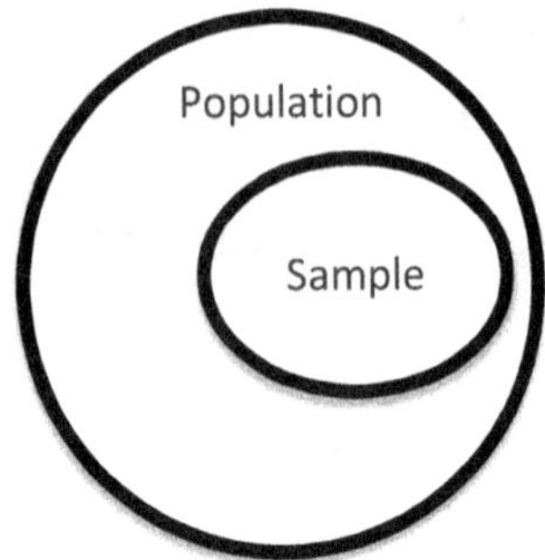

8.3 Obtaining Information

Any statistical analysis can be performed to verify a claim. Data is required for all sort of analysis. The data in unarranged form is called as ***information***. The information regarding an event can be obtained either from a sample ***survey or from a complete enumeration (census).***

8.3.1 Sample surveys

Sample surveys collect information from a fraction of the total population, whereas census collects information based on the whole population.

Some surveys such as economic surveys, health surveys etc. are conducted regularly to get updates in the specific sectors while some surveys are need-based and are conducted when some need arises.

For example:
- Student's satisfaction and feedback survey are conducted for the response of the students for the developed platform for joining the online classes.
- Survey of job satisfaction is conducted time to time by the companies to make amendments in the policies.

8.3.2 Census or Complete Enumeration

The complete count of the population is called a census. The observations of all the sampling units in the population are collected in the census.

For example:

- In India, the census is conducted at every tenth year, in which information on various aspects is collected about all the persons staying in India.
- Data collected from each and every employee of an industry regarding health insurance policy for the employees is complete enumeration.

8.4 Sampling

Sampling is defined as a procedure of selecting a sample from a population and estimating the parameter of population from statistic of sample. It is essential to estimate the parameters of population when census is not possible. In most of the investigations, it is not possible to approach each and every unit in a population hence sampling is used, that saves both time and money.

For example:

Consider the sampling to analyze the average marks of the graduate student in Punjab state of India. As in Punjab there are number of universities and colleges where the students are doing their graduation. Hence it is not feasible to approach all the graduate students. Thus, some universities and colleges can be selected to represent all the students and hence act as a sample.

8.4.1 Sampling Design Process

To collect information from sampling, the ***target population must be defined*** and then the appropriate sampling technique is used to take the sample. For this the ***sample size must be determined*** in such a way that the selected sample represents the whole group. There are various methods of collecting sample from the population some of which are mentioned below:

8.5 Types of sampling methods

There are two types of sampling methods: ***Probability sampling and non-probability sampling.***
Also called as ***random and non-random sampling*** respectively.

In a probability or random sampling, each unit of the population has the same probability (chance) of being selected in the sample. It is mainly used in quantitative research. It produces results that are representative of the whole population. However, the random sampling is not always feasible, then non-random sampling methods are applied to collect the sample.

As compared to random sampling, in non-random sampling, every unit of the population does not have the same chance of being selected in the sample. ***In non-random sampling, members of the sample are selected on convenience base.*** Hence in non-random sampling the collection of data is easy as compared to the random sampling but the chances of selection of units are not same.

8.5.1 Types of probability sampling

There are four main types of probability sampling as simple random sampling, systematic sampling, stratified sampling and cluster sampling discussed in brief with examples as follows:

A. Simple random sampling:

A random sample in which every member of the population has an equal chance of being selected is called a ***simple random sample*** and the process called as simple random sampling.

In this sampling method a list of all the members of the population is prepared by assigning each element a distinct number from 1 to N. Then n items are selected using either a random number table, the random number generator or lottery approach. Random number can be generated from the computer using software commands For example: In Excel software rand ( ) is the command to generate the random numbers. While in a lottery, a number of slips are kept in a bowl with a possible selection of one or two slips to declare the lucky winner.

For example:
To select a simple random sample of 100 employees of company, a number is assigned to every employee in the company database from 1 to N, and then using a random number generator 100 employees can be selected.

B. Systematic sampling

Systematic sampling approach is similar to simple random sampling, but is comparatively easier to conduct and follows a systematic approach. To collect a sample in this approach, every member of the population is listed with a number, but instead of randomly generating numbers, ***individuals are chosen at regular intervals in terms of time, order, or space***.

For obtaining samples in systematic sampling, a sample fraction $k = N/n$ is calculated, where N is the total number of units in the population and n is the sample size. The first member of the sample can be selected randomly between 1 and k, and after that every k^{th} member of the population is included in the sample.

For example:

To select 40 employees of a company from 2000 employees. A starting point can be selected as any number between 1 to 40. Let the initial number is 6. From number 6 onwards, every 50th (=2000/40) person on the list is selected as 56, 106, 156, 206, and end up with a sample of 40 people.

C. Stratified sampling

Stratified sampling involves ***dividing the population into subpopulations having different characteristics***. It allows every subgroup to be properly represented in the sample. In this sampling method, the population is divided into subgroups called as *strata* based on the relevant characteristic.

For example:
gender, age range, income bracket, job role etc.

Based on the overall proportions of the population, units can be selected as a sample from each subgroup using random or systematic sampling.

Stratified sampling is based on the concept of homogeneity and heterogeneity.

For example:
To investigate the students' preference for new developed software for accounting, sample of students and faculty is selected from the different universities. But this population contains students and faculty from different age groups, education level and stream. Hence, there is a need of selecting the students and faculty of Economics only which is a strata in this case. Therefore, ***in stratified sampling instead of selecting people directly from the population, strata are created to divide this heterogeneous population into homogenous groups***, and then simple random sampling procedure can be used to obtain the samples from these homogenous groups.

D. Cluster sampling

It also ***divides the population into subgroups, but each subgroup should have similar characteristics to the whole sample***. Instead of sampling individuals from each subgroup entire subgroup is selected randomly. While in stratified sampling, strata happen to be homogenous but in cluster sampling, clusters are internally heterogeneous.
This method is good for dealing with large and dispersed populations, but there is more risk of error in the sample, as there could be substantial differences between clusters.

For example:
If a company wants to conduct a survey for feedback of a new product in the country. The country can be divided into clusters of cities and the city can be divided into clusters of blocks and then the feedback can be taken from the customers randomly from the blocks.

8.5.2 Types of Non-probability sampling

There are four main types of non-probability sampling methods as quota sampling, judgment sampling, snowball sampling and convenience sampling.

A. Quota Sampling

Quota sampling is similar to stratified random sampling with groups. However, in quota sampling, a non-random sampling method is used. A quota is generally based on the proportion of sub-classes in the population.

For example: To select a sample of 100 students from a population of 500 students with 200 girls and 300 boys. Quota sampling can be assigned in the sample according to the population proportion. Hence, in a sample of 100 students 40 girls and 60 boys can be selected as per the population proportion.

B. Judgment sampling

In judgment sampling, the selection of the sampling unit is based on the judgment of the analyst who is looking for the information. *Judgment sampling involves the selection of the respondents to provide the desired information easily and correctly*. To select a representative sample by using judgment, the survey become time and cost efficient and hence more accurate than simple random sampling.

For example: If manager of a company is looking for the feedback of a new health insurance scheme for the employees. Analyst can fix a meeting of the manager with those employees who can discuss about the pros and cons of the scheme more efficiently than the employees of whom he is not aware about. Hence the selection of appropriate sample is done on based of judgment of the analyst.

C. Snowball Sampling

In snowball sampling, survey respondents are selected on the basis of referrals from other survey respondents. It is also useful when the information about the product or person is not directly available but can be available indirectly.

For example: To know about the person who made an offence, the information can be collected from the neighbour or relatives of the person who witnessed the crime scene.

D. Convenience Sampling

In this sampling the units included in the sample are selected at the convenience of the investigator. Convenience samples are easy to collect data on a particular issue. But, precautions should be taken in interpreting the results to make inferences about a population.

For example: To find the average marks obtained by the students in Statistics competitive exam, a student can collect the information of his/her own friends in the college because they are ready to share the information at no cost. Similarly, to analyze the public opinion on a social issue the data can be collected by the public near the railway station; bus stop, or in a market.

.

8.6 Sampling distribution of mean

For a large population, census method is not feasible to calculate population parameter. Hence to draw a valid conclusion for the population parameter, sampling is used to draw samples of a given size repeatedly from the population and the required 'statistic' is calculated for each sample. The obtained statistic value can be different from sample to sample due to randomness involved.
The distribution of the obtained values of the statistic is called a sampling distribution.

Sampling can be done with and without replacement of the units. Based on either the units are selected with or without replacement, the number of samples varies and results in the sampling distribution.

8.6.1 Sampling distribution of mean with replacement

The number of possible samples of size n from population of size N when taken with replacement is N^n.
If $x_1, x_2, x_3, \ldots, x_k$ are k random sample of size n from a finite population of size N having mean $\overline{x_1}, \overline{x_2}, \overline{x_3}, \ldots, \overline{x_k}$.
The mean of the sample means is the estimate of the population mean μ given as:

$$\mu = \frac{\overline{x_1} + \overline{x_2} + \overline{x_3} + \ldots + \overline{x_k}}{k}$$

and the standard deviation of the sample means is s= $\sigma / \sqrt{N}$.

Here, σ is the standard deviation of population and N is the number of items in the population

Thus,
- If a population has a mean μ, then the mean of the sampling distribution of the mean is also μ.
- The standard deviation of the population is $\sqrt{N}$ times the standard deviation of the sampling distribution.

Example:
For a small population of three candy bags with weight at packaging as 10, 12, 14 gms, ($N = 3$) if samples of size 2 are taken with replacement. Find the total number of samples and show that the
a) Mean of population is same as mean of sample means
b) Standard deviation of the population is $\sqrt{N}$ times the standard deviation of the sampling distribution. Here, N is the number of items in the population.

Solution: Collecting samples with replacement the total number of samples are 3^2 given as:

Samples	(10,10)	(10,12)	{10,14)	(12,10)	(12,12)	(12,14)	(14,10)	(14,12)	(14,14)
Mean	10	11	12	11	12	13	12	13	14

Here, the mean of population is

$$\mu = \frac{10 + 12 + 14}{3} = 12$$

The mean of sample mean is thus calculated as the sum of nine samples means S=108 divided by number of samples n=9.

Thus, mean of sample mean=mean of population=12

$$\sigma = \sqrt{\frac{(x - \bar{x})^2}{N - 1}}$$

The standard deviation of the population is   calculated below:

x	$x - \bar{x}$	$(x - \bar{x})^2$
10	-2	4
12	0	0
14	2	4
Total	0	$(x_i - \bar{x})^2 = 8$

The standard deviation of the population is thus calculated as:

$$\sigma = \sqrt{\frac{(x - \bar{x})^2}{N - 1}}$$

$$\sigma = \sqrt{\frac{8}{2}} = 2$$

The standard deviation of the samples is calculated below:

x	$x - \bar{x}$	$(x - \bar{x})^2$
10	-2	4
11	-1	1
12	0	0
11	-1	1
12	0	0
13	1	1
12	0	0
13	1	1
14	2	4
Total	0	$(x_i - \bar{x})^2 = 12$

The standard deviation of the sample means is thus calculated as:

$$s = \sqrt{\frac{(x - \bar{x})^2}{n}} = \sqrt{\frac{12}{9}}$$

$$s = 1.154$$

As per the relation $\sigma = \sqrt{N}\, s$

Thus, $\sigma = \sqrt{3} \times 1.154 = 2$.

8.6.2 Sampling distribution of mean without replacement

The number of possible samples of size n drawn from a population of size N without replacement.are $^{N}C_{n} = N!/n!\,(N-n)!$.

In sampling without replacement

- The mean of the sample means is the estimate of the population mean μ.
- The standard deviation of the sampling distribution is related to the standard deviation of the population as $s = \sigma\sqrt{\dfrac{1}{n}\left(\dfrac{N-n}{N}\right)}$ where, N is the population size, n is the sample size.

Example: For above considered population selecting samples of size 2 without replacement, there are only $^{3}C_{2} = 3$ possible samples as $\{(10,12),(10,14),(12,14)\}$ with their sample means 11, 12 and 13 respectively. Show that mean of population is same as mean of sample means and the standard deviation of the sampling distribution given by $s = \sigma\sqrt{\dfrac{1}{n}\left(\dfrac{N-n}{N}\right)}$.

Solution:

The mean of sample means is $(11+12+13)/3$ as 12, which is same as population mean. The standard deviation of the population is $\sigma = 2$.

The standard deviation of the sample is calculated as:

x	$x - \overline{x}$	$(x - \overline{x})^2$
11	-1	1
12	0	0
13	1	1
Total		2

The standard deviation of the mean of the means is calculated as

$$s = \sqrt{\frac{(x-\overline{x})^2}{n}} = \sqrt{\frac{2}{3}}$$

As per the relation, $s = \sigma\sqrt{\dfrac{1}{n}\left(\dfrac{N-n}{N}\right)}$

Here, $n = 2$ and $N = 3$. Thus,

$$s = 2\sqrt{\frac{1}{2}\left(\frac{3-2}{3}\right)} = \sqrt{\frac{2}{3}}$$

8.6.3 Interpretation of sampling distribution

When a sample statistic is used to estimate a population parameter, some statistics target the population parameter and are therefore likely to yield good results. Such statistics are called **unbiased estimators**. Statistics that target population parameters are **mean, variance, proportion**. Statistics that do not target population parameters: **median, range, standard deviation**.

Thus, the mean of the sample means is the population mean μ while the standard deviation of all sample means is $s/\sqrt{n}$. The standard deviation of a sampling distribution of a statistic is known as **standard Error (S.E).**

Chapter based Quiz

A) MCQs

1. The statistical constants such as mean and variance for a sample are called
a) statistics
b) parameters
c) characteristics
d) None of the above

2. The statistical constants such as mean and variance for a population are called
a) statistics
b) parameters
c) characteristics
d) None of the above

3. If a sample of size n is drawn from a finite population of size N, then the total number of possible samples are given by:
a) $^{N}C_n$
b) C_n
c) nN
d) None of the above

4. The standard deviation of the sampling distribution of a statistic is called
a) mean
b) sampling
c) standardization
d) standard error

5. If standard deviation is 1 for sample of size 400. What is the value of standard error?
a) 0.01
b) 0.02
c) 0.03
d) 0.05

6. For a sample if the standard error is 0.01, standard deviation is 0.5. What is the sample size?
   a) 50
   b) 500
   c) 250
   d) 2500

7. If 10,12,15,25 are the mean values for 4 samples. What is the mean of sampling distribution?
a) 10.5
b) 12.5
c) 15.5
d) 18.5

8. Which of the following is a statistic that do not target population parameter?
a) mean
b) range
c) variance
d) proportion

9. Which of the following sampling methods is a probability method?
a) Judgement
b) Quota
c) Simple random
d) Convenience

10. Which sampling technique is needed to make a list of voters for the election?
a) sampling
b) random
c) census
d) simple random sampling

11. If the sample size is increasing then the sampling error will__________.
a) increase
b) reduce
c) no effect
d) become infinity

12. A population consists of the values 1, 2, 3 and 5. What are the number of possible samples if samples of size 2 are selected with replacement?
a) 16
b) 18
c) 20
d) 24

13. Which distribution is created by considering all possible values of a statistics?
a) Hypergeometric distribution
b) Normal distribution

c) Sampling distribution
d) Binomial distribution

14. Which of the following is not a random sampling technique?
a) Simple random sampling
b) Systematic sampling
c) Stratified sampling
d) Quota sampling

15. In cluster sampling. Population is divided into clusters or groups which are _________in nature.
a) Homogeneous
b) Heterogeneous
c) Correlated
d) Qualitative

Answers:

1-a	**2-b**	**3-a**	**4-d**	**5-d**
6-d	**7-c**	**8-b**	**9-c**	**10-c**
11-b	**12-a**	**13-c**	**14-d**	**15-a**

B) True or False

1. A sample is a representative unit of the population.
2. Dividing a heterogeneous population into homogeneous groups and then drawing samples from each group is called Stratified sampling.
3. In a non-probability sampling all the units of the population have an equal chance of being included in the sample.
4. The size of the population has no effect on selecting a sampling technique.
5. Target population refers to those elements from which samples are specifically chosen for sampling.
6. The smallest entity of the population is called an element or a unit.
7. The population to be sampled is divided into units which are known as sampling frame.
8. Sampling error is present in census survey.
9. In stratified sampling the population is divided into different strata and sample is taken from different strata.
10. In purposive or judgmental sampling, the investigator chooses his sample according to his desire.

Answers:

1-T	**2-T**	**3-F**	**4-F**	**5-T**
6-T	**7-F**	**8-F**	**9-T**	**10-T**

C) Fill in the blanks

1. The cluster sampling, stratified sampling and systematic sampling are type of_________________.

2. The value that represents the whole population is called as________________.
3. If mean of population is 25 then the mean of sampling distribution is________.
4. The type of sampling in which the desired and useful information is gathered from the best position holder is known as________________.
5. In case of random sampling, the chances of selection of all units are________.
6. Convenience Sampling is a type of ________________.
7. Dividing the population into different groups and then selecting sample on the basis of proportion of each group is called as ____________________.
8. Population is called as ____________ where the members are identical to one another.
9. As the sample size increases, the sampling error____________.
10. The aggregate of all the units pertaining to a study is called____________.

Answers:

1- random sampling	2-parameter	**3-25**	4-judgment sampling	5-same
6-non-random sampling	7-Quota sampling	8-homogeneous	9-decreases	10-population

NOTES:

Chapter 9

Hypothesis Testing

Estimations are required to analyze and perform various types of tasks. Parents estimates budget, students estimate their marks after their exam performance, a bank manager often estimates the amount of loan being sanctioned in a year, and a manager of a car manufacturing company estimates the average life of car on a specific fuel. Since the estimate cannot be done on the whole population a sample is often taken to estimate the considered fact. The considered fact here is the hypothesis for which claims need to be verified. As it is not always possible to analyze the matter from the whole population under study, often samples are taken from the population.

For example:

- In kitchen, a chef just takes a spoon of cooked recipe to estimate the taste.
- A manufacturer of bulb just takes a sample of bulbs to estimate the average life of bulbs in hours and days.

In statistics, the concept of probability is used to make scientific predictions about population parameters using sample statistics. To make such decisions some assumptions are made. Such assumptions that may or may not be true are called the ***statistical hypothesis***. With the help of testing of hypothesis can be accepted or rejected.

For example:
- A farmer uses a fertilizer to a crop with assumption (hypothesis) that fertilizer is helpful in growth of the crop. This hypothesis can be verified on comparing the crop yield with the yield without fertilizer.
- A technician can claim the efficacy of an installation method to install a webcam in a computer system assuming that the method is capable of being installed in all operating system.

To test such claims or assertions statistically, sample data needs to be collected and analyzed, based on which the hypothesis can either be accepted or rejected.

9.1 Hypothesis

In statistics, *a hypothesis is a claim or statement about a parameter of a population*. It can be verified using a standard procedure called as *hypothesis testing*.

9.1.1 Types of hypotheses

There are two types of hypotheses:

i.   Null hypothesis (H_0)
ii. Alternative Hypothesis (H_1)

The *null hypothesis* (denoted by H_0) is a statement that the value of a population parameter is equal to some claimed value. The null hypothesis is tested directly for the possible acceptance or rejection. The symbolic form of the null hypothesis must include equality. It can be either: $=, \leq, \geq$.

The *alternative hypothesis* (denoted by H_1 or H_a or H_A) is the statement that the parameter has a value that somehow differs from the null hypothesis.

The symbolic form of the alternative hypothesis must use one of these symbols: $\neq, <, >$.

9.1.2 Testing of hypothesis

The process that enables a decision maker to verify the hypothesis for the possible acceptance or rejection is called *testing of hypothesis*. It involves analyzing the difference between the value of sample statistic and the corresponding hypothesized population parameter value i.e., calculating the probability of getting the observed value of statistic based on sample. If this value is less than some standard value, the hypothesis will be rejected otherwise accepted.

The procedure of testing a hypothesis is discussed in the steps as follows:

Step 1: Null and alternative hypothesis

The initial step for testing a hypothesis is to finalize the null hypothesis which is tested for possible rejection under the assumption that it is true.

For example:

- To test whether a population mean is equal to 120, a null hypothesis can be taken as
  H_0: Population mean is equal to 120
  $$H_0: \mu = 120$$
  The alternative hypothesis can be taken as population mean is not equal to 120.
  $$H_1: \mu \neq 120$$

- To test whether a population mean is greater than 120, a null hypothesis can be taken opposite of the claim as it does not involve equality. Hence,
  H_0: Population mean is less than or equal to 120
  $$H_0: \mu \leq 120$$

The alternative hypothesis is thus, population mean is greater than 120.

$$H_1: \mu > 120$$

- To test whether a population mean is less than 120, a null hypothesis can be taken opposite of the claim as it does not involve equality. Hence,

  H_0: Population mean is greater than or equal to 120

  $$H_0: \mu \geq 120$$

  The alternative hypothesis is that the population mean is less than 120.

  $$H_1: \mu < 120$$

Step 2: Test statistics

After writing the hypothesis, an appropriate statistical test (test statistics) needs to be chosen to analyze the hypothesis. The test statistics can be decided based on the data values (sample size and type) and the measure of central tendency or dispersion.

For choosing a particular test these four criteria can be considered:

(a) The number of samples in the data (one sample, two samples, or k samples)
(b) The provided samples used are independent or dependent.
(c) The measurement scale of data values. (Nominal, ordinal, interval, or ratio)
d) The sample size of the provide sample(s).

Step 3: The level of significance

The probability level below which the hypothesis is rejected is called the level of significance even when it is true.
It can be taken as the size of the rejection or critical region.

The area of the normal curve is divided into two mutually exclusive regions (areas) called as the **acceptance region and the rejection (or critical) region.**
If the computed value of the test statistic falls in the acceptance region, the null hypothesis is accepted, otherwise it is rejected.
For finding the acceptance or rejection of the null hypothesis, the value that separates the rejection region from the acceptance region is called the **critical value**. Example discussed in the **section 9.3.1**.
The determination of critical value depends on the level of precision which a decision maker wants to maintain while estimating the population parameter. The tails in a distribution are the extreme regions bounded by critical values.

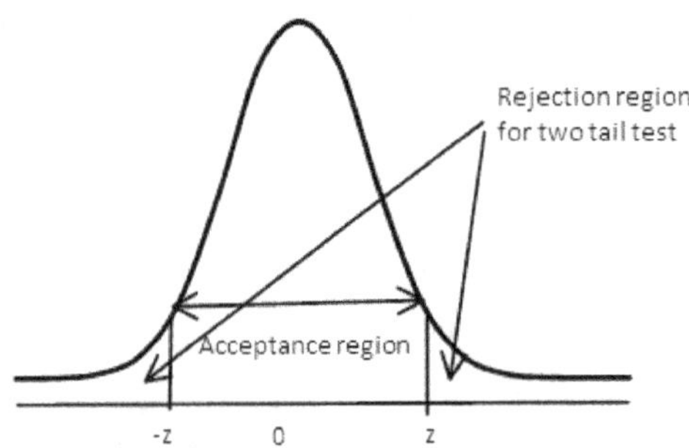

The significance level is also called as probability of Type-I Error (denoted by α). In other words, level of significance is the probability that the test statistic will fall in the rejection region when the null hypothesis is actually true. The most frequently used level of significance is 0.01, 0.05 and 0.10 that can be written as 1%, 5% and 10% level of significance.

The probability to accept a null hypothesis is called the confidence level and is given as $1-\alpha$.

<u>Step 4: Decision Making</u>

After deciding the level of significance decision to accept or reject a null hypothesis depends on the acceptance and the rejection region. If a hypothesis is tested for claim at 5% level of significance and the hypothesis is rejected, it signifies that the difference between the sample statistic and the hypothesized population parameter is significant.

In other words, the hypothesis is accepted or rejected based on the standard value of the test statistics at the given level of significance.

If the calculated value of the test statistic is less than the standard value, the hypothesis is accepted else it is rejected.

9.1.3 Errors

When a hypothesis is tested, it can be rejected or accepted.

If a hypothesis is rejected when it should have been accepted, then an error has been committed, known as **Type I error (α).**

If a hypothesis is accepted while it should have been rejected, another error has been made and this error is known as **Type-II error (β).**

The aim of statistical testing of hypothesis is to limit the Type-I error to a pre-assigned value (say: 1% or 5%) and to minimize the Type-II error.

Both types of errors can be reduced by increasing the sample size.

Types of errors can be summarized as follows:

	H_0 is True	H_0 is False
H_0 Rejected	**Type-I error**	Correct Decision

H_0 Accepted	Correct Decision	**Type-II error**

9.2 Two tail and One tail test

There are two types of tests of hypothesis: one-tailed test and two-tailed test.

a) Two tail tests

When the hypothesis testing is made on the basis of rejection region represented by both side of the normal curve, the test is called a **two-tailed test**.

Thus, a null hypothesis will be rejected if the computed sample statistic is significantly higher than or lower than the hypothesized population parameter (considering both the tails). The test is a two tailed test if the hypothesis has the following combination of H_0 and H_1:

$$H_0: \mu = \mu_0.$$
$$H_1: \mu \neq \mu_0.$$

If the level of significance is α, then the rejection region will lie on both the tails of the normal curve with $\alpha/2$ area.

For example: To test a hypothesis at 5% level of significance, the rejection region on both the tails is 0.05 which is equally distributed on both sides as 0.025.

Similarly, for testing a hypothesis at 1% level of significance, the size of rejection region on both the tails is 0.01 which is equally distributed on both sides as 0.005.

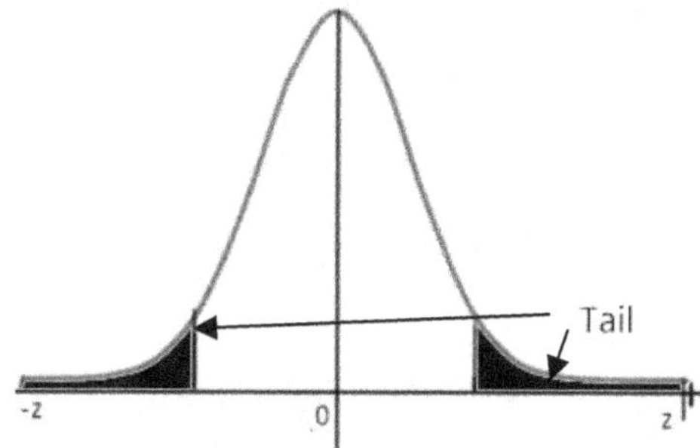

b) One tail test

When the hypothesis testing is made on the basis of rejection region represented by either of one side of the normal curve, the test is called a **one-tailed test**.

Rejection region can be on the left or the right side of the curve.

In case of a *left-tailed test,* the null hypothesis is rejected if the computed sample statistic is significantly lower than the hypothesized population parameter (considering the left side of the curve).

In the case of a *right-tailed test,* null hypothesis is rejected if the computed sample statistic is significantly higher than the hypothesized population parameter (considering the right side of the curve).

The test will be a one tailed test if the hypothesis has the following combination of H_0 and H_1:

Left tail test:

$$H_0: \mu \geq \mu_0, \; H_1: \mu < \mu_0$$

Right tail test:

$$H_0: \mu \le \mu_0, \; H_1: \mu > \mu_0$$

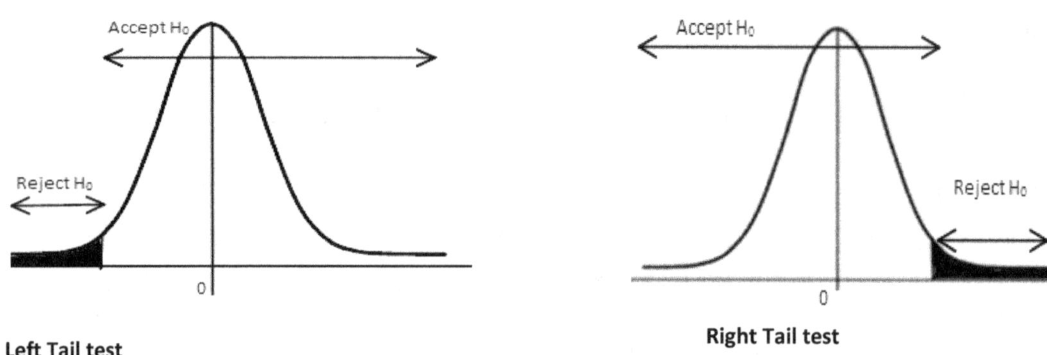

Left Tail test

Right Tail test

9.3 z-Statistic

9.3.1 Testing a hypothesis for a single large population mean

For testing hypothesis about a single population mean, z-statistics can be applied if following conditions are fulfilled:

1. The sample should be a simple random sample.
2. The value of the population standard deviation, σ must be known.
3. Either or both of these conditions should satisfy: The population is normally distributed or n > 30.

For testing a hypothesis for a large sample (n >30) it is assumed that the population, from which the sample is drawn has a normal distribution.

The formula for calculating the z-statistics for H_0 versus H_1 is given as:

$$z = \frac{\bar{x} - \mu}{\sigma/\sqrt{n}}$$

Here, μ is the population mean, σ is the population standard deviation, n the sample size, and $\bar{x}$ is the sample mean.

If the standard deviation σ is not known for the population, it is approximated by the sample standard deviation (s) and hence the formula become:

$$z = \frac{\bar{x} - \mu}{s/\sqrt{n}}$$

Following is the list of critical values of z to make the decision at the given level of significance based on either the test is a two tailed test or a one tailed test.

Critical value concept has been discussed **in section 9.1.2 under step 3 of level of significance**. It can be seen from the table given below that for 1% level of significance the critical value for two tail is 2.58. It means that if the calculated value of z lies from -2.58 to 2.58 the hypothesis is accepted else rejected. Similarly, the critical value for 5% level of significance at two tail is 1.96 and for one tail is 1.645.

Critical value (z_α)	Level of significance (α)		
	1%	5%	10%
Two tail	|z|=2.58	|z|=1.96	|z|=1.645
One tail	|z|=2.33	|z|=1.645	|z|=1.28

Following are the values of z corresponding to how much area is covered under the acceptance region:

$z_{\alpha/2}$	Area Covered
1.645	90%
1.96	95%
2.33	98%
2.58	99%

Note: In testing a hypothesis, if the level of significance is not mentioned then it should be taken as 5% .

Example 1: A sample of 200 items was drawn and the sample mean was found to be 98. Test whether this sample could have come from a normal population with mean 100 and standard deviation 10 at 5% level of significance.

Solution:

$$Given: n = 200, \bar{x} = 98, \mu = 100, \sigma = 10$$

$$Null\ Hypothesis: H_0{:}\mu = 100,\ Alternative\ Hypothesis: H_1{:}\mu \neq 100$$

$$Test\ statistic:$$

$$z = \frac{\bar{x} - \mu}{\sigma/\sqrt{n}} = \frac{98 - 100}{10/\sqrt{200}} = -2.82$$

$$\Rightarrow |z| = 2.82$$

$$At\ 5\%\ level\ of\ significance (Two\ Tailed)\ z_{\alpha/2} = 1.96$$

$$\because |z| > |z_{\alpha/2}|$$

$$Hence\ null\ hypothesis\ is\ rejected.$$

$$Thus,\ sample\ has\ not\ been\ drawn\ from\ the\ population\ with\ mean\ 100\ and\ s.d.\ 10.$$

Example 2: The mean life of 400 LED produced by a company is found to be 1550 hours with standard deviation of 450 hours. Test the hypothesis that the mean life of LED produced by the company is more than 1600 hours at 1% level of significance.

Solution:

$$Given: n = 400, \bar{x} = 1550, s = 450, \mu = 1600$$

$$Null\ Hypothesis: H_0{:}\mu \leq 1600,\ Alternative\ Hypothesis: H_1{:}\mu > 1600$$

$$Test\ statistic{:}$$

$$z = \frac{\bar{x} - \mu}{\sigma/\sqrt{n}} = \frac{1550 - 1600}{450/\sqrt{400}} = -2.22$$

$$\Rightarrow |z| = 2.22$$

$$At\ 1\%\ level\ of\ significance (One\ Tailed)\ z_\alpha = 2.33$$

$$\because |z| < |z_\alpha|$$

$$Hence\ null\ hypothesis\ is\ accepted.$$

$$Thus, the\ mean\ life\ of\ LED\ produced\ by\ the\ company\ is\ more\ than\ 1600\ hours.$$

Example 3: An entrepreneur randomly samples 144 gadgets similar to her own and finds that the average selling price of the similar gadgets available in the market is 2,000 with a standard deviation of 500. Is this sufficient evidence to conclude that the average selling price is less than 2500 at 5% level of significance?

Solution:

$$Given: n = 144, \bar{x} = 2000, s = 500, \mu = 2500$$

$$Null\ Hypothesis: H_0{:}\mu \geq 2500,\ Alternative\ Hypothesis: H_1{:}\mu < 2500\ Test\ statistic{:}$$

$$z = \frac{\bar{x} - \mu}{s/\sqrt{n}} = \frac{2000 - 2500}{500/\sqrt{144}} = -12$$

$$At\ 5\%\ level\ of\ significance (One\ tailed)\ z_{\alpha/2} = 1.645$$

$$\because |z| > |z_{\alpha/2}|$$

$$Hence\ null\ hypothesis\ is\ rejected.$$

$$Thus, the\ average\ selling\ price\ is\ more\ than\ 2500\ .$$

9.3.2 Testing a Hypothesis for difference between two large population mean

Often there exists the hypothesis to be verified for two samples from two different populations or two samples from the same population. In either of this case, hypothesis is to be analyzed using the two-sample z-test.

For example, a teacher may want to find out the difference between the performances of two different sections.

In order to analyze the performance of two different sections, samples can be taken from the sections and the z-statistics for two population can be applied.

 The z-test can also be applied to two samples from the same section to analyze if the difference between the two-sample means is just by chance or it really exists.

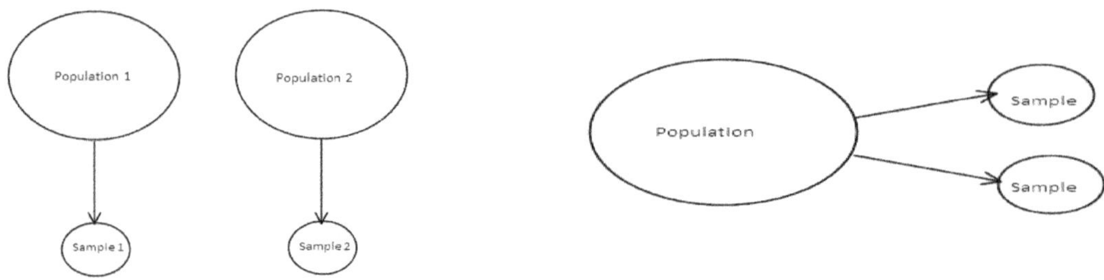

Let, two random samples of size n_1 and n_2 are taken from the two populations with mean μ_1 and μ_2 and the variance σ_1^2 and σ_2^2.

The testing of hypothesis for the difference between the two population mean (two tail) is given by:

$H_0{:}\mu_1 = \mu_2\ versus\ H_1{:}\mu_1 \neq \mu_2$ The hypothesis can be framed as per the requirement in case of one tail test.

Test statistic is given by:

$$z = \frac{\bar{x}_1 - \bar{x}_2}{\sqrt{\dfrac{\sigma_1^2}{n_1} + \dfrac{\sigma_2^2}{n_2}}}, if\ population\ s.d\ is\ known$$

$$z = \frac{\bar{x}_1 - \bar{x}_2}{\sqrt{\dfrac{s_1^2}{n_1} + \dfrac{s_2^2}{n_2}}}, if\ sample\ s.d.\ is\ given\ and\ population\ s.d\ is\ not\ known$$

Example 1: A survey was conducted to analyze the performance of the students in a graduate course based on their residential status. Data is collected from the students living in hostel and those living in either a PG or at their home. A sample taken from the 100 hosteller students has mean marks 45 with standard deviation of 11.5. Another sample of 150 students coming from outside the university reported the mean marks 42 with a standard deviation of 13. Are the two means statistically different at 5% level of significance?

Solution:

$$Given{:}\ n_1 = 100, \bar{x}_1 = 45, s_1 = 11.5, n_2 = 150, \bar{x}_2 = 42, s_2 = 13$$

$$Hypothesis{:}$$

$$H_0{:}\mu_1 = \mu_2$$

$$H_1{:}\mu_1 \neq \mu_2$$

$$Test\ statistic{:}\ z = \frac{\bar{x}_1 - \bar{x}_2}{\sqrt{\dfrac{s_1^2}{n_1} + \dfrac{s_2^2}{n_2}}}$$

$$= \frac{45 - 42}{\sqrt{\dfrac{11.5^2}{100} + \dfrac{13^2}{150}}} = 1.91$$

$$\Rightarrow |z| = 1.91$$

$$At\ 5\%\ level\ of\ significance\ (Two\ tailed)\ Z_{\alpha/2} = 1.96$$

$$\because |z| < |z_{\alpha/2}|$$

$$Hence\ null\ hypothesis\ is\ accepted$$

$$Thus,\ the\ performance\ of\ the\ students\ has\ not\ been\ effected\ by\ their\ residential\ status.$$

Example 2: From a state, sample of 60 plots has the mean yield 70 kg with a standard deviation of 11 kg. In another sample of 50 plots mean yield is 80 kg with standard deviation of 12 kg. Test whether there is any significant difference between the yields of crops from two samples at 1% level of significance.

Solution:

$$Given: n_1 = 60, \bar{x}_1 = 70, s_1 = 11, n_2 = 50, \bar{x}_2 = 80, s_2 = 12$$

$$Hypothesis:$$

$$H_0: \mu_1 = \mu_2$$

$$H_1: \mu_1 \neq \mu_2$$

$$Test\ statistic:\ z = \frac{\bar{x}_1 - \bar{x}_2}{\sqrt{\dfrac{s_1^2}{n_1} + \dfrac{s_2^2}{n_2}}}$$

$$= \frac{70 - 80}{\sqrt{\dfrac{11^2}{60} + \dfrac{12^2}{50}}} = -4.52$$

$$\Rightarrow |z| = 4.52$$

$$At\ 1\%\ level\ of\ significance\ (Two\ tailed)\ z_{\alpha/2} = 2.58$$

$$\because |z| > |z_{\alpha/2}|$$

Hence null hypothesis is rejected.

Thus, there is a significant difference between the yields of crops from two samples.

9.3.3 Testing a Hypothesis for a single large population proportion

Above section discusses the hypothesis testing procedures for the population mean, in a similar way the hypothesis can be tested for a population proportion.

Proportion is a fraction of values to investigate a part of the population or sample with common attributes.

The sample proportion can be calculated as,

$$\hat{p} = x/n,$$

where n is the sample size and x are the values in favor of an outcome.

The test-statistics for population proportion assumes that the sampling distribution of a proportion follows a standardized normal distribution.

The value for the z-test statistic for a single large can be defined as follows:

$$z = \frac{\hat{p} - p}{\sqrt{\dfrac{pq}{n}}}$$

Where, p is the population proportion, $\hat{p}$ is sample proportion and n is the sample size.

It can be noted that sometimes the value of proportion can be given directly and sometime it needs to be calculated.

For example:

- If 12% of the students has reported late then the proportion is $\hat{p} = 0.12$
- 15 students out of 60 have passed the competition then the proportion can be calculated as $\hat{p} = 15/60$.

The comparison of the calculated z-test statistic value with its standard value at a given level of significance leads to the decision for the population proportion.

Example 1: A floor manufacturing company *AMPRA* claims that 60 percent of the popular chefs prefer their brand. A random sample of 100 chefs has been surveyed to investigate this claim. It was observed that 45% chefs prefer *AMPRA* brand floor in cooking. At 5 % level of significance, test the claim of the company.

Solution:

Given: $p = 0.60, n = 100, x = 45, q = 1 - p = 0.4$

$$Hypothesis: H_0:p = 0.60;$$
$$H_1:p \neq 0.60$$

$$Test\ statistic:\ z = \frac{\hat{p} - p}{\sqrt{\dfrac{pq}{n}}}$$

$$Here, \hat{p} = x/n = 0.45;$$

$$Hence, z = \frac{0.45 - 0.60}{\sqrt{\dfrac{0.6 \times 0.4}{100}}} = -3.06$$

$$\Rightarrow |z| = 3.06$$

At 5% level of significance (Two tailed) $z_{\alpha/2} = 1.96$

$$\because |z| > |z_{\alpha/2}|$$

Hence, the null hypothesis id rejected. Thus, the percentage of chefs who prefer using *AMPRA* floor is significantly different from the claimed value.

Example 2: A teacher claims that only 2% of the answers provide in the answer key can be incorrect. To test this claim, a random sample of 200 answers is checked and 5 are found to be incorrect. At 1 % significance level, test whether the claim of teacher is supported by the sample evidence.

Solution:

Given: $p = 0.02, n = 200, x = 5$

Hypothesis: $H_0:p = 0.02; H_1:p \neq 0.02$

$$Test\ statistic:\ z = \frac{\hat{p} - p}{\sqrt{\dfrac{pq}{n}}}$$

$$Here, \hat{p} = \frac{x}{n} = 0.025;$$

$$As,\ p = 0.02 \Rightarrow q = 1 - p = 0.98$$

$$Hence, z = \frac{0.025 - 0.02}{\sqrt{\dfrac{0.02 \times 0.98}{200}}} = 0.5050$$

$$\Rightarrow |z| = 0.5050$$

At 1% level of significance (Two Tailed) $z_{\alpha/2} = 2.58$

$$\because |z| < |z_{\alpha/2}|$$

Hence null hypothesis is accepted. Thus, the claim of teacher is supported by the sample evidence.

9.3.4 Testing a Hypothesis for two large population proportion

The hypothesis for one population proportion can be extended to test whether there is any difference between the two proportions of the populations or the two proportions from the two populations.

For testing the hypothesis for the difference between two population proportions it is assumed that the population proportions are normally distributed.

The hypotheses for two tails are:

$H_0{:}p_1 = p_2, H_1{:}p_1 \neq p_2$

In most of the cases when the two population proportions are compared, the hypothesis testing follows two tail tests. But it can vary as per the requirement.

The z-statistic is given as:

$$z = \frac{\hat{p}_1 - \hat{p}_2}{\sqrt{\hat{p}\hat{q}\left(\dfrac{1}{n_1} + \dfrac{1}{n_2}\right)}}$$

Here, $\hat{p}$ is the pooled proportion given as:

$$\hat{p} = \frac{n_1\hat{p}_1 + n_2\hat{p}_2}{n_1 + n_2}$$

and $\hat{q} = 1 - \hat{p}$

Example 1: In a random sample of 1000 students from a country, 810 were found to be using the kindle software for reading the eBooks. In another sample of 800 students from a country, 700 were found to be the user of kindle software. From the data can it be concluded that there is a significant difference in kindle users between two countries?

Solution:

Given: $n_1 = 1000, x_1 = 810, n_2 = 800, x_2 = 700$

$Hence, \hat{p}_1 = 810/1000 = 0.81$ $\qquad\qquad \hat{p}_2 = 700/800 = 0.875$

Hypothesis: $H_0{:}p_1 = p_2, \ H_1{:}p_1 \neq p_2$

$$\hat{p} = \frac{n_1\hat{p}_1 + n_2\hat{p}_2}{n_1 + n_2} = \frac{1000 \times 0.81 + 800 \times 0.875}{1800} = 0.838$$

$$Test\ statistic{:}\ z = \frac{\hat{p}_1 - \hat{p}_2}{\sqrt{\hat{p}\hat{q}\left(\dfrac{1}{n_1} + \dfrac{1}{n_2}\right)}}$$

$$z = \frac{0.81 - 0.875}{\sqrt{0.838 \times 0.162\left(\dfrac{1}{1000} + \dfrac{1}{800}\right)}} = -3.717$$

$$\Rightarrow |z| = 3.717$$

At 5% level of significance(Two tailed) $z_{\alpha/2} = 1.96$

$$\because |z| < |z_{\alpha/2}|$$

Hence null hypothesis is rejected.

Thus, there is a significance difference in kindle users between two countries.

Example 2: A quality manager checked that there are 10 defective units in a sample of 500 units. The batch was returned and refilled. This time during inspection, officer found that now there are 4 defective units in a sample of 200 units. Has the package been improved?

Solution:

$Given: n_1 = 500, x_1 = 10, n_2 = 200 x_2 = 5$

$Hence, \hat{p}_1 = 10/500 = 0.02$

$\hat{p}_2 = 5/200 = 0.025$ $Hypothesis: H_0{:}p_1 \le p_2, H_1{:}p_1 > p_2$

$$\hat{p} = \frac{n_1\hat{p}_1 + n_2\hat{p}_2}{n_1 + n_2} = \frac{10 + 5}{700} = 0.0215$$

$$Test\ statistic: z = \frac{\hat{p}_1 - \hat{p}_2}{\sqrt{\hat{p}\hat{q}\left(\dfrac{1}{n_1} + \dfrac{1}{n_2}\right)}} = -0.4127$$

$$\Rightarrow |z| = 0.4127$$

$At\ 5\%\ level\ of\ significance (One\ tailed)\ z_\alpha = 1.645$

$$\because |z| < |z_\alpha|$$

Hence null hypothesis is accepted.

Thus, the package has not been improved in terms of defective samples.

9.4 Testing a Hypothesis for a Single small population mean (t-Statistic)

Due to constraints of time, money and computational complexity of data, sometimes a researcher takes a sample of small size $(n \le 30)$. When the sample size is small (equal to or less than 30), the estimation and testing procedures studied earlier are not appropriate. Also, for the large sample test when the standard deviation of population is not known, the standard deviation is approximated by the sample standard deviation but the resulting statistic is not normal.

In any such situation when the sample size is small or the population standard deviation is not known, there is an equivalent small sample test procedure known as t-statistic with n-1 degrees of freedom.

The t-statistics for testing a hypothesis H_0 versus H_1 for mean follows the same procedure as for the large sample size and is given as:

$$t = \frac{\bar{x} - \mu}{s/\sqrt{n}}$$

Rejection region is based on degree of freedom, $df = n - 1$ with the standard deviation calculated from the sample using formula:

$$s = \sqrt{\frac{\Sigma(x - \bar{x})^2}{n - 1}}$$

The t-statistics follows the t-distribution with properties as follows:

9.4.1 Properties of t -distribution

1. The curve of the t -distribution is mound-shaped.
2. The t -distribution is a symmetric distribution with mean zero.
3. The t -distribution extends to infinity on either side.
4. The curve of the t -distribution is more variable than the normal curve, with "heavier tails".
5. Shape of the curve depends on the sample size n or the degrees of freedom, n-1.

6. As sample size increases, the shapes of the t and z distributions become almost identical.

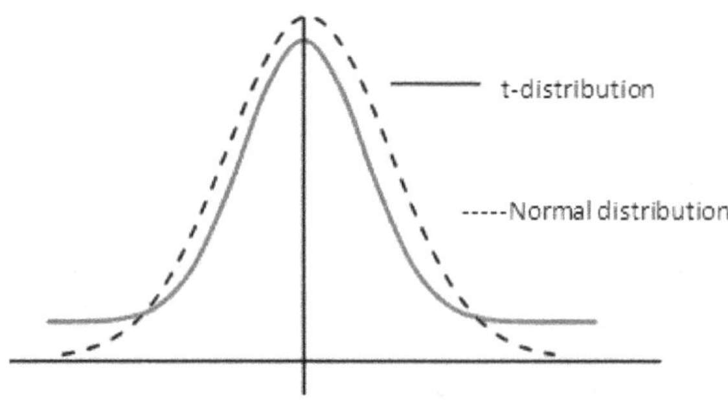

Example 1: Nine packs of rice are taken at random from a packing machine in an industry. The mean weight of the packs is 19.8 kg and the standard deviation is 0.50 kg. Does the sample mean differ significantly from the intended weight of 20 kg?

Solution:

$Given: n = 9, \bar{x} = 19.8, s = 0.50, \mu = 20$

$Hypothesis: H_0{:}\mu = 20, H_1{:}\mu \neq 20$

$$Test\ statistic: t = \frac{\bar{x} - \mu}{s/\sqrt{n}}$$

$$= \frac{19.8 - 20}{0.5/\sqrt{9}}$$

$$= \frac{-0.2}{0.1667} = -1.2$$

$$\Rightarrow |t| = 1.2$$

$At\ 5\%\ level\ of\ significance (Two\ tailed)\ t_{\alpha/2,8} = 2.306$

$$\because |t| < |t_{\alpha/2}|$$

$Hence\ null\ hypothesis\ is\ accepted.$

$The\ weight\ of\ sample\ is\ same\ as\ the\ intended\ weight.$

Example 2: A sample of nine items from the population has the following values:

25	27	27	24	28	25	29	30	28

The mean is observed as 27 and the sum of the square of the deviation from mean is 32. Can this sample be regarded as taken from the population having mean 30?

Solution: $Given: n = 9, \bar{x} = 27,$

$sum\ of\ square\ deviation = \sum(x - \bar{x})^2 = 32, \mu = 30$

$Hypothesis: H_0{:}\mu = 30, H_1{:}\mu \neq 30$

$$Test\ statistic: t = \frac{\bar{x} - \mu}{s/\sqrt{n}}$$

$$Here, s = \sqrt{\frac{\sum(x - \bar{x})^2}{n - 1}} = \sqrt{\frac{32}{8}} = 2$$

$$Hence, t = \frac{27 - 30}{2/\sqrt{9}}$$

$$= \frac{-3}{(2/3)} = -4.5$$

$$\Rightarrow |t| = 4.5$$

At 5% level of significance(Two tailed) $t_{\alpha/2,8} = 2.306$

$$\because |t| > |t_{\alpha/2}|$$

Hence null hypothesis is rejected.

The sample cannot be regarded as taken from the population having mean 30.

Example 3: The diastolic blood pressure of a man on different days in a month is found to be 69, 65, 77, 70, 69, 71, 70, 73, 69, 78. From the data can it be concluded that the mean blood pressure of man in this month is 70 at 10% level of significance?

Solution:

Given: $n = 10, \mu = 70$

From the data $\bar{x} = \frac{711}{10} = 71.1, s = 3.928$

Hypothesis: $H_0{:}\mu = 70, H_1{:}\mu \neq 70$

Test statistic: $t = \dfrac{\bar{x} - \mu}{s/\sqrt{n}}$

$$Hence, t = \frac{71.1 - 70}{3.928/\sqrt{10}}$$

$$= 0.8855$$

$$\Rightarrow |t| = 0.8855$$

At 10% level of significance(Two tailed) $t_{\alpha/2,9} = 1.383$

$$\because |t| > |t_{\alpha/2}|$$

Hence null hypothesis is accepted.

Thus, the mean blood pressure of man in this month can be considered as 70.

9.4.2 Testing a hypothesis for a two small population mean

Let, two random samples of size $n_1 and n_2$ (both small) are taken from the two populations with mean μ_1 and μ_2. Let, the two-sample means are given by $\bar{x}_1$ and $\bar{x}_2$ with the sample variance as s_1^2 and s_2^2.

The hypothesis for the difference between the two population mean for two tail test is given by:

$H_0{:}\mu_1 = \mu_2, H_1{:}\mu_1 \neq \mu_2$

Similarly, the hypothesis can be framed for the one tail test.

In the small population, it is assumed that the two population variances are unknown but equal. Under this assumption the pooled sample variance is calculated as:

$$s^2 = \frac{s_1^2(n_1 - 1) + s_2^2(n_2 - 1)}{n_1 + n_2 - 2}$$

Hence the t-statistics is given by:

$$t = \frac{\bar{x}_1 - \bar{x}_2}{\sqrt{s^2\left(\dfrac{1}{n_1} + \dfrac{1}{n_2}\right)}},$$

with degree of freedom $n_1 + n_2 - 2$

Example 1: Two filtration procedures are compared by measuring the time taken. From the given data can it be concluded that the two methods are significantly different? Assume equal standard deviations of two populations at 5% level of significance.

	Method 1	Method 2
Sample size	15	12
Mean(sec)	40	55
Std dev.	2.5	3.2

Solution:

$Given\text{: } n_1 = 15, n_2 = 12, \bar{x}_1 = 40, \bar{x}_2 = 55, s_1 = 2.5, s_2 = 3.2\,Hypothesis\text{: } H_0\text{:}\mu_1 = \mu_2 \text{ ;} H_1\text{:}\mu_1 \neq \mu_2$

Calculation of the pooled variance:

$$s^2 = \frac{s_1^2(n_1 - 1) + s_2^2(n_2 - 1)}{n_1 + n_2 - 2}$$

$$s^2 = \frac{2.5^2(14) + 3.2^2(11)}{25}$$

$$= 8.0056$$

Hence using the t-statistics:

$$t = \frac{\bar{x}_1 - \bar{x}_2}{\sqrt{s^2\left(\dfrac{1}{n_1} + \dfrac{1}{n_2}\right)}} = \frac{40 - 55}{\sqrt{8.0056\left(\dfrac{1}{15} + \dfrac{1}{12}\right)}} = -13.688$$

$$\Rightarrow |t| = 13.688$$

$At\ 5\%\ level\ of\ significance (Two\ tailed)\ t_{\alpha/2,25} = 2.06$

$$\because |t| > |t_{\alpha/2}|$$

$Hence\ null\ hypothesis\ is\ rejected.$

$Thus, there\ is\ a\ significance\ difference\ in\ the\ two\ procedures.$

Example 2: Tyres of two brands were tested for length of life. Following are the observations:

	Type A	Type B
Sample size	12	10
Sample mean (months)	36	40
Sample std dev.	4.5	5

From the given data can it be concluded that type-A tyres are superior to type-B, assuming equal standard deviation from the two populations at 10% level of significance.

Solution:

Given: $n_1 = 12, n_2 = 10, \bar{x}_1 = 36, \bar{x}_2 = 40, s_1 = 4.5, s_2 = 5.0$ *Hypothesis:* $H_0 : \mu_1 \leq \mu_2 \; ; \; H_1 : \mu_1 > \mu_2$

Calculating the pooled variance as:

$$s^2 = \frac{s_1^2(n_1 - 1) + s_2^2(n_2 - 1)}{n_1 + n_2 - 2}$$

$$s^2 = \frac{4.5^2(11) + 5^2(9)}{20} = 22.3875$$

Hence the t-statistics is given by:

$$t = \frac{\bar{x}_1 - \bar{x}_2}{\sqrt{s^2\left(\dfrac{1}{n_1} + \dfrac{1}{n_2}\right)}} = \frac{36 - 40}{\sqrt{22.3875\left(\dfrac{1}{12} + \dfrac{1}{10}\right)}} = -1.9744$$

$$\Rightarrow |t| = 1.9744$$

At 10% *level of significance (One Tailed)* $t_{\alpha,25} = 2.552$

$$\because |t| < |t_{\alpha/2}|$$

Hence null hypothesis is accepted.

Thus, type – A tyres are superior to type – B tyres.

9.5 Testing a hypothesis to compare population with matched pairs (paired t-test)

The above discussed procedures of hypothesis testing are to make decision about the hypothesis for two mean and proportion. But if the ***samples dependent of each other and with small sample size, the hypothesis testing is referred as a paired t-test or a matched paired test.***
This test is commonly implemented to ***study the pre-and post-training measures.***
The t-statistics to test the difference between the means of two related populations (matched pairs) is given as:

$$t = \frac{\bar{d}}{s_d/\sqrt{n}}$$

with $n - 1$ degree of freedom.
Here, n is the number of pairs of difference, $\bar{d}$ is the mean of difference and s_d is the standard deviation of the sample difference.
The hypothesis for this test can be framed as:

$$H_0 : \mu_1 = \mu_2, \; H_1 : \mu_1 \neq \mu_2$$

$$or$$

$$H_0 : \mu_d = 0, \; H_1 : \mu_d \neq 0$$

Example 1: A study was conducted to investigate the effect of a drug in controlling the blood pressure level. Results of the blood pressure collected from ten randomly selected patients after and before taking the pill are:

Patient	1	2	3	4	5	6	7	8	9	10
Before	75	68	69	70	78	82	58	69	80	79
After	80	75	78	68	80	68	68	70	75	80

From the data can it be concluded that the drug is effective in controlling the blood pressure at 5% level of significance?

Solution:

Calculating the difference between the sample values before and after taking the pill provides the difference values as:

Before	75	68	69	70	78	82	58	69	80	79
After	80	75	78	68	80	68	68	70	75	80
Difference(d)	-5	-7	-9	2	-2	14	-10	-1	5	-1

The mean and the standard deviation of the difference values are obtained as:

$$\bar{d} = \frac{-14}{10} = -1.4; s_d = 7.1987$$

The paired t-test can be applied for the hypothesis

$$H_0 : \mu_1 = \mu_2 \ versus \ H_1 : \mu_1 \neq \mu_2$$

$$or$$

$$H_0 : \mu_d = 0 \ versus \ H_1 : \mu_d \neq 0$$

The t-statistics for the paired samples can thus be calculated as:

$$t = \frac{\bar{d}}{s_d/\sqrt{n}} = \frac{-1.4}{7.1987/\sqrt{10}} = -0.615$$

At 5% level of significance (Two tailed) $t_{\alpha/2,9} = 2.262$

$$\because |t| < |t_{\alpha/2}|$$

Hence the null hypothesis is accepted. Thus, there is no significance difference in the blood pressure after the consumption of drug.

Example 2: A school principal wants to check difference in the performance of the students before and after training sessions. For this purpose, a random sample of 6 students is taken and the scores are noted after and before training. At 10% level of significance determine whether there is a significant change in the scores obtained by the students after the training.

Student	1	2	3	4	5	6

Before	7	6	8	7	6	7
After	9	7	10	9	8	10

Solution:

Calculating the difference between the sample values provides the difference values as:

Student	1	2	3	4	5	6
Difference (d)	-2	-1	-2	-2	-2	-3

The mean and the standard deviation of the difference values are obtained as:

$$\bar{d} = \frac{-12}{6} = -2; s_d = 0.6324$$

The t-test for the paired test can be applied for the hypothesis
$H_0{:}\mu_1 = \mu_2, H_1{:}\mu_1 \neq \mu_2$

The t-statistics for the paired samples can thus be calculated as:

$$t = \frac{\bar{d}}{s_d/\sqrt{n}} = \frac{-2}{0.6324/\sqrt{6}} = -7.746$$

At 10% level of significance (Two tailed) $t_{\alpha/2,5} = 2.015$

$$\because |t| > |t_{\alpha/2}|$$

Hence the null hypothesis is rejected. Thus, there is a significance difference in the scores obtained by the students after the training program.

9.6 Testing a Hypothesis to compare population variances (F-test)

To make a comparison of the variance between the two data sets the above discussed hypothesis test cannot be used.

The hypothesis for comparing variances can be defined as:

$H_0{:}\sigma_1^2 = \sigma_2^2 \text{ or } \sigma_1^2 \leq \sigma_2^2 \text{ or } \sigma_1^2 \geq \sigma_2^2$ *(variances difference are not significant)*

$$H_1: \sigma_1^2 \neq \sigma_2^2 \text{ or } \sigma_1^2 > \sigma_2^2 \text{ or } \sigma_1^2 < \sigma_2^2$$

To make inferences about the population variances two independent random samples of size n_1 and n_2 are taken assuming normal distributions. The ratio of the two sample variances are compared and the ratio is called as F-value that follows the F-distribution. The F-statistic can hence be defined as:

$$F = \frac{S_1^2}{S_2^2}$$

with degrees of freedom $n_1 - 1, n_2 - 1$.

Here numerator value should be the larger of the two estimated values.

If the data is provided, the standard deviation of the two samples needs to be obtained using the formula:

$$S = \sqrt{\frac{\Sigma(x - \bar{x})^2}{n - 1}}$$

If the standard deviation or the variances of samples are provided, estimators for the sample variance are given as:

$$S_1^2 = \frac{n_1 s_1^2}{n_1 - 1} \; ; \; S_2^2 = \frac{n_2 s_2^2}{n_2 - 1}$$

where, s_1^2 and s_1^2 are the given sample variance.

Properties of the F-Distribution

1. F-distribution is based on the assumption that the populations from which samples are drawn are normally distributed.
2. The F-distribution is not symmetric.
3. Values of the F-distribution cannot be negative.
4. The exact shape of the F-distribution depends on two different degrees of freedom.
5. F-distribution follows reciprocal property. The value of F at m, n degree of freedom at α level of significance can be obtained using F value at n, m degree of freedom as:

$$F_{\alpha,(m,n)} = \frac{1}{F_{1-\alpha,(n,m)}}$$

While using the F distribution table, the numerator degrees of freedom are always given first, as switching the order of degrees of freedom changes the distribution (e.g., F (10,12) is not same as F (12,10)).

Example 1: Two samples A and B of size 6 and 10 have the following observations:

A	11	12	14	15	19	16				
B	12	11	13	14	11	14	15	12	13	11

Test the equality of sample variance. The F-value at 5,9 degree of freedom is 3.48.

Solution:

For given data $n_1 = 6; n_2 = 10$ and the average is calculated as 14.5 and 12.6. For the given samples the variance can be obtained as:

A	Square of deviation	B	Square of deviation
11	(11-14.5)2=12.25	12	0.36
12	6.25	11	2.56
14	0.25	13	0.16
15	0.25	14	1.96
19	20.25	11	2.56
16	2.25	14	1.96
		15	5.76
		12	0.36
		13	0.16
		11	2.56
Sum =87	Sum of sq deviation=41.5	Sum=126	Sum of sq deviation=18.4

Mean $=14.5$ Variance $=8.3$	Mean$=12.6$ Variance $=2.04$

Hence, $S_1^2 = 8.3, S_2^2 = 2.04$

For hypothesis:

$H_0{:}S_1^2 = S_2^2 \quad H_1{:}S_1^2 \neq S_2^2$ The test statistic:

$$F = \frac{S_1^2}{S_2^2} = 4.086$$

Since, $F < 3.48 (tabulated\,value)$

$Hence, H_0\,is\,rejected.$

Example 2: Two samples of size 9 and 8 has the standard deviation 4 and 6.3. Can the samples be regarded as drawn from the normal population with equal variance? F-value from table 8 and 7 at degrees of freedom is 3.73.

Solution: The F-test for the equality of variance has the hypothesis as:

$H_0{:}S_1^2 = S_2^2 \quad H_1{:}S_1^2 \neq S_2^2$

For given data $n_1 = 9; n_2 = 8$

For, $s_1^2 = 16, s_2^2 = 39.69$

$$S_1^2 = \frac{n_1 s_1^2}{n_1 - 1} = \frac{9 \times 16}{8} = 18;$$

$$S_2^2 = \frac{n_2 s_2^2}{n_2 - 1} = \frac{8 \times 39.69}{7} = 45.36 \qquad F = \frac{S_1^2}{S_2^2} = 0.3968$$

Test statistics:

$F < 3.73 (tabulated\,value)$

$Hence, H_0\,is\,accepted.$

Summary:

Following is the summary of the hypothesis test for the population mean for large and small sample size

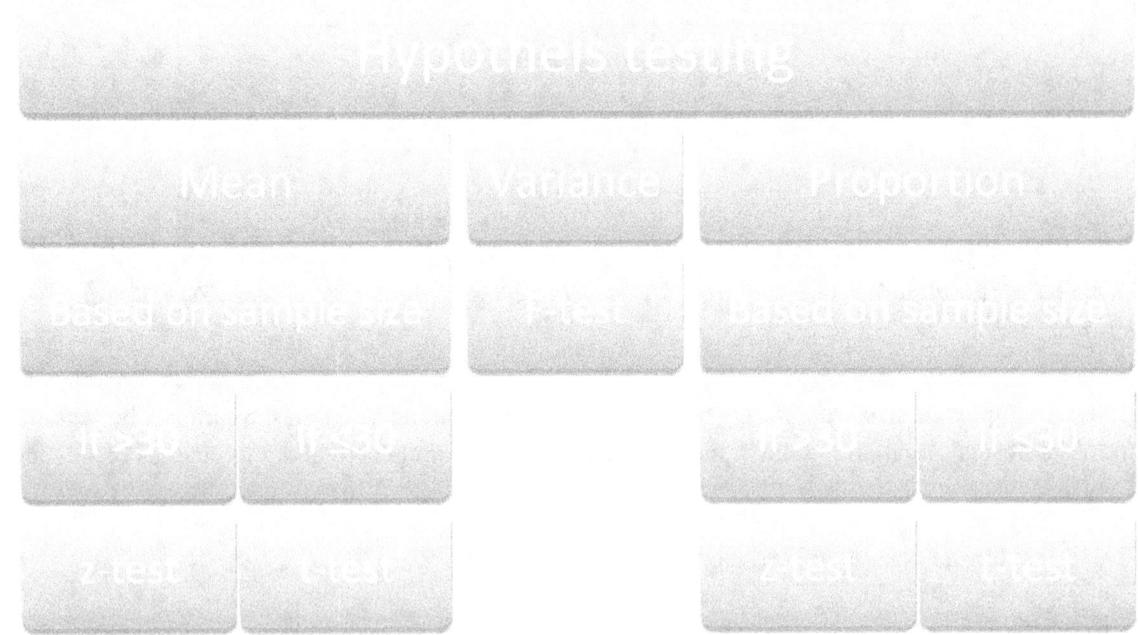

<u>Chapter based Quiz</u>

A) MCQs

1. What is the shape of the curve in t-distribution?
a) Mound shape
b) Ring shape
c) Bell shape
d) A parabola shapes

2. Which of the following statements are correct?
A. Shape of the curve in normal distribution is bell shaped.
B. Shape of the curve in t-distribution is bell shaped.
C. t-distribution is applicable for sample size >30.
D. Normal distribution is applicable for sample size >30.

a) A and D
b) C and D
c) A and C
d) B and D

3. Which measure is use to find the spread of data values from their mean with same unit as that of data?
a) Variance
b) Standard deviation
c) Range
d) Correlation

4. Match the correct options
A) The acceptance of null hypothesis, when it is actually false   1) Type-1 error

B) The rejection of null hypothesis, when it is actually true   2) Type-2 error

    a) A-1, B-2
    b) A-2, B-1
    c) A-1, B-1
    d) A-2, B-2

5. Which tail test is needed for testing a hypothesis that the mean life of bulb produced is 800 hours with an alternative hypothesis that it is greater than 800 hours?

a) One tailed test
b) Two tailed tests
c) Three tailed tests
d) Four tail tests

6. On testing a hypothesis that means life of bulb produced is 800 hours with an alternative hypothesis that it is greater than 800 hours. If the value of calculated z is less than the standard value of z. What is the decision for the null hypothesis?

a) Accepted
b) Rejected
c) Not able to make decision
d) Two tail tests

7. What is the mean and variance of given data 4, 10, 16, 12?

a) 20.5, 26
b) 10.5, 30
c) 30.6, 10
d) 10.5, 25

8. What is the mean and variance of given data 1, 3, 8, 10?

a) 4.5, 4.2
b) 5.5, 3.5
c) 5.5, 4.2
d) 4.5, 1.2

9. Four participants take Mathematics and English quiz. Which test statistics is appropriate to verify the claim that the overall performance of students is the same in both courses?

Student	1	2	3	4
Mathematics	80.00%	72.60%	99.00%	91.30%
English	85.50%	71.00%	93.20%	93.00%

a. Two-tailed two-sample paired/dependent t-test of means
b. Regression
c. Two-tailed two-sample independent z-test of means
d. One-tailed two-sample z-test of mean

10. What is the degree of freedom for 10 data values in a sample?

a) 7
b) 8

c) 9

d) 10

11. Which tail test can be used to verify a claim $H_0: \mu = 10$ with $H_1: \mu \neq 10$?

a) One tailed test

b) Two tailed tests

c) Three tailed tests

d) Four tailed tests

12. What is the value of z at 5% level of significance for 2 tails?

a) 1.52

b) 1.645

c) 1.96

d) 2.58

13. What is the value of z at 1% level of significance for 1 tail?

a) 1.645

b) 1.96

c) 2.33

d) 2.58

14. The tail of the t-distribution is _____ than the tails of the curve in normal distribution.

a) Heavier

b) Light

c) Thick

d) Dense

15. The ___________ distribution approaches __________ distribution as sample size increases.

a) normal, t

b) normal, Poisson

c) normal, binomial

d) t, normal

16. If $|z|$ calculated value is more than $|z|$ standard value then the H_1 is_____.

a) rejected

b) accepted

c) information is incomplete

d) not available.

17. In z-test, which one of the following is not an assumption?

a) Sample size is less than 30.

b) The sample is a simple random sample.

c) The value of the population standard deviation is known.

d) The population is normally distributed

18. What are the two types of hypotheses?

a) Positive and negative hypothesis
b) Skewed and normal hypothesis
c) Null and alternative hypothesis
d) Null and complete hypothesis

19. What is the shape of curve in normal distribution?
a) Circle
b) Bell
c) Parabola
d) Mound

20. What is described by variance of a given data?
a) Spread of data values from their mean
b) Sum of all the value of a given data
c) Square root of standard deviation
d) Measure of skewness of the data

21. Which of the following is a WRONG assumption for Z-test?
a) Sample size must be more than 30
b) Data must have a standard deviation more than 10
c) Data must be randomly distributed
d) Sample must be a simple random sample

22. For the statement, "Average marks obtained by students in a class is atmost 10", which of the following is correct as null hypothesis?
a) $H_0 : \mu = 10$
b) $H_0 : \mu \geq 10$
c) $H_0 : \mu \leq 10$
d) $H_0 : \mu > 10$

23. The symbol _____ is used to represent the probability of a type I error.
a) α
b) β
c) γ
d) δ

24. The rejection of null hypothesis, when it is actually true leads to _____ error.
a) Type A
b) Type B
c) Type |
d) Type ||

25. The acceptance of alternative hypothesis, when it is actually false leads to _____ error.
a) Type A
b) Type B
c) Type |

d) Type ||

26. If the calculated value of z=1.23 and the decision is to be done at 95% level of significance for two
    tailed test. What is the decision for null hypothesis?
a) Rejected
b) Accepted
c) Required to investigate for decision
d) 95%

27. Choose the correct match for the shape of the curve

A) Z-distribution	i) Depend on the degree of freedom
B) t-Distribution	ii) Bell-shaped
C) F-distribution	iii) Mound shape

a) A-ii; B-iii; C-i
b) A-i; B-ii; C-iii
c) A-ii; B-i; C-iii
d) A-I; B-iii; C-ii

28. Which of the following is INCORRECT in t-distribution?
a) Tail in t-distribution is heavier as compared to normal distribution
b) t-distribution approaches normal distribution with increase in sample size
c) t-distribution curve is unsymmetrical about the axis.
d) t-test is applied when sample size is less or equal to 30

29. For t-test the standard value depends upon which of the following?
a) Level of significance
b) Degree of freedom
c) Tailed test
d) All of the above

30. For z-test the standard value depends upon which of the following?
a) Level of significance and Tailed test
b) Degree of freedom
c) Tailed test
d) All of the above

31. Which of the following is a test to compare two population variances?
a) Z-test
b) t-test
c) F-test
d) Chi-Square-test

32. For F-test the standard value depends upon which of the following?
a) The significance levels
b) Numerator degrees of freedom = $n_1 - 1$
c) Denominator degrees of freedom = $n_2 - 1$

d) All of the above

33. Which of the following distribution is not symmetric?
a) Normal distribution
b) t-distribution
c) F- distribution
d) None of the above

34. If the critical value of Z is 1.645. What is the level of significance of two tail test?
a) 10%
b) 1%
c) 2%
d) 5%

35. If X is a normal variable with mean=50 and standard deviation=10. What is the value of P(30<X<80)?
a) P(3<Z<8)
b) P(-2<Z<8)
c) P(-3<Z<3)
d) P(-2<Z<3)

36. What is presented by the degree of freedom?
a) The number of variables
b) The number of independent variables
c) Difference between mean and standard deviation
d) None of these

37. Which test can be used for small samples?
a) Student's t-test
b) Z-test
c) KD test
d) All of the above

38. What are the parameters of binomial distribution with mean=8 and variance=4?
a) n=20, p=0.2
b) n=16, p=0.5
c) n=4, p=0.5
d) n=16, p=0.2

39. What are the parameters of binomial distribution with mean=10 and variance=7.5?
a) n=20, p=0.2
b) n=40, p=0.5
c) n=8, p=0.2
d) n=40, p=0.25

40. If X is a normal variable with mean=40 and standard deviation=10. What is the value of P(20<X<50)?

a) P(3<Z<8)
b) P(5<Z<8)
c) P(-2<Z<1)
d) P(-3<Z<1)

Answers:

1-a	2-a	3-b	4-b	5-a	6-a	7-d	8-c	9-a	10-c
11-b	12-c	13-c	14-a	15-d	16-b	17-a	18-c	19-b	20-a
21-b	22-c	23-a	24-c	25-d	26-b	27-a	28-c	29-d	30-a
31-c	32-d	33-c	34-a	35-d	36-b	37-a	38-b	39-d	40-c

B) Fill in the blanks

1. The rejection of null hypothesis, when it is actually true leads to ___________error.
2. The acceptance of alternative hypothesis, when it is actually false leads to ___________error.
3. Area under the probability distribution curve is ________.
4. The t-distribution approaches normal distribution with __________in sample size.
5. The normal distribution curve is _________about the x axis.
6. Z-test is applied when sample size _________30.
7. If sample size in an experiment is 21, the degree of freedom is_________.
8. Variance of given data 6,8,10,12,14 is_________.
9. A group of 14 employees was selected for a training of stress relief. The statistical test for the comparison of stress level of the employees as compared to the other employees requires ____________.
10. A group of 10 employees was selected for a training of writing. The statistical test used for the comparison of the writing styles of employees before and after training requires _____________.
11. Null hypothesis is rejected in a right tail test if the calculated value of the statistic is ______then the standard value.
12. The mean salary of a fresh graduate student is $ 5000. This value is a ______(statistic/parameter) because it is a numerical measurement describing some characteristic of a population.
13. When the level of significance of a hypothesis test is increased, the probability of committing a Type I error is ________.
14. Two samples of size 22 and 24 are drawn from the two normal populations, with the unknown variances assumed to be equal. The degree of freedom for the equal variance t-test statistics is_____
15. The null hypothesis in F-test for comparing two sample variances states that the two sample variances are __________.
16. The degree of freedom for F-test has _______(one/two) values.
17. When comparing the performance of same participant before and after training __________ test is employed.
18. Value of z at 5% level of significance for one tail is_________.
19. Value of z at 10% level of significance for two tail is_________.
20. Value of z at 10% level of significance for one tail is_________.

Answers:

1- Type I	2- Type II	3-one	4- increase	5- symmetrical
6- more than	7-20	8-10	9- t test	10-paired t-test
11-more	12- statistic	13-increased	14-44	15-equal
16-2 values	17-paired t-test	18-1.645	19-1.645	20-1.28

NOTES:

Chapter 10

Experimental Design: ANOVA

Various techniques of analyzing data related to means and proportions for one or two samples have been discussed in the previous chapters. To compare three or more than two sample means the previous learned concepts are not applicable.

Analysis of variance (ANOVA) is a method that can be used to compare three or more population means.

For example: To measure the change in the average salary structure in four organizations.

The null hypothesis can be: The average salary in the four organization is equal i.e., there is no significant difference in the average salary of the employees in four organizations against the alternative hypothesis that at least one of the means is different from the others.

The concept of analysis of variance (ANOVA) has many applications in real life and has been designed to study the difference in the values with respect to the variances of the data values.

For Example: ANOVA can be implemented to study:

- Heights of animals of a specific genus based on habitat.
- Comparing birth weights of children under different circumstances.
- Comparing the recovery rate of patients being operated using different techniques.
- Comparing attention spans of graduate students while learning in online mode.

10.1 Experimental design

An experimental design is the logical construction of an experiment to test a hypothesis in which the researcher either controls or manipulates one or more variables. There are three basic principles of experimental designs: randomization, replication, and local control.

Randomization

Randomization is the first principle of an experimental design.

Randomization is a proses of assigning the treatments randomly to the experimental units.

It implies that there is an equal probability of allotment of treatments to the units. The purpose of randomizations is to remove biasedness and other sources of uncontrollable variation.

Replication

This is the second principle of an experimental design.

Replication means repetition of the basic experiment to remove the errors occurring by chance.

The variation in the values of the outcomes can be removable by using a number of experimental units and repeating the experiment a number of times. Thus, replication helps in obtaining an accurate estimate of the experimental values; decreasing the experimental error, thereby increasing precision; and obtaining a more precise estimate of the mean treatment effect.

Local Control

All extraneous sources of variation cannot be controlled either by randomization or replication.

To remove the errors, balancing and blocking of the experimental units are done called as local control.

Balancing implies that the treatments should be assigned to the experimental units in a pre-defined way and blocking means collecting similar experimental units together to form a relatively homogeneous group.

Thus, the main purpose of local control is to increase the efficiency of an experimental design by minimizing the experimental error.

10.2 Important Terms

Some of the widely used terms to discuss experimental designs are as follows:

1. **Treatment variable:** This is a variable which is controlled or modified by the researcher in the experiment.

   For example: In agriculture, the different fertilizers or the different methods of cultivation are the treatments.

2. **Classification variable:** Classification variable is the characteristics of the experimental subject that are present prior to the experiment and not a result of the researcher's manipulation or control.

   For example: In agriculture, the condition or quality of the soil is a classification variable.

3. **Experimental Units:** The smallest divisions of the experimental material to which treatments are applied and observations are made are referred to as experimental units.

   For example: In agriculture, the seeds of a crop which are investigated for the maximum yield by providing the different sets of treatments.

4. **Factor:** A factor refers as a set of treatments of a single type. In most situations, a researcher may be interested in studying more than one factor.

   For example: In agriculture, the two factors under study can be the effect of fertilizers and the type of irrigation. The classifications of the types of fertilizer as A, B, C are the treatments. Hence, factor is a set of treatments applied to the units in an experiment.

10.3 ANOVA

Analysis of variance (ANOVA) is a technique of testing hypothesis for several populations means. This is an extension of the two independent samples t-test.

10.3.1 Assumptions of ANOVA

Analysis of variance (ANOVA) is based on some assumptions to be satisfied for its application to test the significance difference between the population mean of more than two samples.

1. *Normality*: Each population should have a normal distribution.

2. *Independence of cases*: Samples should be randomly drawn from the population and should be independent of each other.

3. *Equality (or "homogeneity") of variances*: All populations must have an equal variance.

10.3.2 Hypothesis of ANOVA

If there are k samples to be analyzed for the difference between their mean having different or same number of units, then the null and alternative hypotheses can be defined as follows:

$$H_0 : \mu_1 = \mu_2 = \mu_3 = ... = \mu_k \ (\text{All sample means are same})$$
$$H_1 : \text{All sample means are not same}$$

10.3.3 Variance between the samples and Variance within the samples

In ANOVA, the total variation in the sample data can be divided in to two components:
1. variance between samples
2. variance within samples.

Variance between samples is due to the difference among the sample means. This variance is due to some assignable causes.

Variance within the samples is the difference due to chance or experimental errors.

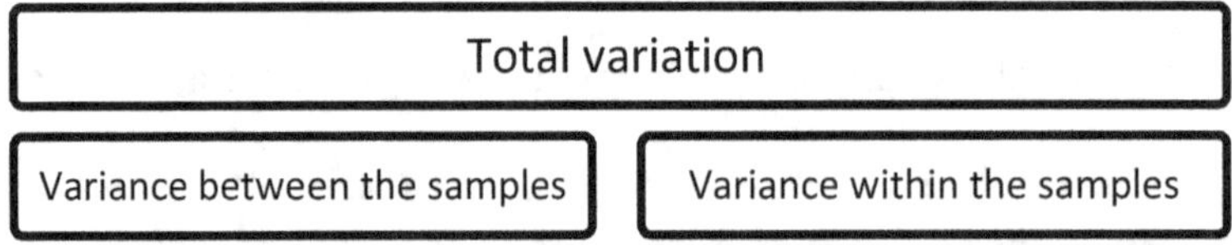

For example: Three branches of a company can be analyzed for profit. The difference in the profit of the three branches is the variance between samples. The profits in the same branch can also be different for different sections. This is the variance within the samples, as change is due to chance.

The analysis of variance can be categorized based on the number of treatments and factors as:

- Completely randomized design (CRD)
- Randomized block design (RBD)
- Latin square design (LSD)

Each of these types of ANOVA is different from one another in terms of the calculation of variances considered under the different conditions. The brief description of the CRD and RBD ANOVA is discussed in the sections below:

10.4 Completely randomized design (CRD)

Completely randomized design (CRD) ***involves only one independent variable, with two or more treatment levels or classifications***, hence also called as one-way ANOVA.

Following is the hypothesis for mean of more than two samples.

H_0:$\mu_1 = \mu_2 = \mu_3 = \dots = \mu_c$ All treatment means are equal.

H_1: All treatment means are not equal.

In CRD, the total sum of squares can be divided into two additive and independent parts as SSC (sum of squares between columns) and SSE (sum of squares within samples due to errors).

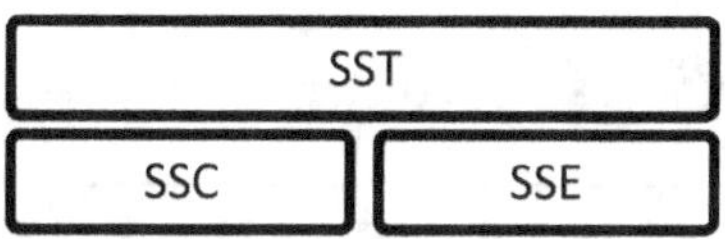

Following are the steps for CRD:

1. Calculate sum of squares between columns (SSC) and sum of squares within samples (SSE). The SSC and SSE are given by relation:

$$SSC = \sum_i (x_{ij} - \overline{x_j})^2, \;\; SSE = \sum_i n_j(\overline{x_j} - \overline{x})^2$$

Detail procedure is defined in example.

2. Using the sum of squares find the mean square (MS) values on dividing by the corresponding degree of freedom.

For k samples, the degree of freedom is $(k-1)$ between column and $(n-k)$ within the samples where n is the total number of units in the experiment.

Hence,

$$MSC = SSC/(k-1)$$

$MSE = SSE/(n-k)$

3. For decision F-test is used which is the ratio of the treatment variance (MSC) by the error variance (MSE), where MSC is the mean square between column and MSE is the mean square due to error.

$F = MSC/MSE$

The F test statistic follows F-distribution with $k-1$ degrees of freedom corresponding to MSC in the numerator and $n-k$ degrees of freedom corresponding to MSE in the denominator.

The null hypothesis is rejected if the calculated F-value is greater than the F-value at $k-1$ degrees of freedom in the numerator and $n-k$ degrees of freedom in the denominator.

Symbolically, for a given level of significance α, the null hypothesis will be accepted if:

$$F_{calculated} < F_{std}$$

Thus, the null hypothesis will be rejected if

$$F_{calculated} > F_{std(k-1, n-k)}$$

The summary table for the CRD can be constructed as follows:

Source of Variation	Sum of Squares (SS)	Degree of freedom (df)	Mean Squares (MS)	F-statistic
Between Column	SSC	$k-1$	$MSC = SSC/(k-1)$	
			$F = MSC/MSE$	
Within Column	SSE	$n-k$	$MSE = SSE/(n-k)$	
Total	SST	$n-1$		

Example: Using the procedure of CRD, investigate difference in marks of the students in the three sections:

A	B	C
13	17	12
12	15	15
13	18	17
14	16	18
15	17	19

Given, the standard F-value at 2,12 degree of freedom is 9.40813.

Solution: To investigate the difference in marks of the students in the three sections, following is the hypothesis: $H_0: \mu_1 = \mu_2 = \mu_3$ mean marks of the three sections are equal with H_1: mean marks of the three sections are not equal.

Following are the detail step procedure to find the entries in the CRD table:

10.4.1 Steps for calculating SSC and MSC

Following are the steps to calculate SSC:

1. *Calculate the mean of each sample category and their grand mean as mean of mean.*
In the above example, the mean of each column is calculated on dividing the sum of column A, B and C respectively by the number of values as 5.
Hence, for each column the mean values are calculated as 13.4, 16.6 and 16.2.
Hence the grand mean is (13.4+16.6+16.2)/3=15.4.

2. *Find the difference between the mean of each sample and grand mean* $(\overline{x_j} - \overline{x})$

3. *Find the square of the terms and multiply by the respective number of observations in each column.* The sum thus provides the SSC as:

$$SSC = \sum_i n_j(\overline{x_j} - \overline{x})^2$$

Here, the sum of square of difference of mean and grand mean are 4, 1.44 and 0.64 for each column and $n_j = 5$.

Hence, SSC = 5 x 4 + 5 x 1.44 + 5 x 0.64 = 30.4.

4. Find $MSC = \dfrac{SSC}{k-1}$

Here $k = 3$, hence the degree of freedom is 2.

Thus, $MSC = 30.4 / 2 = 15.2.$

The whole calculation can be summarized as follows:

	A	B	C
	13	17	12
	12	15	15
	13	18	17
	14	16	18
	15	17	19
Sum	67	83	81
Mean	13.4	16.6	16.2
Grand mean	15.4		
SS	4	1.44	0.64
n*SS	20	7.2	3.2
SSC	30.4		
MSC	15.2		

10.4.2 Steps for calculating SST (Total sum of squares)

To find SST, the difference is calculated between each and every value from the grand mean. Grand mean is already calculated in the earlier step. SST is the sum of square of difference between the values from the grand mean given as:

$$SST = \sum_{i,j} (x_{ij} - \overline{x})^2$$

Here ij is the representation for all the values of the rows as well as column.

Square of the differences of the data values from the grand mean 15.4 generate the following data whose sum is SST.

A	B	C	SSD_1	SSD_2	SSD_3
13	17	12	5.76	2.56	11.56
12	15	15	11.56	0.16	0.16
13	18	17	5.76	6.76	2.56
14	16	18	1.96	0.36	6.76
15	17	19	0.16	2.56	12.96

$$SST = SSD_1 + SSD_2 + SSD_3 = \textbf{71.6}$$

10.4.3 Steps for calculating SSE and MSE

SSE can be calculated by two ways:
  i) Directly using data values.
  ii) Using already calculated SSC and SST.

SSE can be calculated directly from the data values using the formula

$$SSE = \sum_i n_j (\overline{x_j} - \overline{x})^2$$

It is the difference of each value of each column data values from their respective column means.

In this example, there are three columns. The square of the difference of data value from their respective column mean are calculated as follows:

	SE_1	SE_2	SE_3
	0.16	0.16	17.64
	1.96	2.56	1.44
	0.16	1.96	0.64
	0.36	0.36	3.24
	2.56	0.16	7.84
Sum	5.2	5.2	30.8

Hence, $SSE = SD_1 + SD_2 + SD_3 = 41.2$

To calculate SSE using the already calculated SSC and SST, the relation between SSC, SSE and SST is used: SST=SSC + SSE.
Hence,

$$SSE = SST - SSC$$

As calculated earlier, SST=71.6 and SSC=30.4.

Hence, SSE=71.6-30.4=41.2.

Since the total number of samples are 15, hence the degrees of freedom is 15-3=12.

Thus, MSE=41.2 / 12=3.433.

The whole calculation can be summarized as follows:

10.4.4 Summary table of ANOVA

To make the decision the F-value is calculated as the ratio of MSC and MSE. As, MSC=15.20 and MSE=3.433, hence the value of F =15.20/3.43=4.427.

The F standard value at 2,12 degree of freedom is 9.40813 and the calculated F value is 4.427.

Since, $F_{calculated} < F_{std}$. Hence the hypothesis is accepted.

Source of Variation	Sum of Squares (SS)	Degree of freedom (df)	Mean Squares (MS)	F-statistic
Between column	SSC	2	15.20	
				4.427
Within column (due to errors)	SSE	12	3.433	
Total	71.6	14		

10.5 Randomized block design (RBD)

In CRD, the total variation is divided into two components. The variations were taken due to treatments (between the samples or columns) and due to errors (within the samples). But the variation due to error may occur due to some other measurable factors. Hence there exists a need to control additional factors called as BLOCK factors.

For example:
In the above discussed example of CRD ANOVA, the difference in the marks of the students in the three sections can be different due to timings of the class, background of the students etc. Hence by including more factors in the experimental design, the possibility of controlling these variables can be examined.

In RBD, experimental units are divided into blocks and in each block, treatments are assigned randomly.

In RBD, the total sum of squares consists of three parts:

SST (total sum of squares) = SSC (sum of squares between columns) + SSE (sum of squares of errors) + SSR (sum of squares between rows).

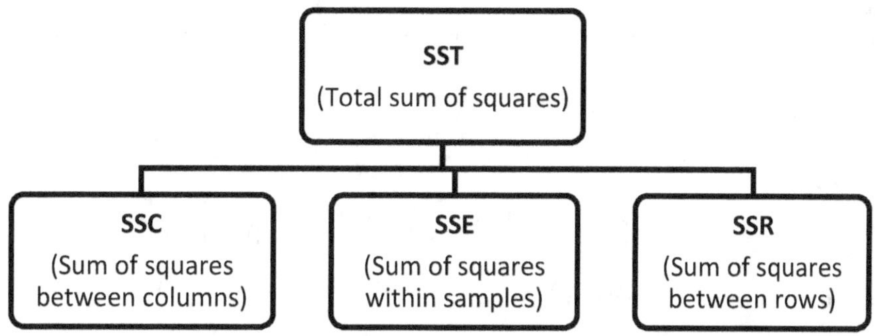

Following are the steps involved in testing hypothesis in RBD:

10.5 .1 Hypothesis

In a randomized block design (RBD) *there are two hypotheses: one for analysing treatment effect and other for locking effect.*

For the **treatment effect,** with c categories as columns and with r rows in each column (the total data values $rc = n$) hypothesis can be stated as:

$$H_0{:}\mu_1 = \mu_2 = \mu_3 = \ldots = \mu_c$$

H_1: All treatment means are not equal.

For **blocking effect,** the hypothesis can be defined as:

$$H_0{:}\mu_1 = \mu_2 = \mu_3 = \ldots = \mu_r$$

H_1: All blocking means are not equal

10.5.2 MSC (Mean sum of squares between columns)

The process of calculating MSC in RBD is same as discussed above in CRD and can be summarized as follows:

1. Calculate the mean of each column.
2. Find grand mean, $\bar{x}$ as mean of mean.
3. Find the square of difference between the mean of each sample and grand mean $(x - \bar{x})^2$.
4. Multiply the square deviation with the respective number of observations in each column. The sum thus provides the SSC as:

$$SSC = r \sum_{j=1}^{c} (\bar{x}_j - \bar{x})^2$$

5. Calculate $MSC = SSC\,/(c-1)$. Here $(c-1)$ is the degree of freedom.

10.5.3 MSR (Mean sum of squares between rows)

The process of calculating MSR is similar as for MSC discussed above but has to be applied for the rows instead of columns and hence can be summarized as:

1. Calculate the mean of each row.
2. Find grand mean, $\bar{x}$ as mean of mean for rows. (Value of grand mean is same as calculated for columns).
3. Find the square of difference between the mean of each sample and grand mean $(x - \bar{x})^2$.
4. Multiply the square deviation with the respective number of observations in each row.

   The sum thus provides the SSR as:

$$SSR = c \sum_{i=1}^{r} (\bar{x}_i - \bar{x})^2$$

5. Calculate $MSR = SSR\,/(r-1)$. Here $(r-1)$ is the degree of freedom.

10.5.4 MSE (Sum of squares within column)

On dividing the sum of squares by the number of degrees of freedom, the result is called mean square (MSE). Hence,

$$MSE = \frac{SSE}{(c-1)\,(r-1)}$$

As discussed in CRD, SSE can be calculated either directly or using the value of SSC and SST.

To calculate SSE directly from the data values, the formula is given as:

$$SSE = \sum_{i=1}^{r}\sum_{j=1}^{c}\left(x_{ij} - \overline{x}_j - \overline{x}_i + \overline{\overline{x}}\right)^2.$$

where c is the number of treatment levels (columns), r the number of observations in each treatment level (number of blocks), $\overline{x}_i$ the sample mean of group i (row means), $\overline{x}_j$ the sample mean of group j (column means), x_{ij} the ith observation in group j, and $\overline{\overline{x}}$ is the grand mean.

To calculate SSE using the already calculated SSC and SST, the relation between SSC, SSE and SST is used given as: SST=SSC + SSE. Hence,

$$SSE = SST - SSC$$

To find SST, the difference is calculated between each and every value from the grand mean (which is already calculated in the earlier step). SST is the sum of square of difference between the values from the grand mean given as:

$$SST = \sum_{i,j}(x_{ij} - \overline{\overline{x}})^2.$$

Here ij represent values of the rows as well as column.

10.5.5 Decision for the claim by F-test

After the calculation of MSC (mean square column), MSR (mean square row) and MSE (mean square error) to make the decision, the F value needs to be calculated for both the treatments as well as blocks as:

$$F_{treatment} = \frac{MSC}{MSE}$$

with $(c-1)$ degrees of freedom for numerator and $(c-1)(r-1)$ degrees of freedom for denominator. Similarly for blocks:

$$F_{block} = \frac{MSR}{MSE}$$

with $(r-1)$ degrees of freedom for numerator and $(c-1)(r-1)$ degrees of freedom for denominator. For a given level of significance α, the null hypothesis will be accepted if:

$$F_{calculated} < F_{std}$$

else the hypothesis is rejected.

10.5.6 Summary table of RBD

Source of Variation	Sum of Squares (SS)	Degree of freedom (df)	Mean Squares (MS)	F-statistic
Between Column	SSC	c-1	MSC=SSC/(c-1)	
				For treatment decision: F=MSC/MSE

Between Rows	SSR	r-1	MSR=SSR/(r-1)
			For block decision: F=MSR/MSE
Due to errors	SSE	(c-1) (r-1)	MSE=SSE/(c-1) (r-1)
Total	SST	n-1	

To understand the working procedure of RBD, consider the following example:

Example: The course of mathematics is offered to the different domains (D_1, D_2, D_3, D_4 and D_5) in the university. To investigate the effect of the stream on the performance of the students, three sections (A, B and C) has been taken from each of the selected five domains. Analyse if there is a change in the number of students getting more than 60%.

	Different domains				
Sections	D_1	D_2	D_3	D_4	D_5
A	12	14	11	10	12
B	11	18	12	16	12
C	10	12	16	12	18

The F standard value at 4, 2 degree of freedom is 3.84 and F standard value at 8, 14 degree of freedom is 4.46.

Solution:

To analyze the hypothesis frame the null and alternative hypothesis both for treatments (columns) as well as for blocks (rows) as:

For the **treatment effect:**
$H_0: \mu_1 = \mu_2 = \mu_3 = \mu_4 = \mu_5$
H_1: All treatment means are not equal.

For **blocking effect:**
$H_0: \mu_1 = \mu_2 = \mu_3$
H_1: All blocking means are not equal.

Following are the calculations to find the value of SSC, SSR, SSE and SST followed by the MSC, MSR and MCE and hence the value of F-statistic to make the decision.

Calculating SSC:

	Different domains				
Sections	D_1	D_2	D_3	D_4	D_5
A	12	14	11	10	12
B	11	18	12	16	12
C	10	12	16	12	18
Total	33	44	39	38	42

Mean	11	14.66667	13	12.66667	14
Grand mean	13.06667				
Deviation	12.81333	7.68	0.013333	0.48	2.613333
SSC	**23.6**				

Calculating SSR:

Sections	D_1	D_2	D_3	D_4	D_5	Sum	Mean	Grand mean	Deviation
A	12	14	11	10	12	59	11.8	13.0666667	8.022222
B	11	18	12	16	12	69	13.8		2.688889
C	10	12	16	12	18	68	13.6		1.422222

SSR=12.13333

Calculating SSE from SST:

SST can be calculated as:

	Different domains					Square of deviation of each value from mean of respective column				
Sections	D_1	D_2	D_3	D_4	D_5					
A	12	14	11	10	12	1.138	0.871	4.271	9.404	1.138
B	11	18	12	16	12	4.271	24.338	1.138	8.604	1.138
C	10	12	16	12	18	9.404	1.138	8.604	1.138	24.338
Total	33	44	39	38	42					
Mean	11	14.667	13	12.667	14			**SST=100.933**		

Hence, SSE=100.933-23.6-12.13333=65.2

Calculating SSE directly:

	Different domains					Square of deviation of each value from grand mean				
Sections	D_1	D_2	D_3	D_4	D_5					
A	12	14	11	10	12	5.138	0.360	0.538	1.960	0.538
B	11	18	12	16	12	0.538	6.760	3.004	6.760	7.471
C	10	12	16	12	18	2.351	10.240	6.084	1.440	12.018
Total	33	44	39	38	42					
Mean	11	14.667	13	12.667	14					
Grand mean	13.066							**SSE=65.200**		

After calculating the sum of square of the variation the next step is to find the mean sum of square of the variation using degree of freedom.

The summary table with the mean square values and hence the F-value is as follows:

Source of Variation	Sum of Square		df	Mean Squares	F-Statistic	F-std
Between Column	SSC	23.600	4	MSC=5.900		
					For treatment decision:	
Between Rows	SSR	12.133	2	MSR=6.067	F=MSC/ MSE=0.724	F=3.84
					For block decision:	
Within Columns (Error)	SSE	65.200	8	MSE=8.150	F=MSR/ MSE=0.744	F=4.46
Total	SST	100.933	14			

The F standard value at 4, 2 degree of freedom is 3.84 and F standard value at 8, 14 degree of freedom is 4.46.

Since, both values of F treatment and F blocks are less than the respective standard values. Hence both the hypotheses are accepted.

Chapter based Quiz

MCQs

1. What are the three principles of experimental design?
   A. Replication
   B. Randomization
   C. Local Control

   a) A and B
   b) A and C
   c) B and C
   d) All of the above

2. Which of the following assumptions must be met to use an ANOVA?
   a) There is homogeneity of variance
   b) Random sampling of cases must have taken place
   c) The data must be normally distributed
   d) All of these

3. Analysis of variance is a statistical method of comparing the _________ of several populations.

a) standard deviations
b) variances
c) means
d) proportions

4. Repeating an experiment to observe the maximum temperature tolerated by a boiler is known as
a) Replication
b) Randomization
c) Local Control
d) Factorization

5. For replication which of the following is **incorrect**?
a) It helps in obtaining an accurate estimate of the experimental error.
b) It helps in decreasing the experimental error.
c) In helps in increasing precision.
d) In helps in estimating yield.

6. Which of the following is **incorrect**?
a) Local control refers to the amount of balancing, blocking and grouping of the experimental units.
b) Randomization means randomly assigning treatments to the experimental units.
c) Blocking means collecting different experimental units together to form small heterogeneous groups.

7. Characteristics of the experimental subject that are present prior to the experiment are called ________.
a) treatment variable
b) classification variable
c) experimental units
d) factor

8. A variable which is controlled or modified by the researcher in the experiment is __________.
a) treatment variable
b) classification variable
c) experimental Units
d) factor

9. Which is a technique of testing hypothesis about the significant difference in several population?
a) ANOVA
b) t-test
c) z-test
d) Chi square test

10. Which of the following are the assumptions of ANOVA?
A. Independence of cases
B. Normality
C. Validation for mean

D. Homogeneity of variances

a) A, B, D
b) A, B, C
c) B, C, D
d) All of the above

11. Which of the following is correct?
A. Variance between samples is attributed to the difference among the sample means.
B. Variance within the samples is the difference due to chance or experimental errors.
C. In analysis of variance the total variation in the sample data can be on account of three components.

a) Only A
b) Only B
c) A and B
d) All of the above

12. In ________ process, the total sum of squares can be divided into two additive and independent parts. SST (total sum of squares) = SSC (sum of squares between columns) + SSE (sum of squares within samples)
a) CRD
b) RBD
c) LSD
d) FD

13. In__________ process, the total sum of squares consists of three parts. SST (total sum of squares) = SSC (sum of squares between columns) + SSR (sum of squares between rows) + SSE (sum of squares of errors)
a) CRD
b) RBD
c) LSD
d) FD

14. For the given data of CRD, what is the value of F statistics?

Source of Variation	Sum of Squares	df	Mean Squares
Between Column	SSC=34	3	
			MSC=11.33
Within Columns	SSE=11	20	
			MSE=0.55
Total	SST=45	23	

a) 20.6
b) 10.2
c) 11.88

d) 25

15. For the given data of CRD what is the value of degree of freedom as x?

Source of Variation	Sum of Squares	df	Mean Squares
Between Columns	SSC=23	3	
Within Columns	SSE=22	x	MSC=7.66
Total	SST=45	23	MSE=1.1

a) 20
b) 8
c) 11
d) 21

16. What is the degree of freedom between column, between rows and within columns (error) for data of 5 employees in 3 different cities.

		Employee			
A	24	30	26	23	32
B	22	32	27	25	31
C	23	28	25	22	32

a) 4,2,8
b) 2,4,8
c) 2,4,15
d) 5,3,15

17. Which of the following is correct formula to compute MSE with c column and r rows in RBD?
a) SSE/(c-1)
b) SSE/(r-1)
c) SSE/(c-1) (r-1)
d) SSE/c x r

18. What is the obtained F-value in the given table of ANOVA?

	SS	df	F
Between	50	5	?
Within column	24	4	

a) 1.266
b) 1.545
c) 4.450
d) 1.667

19. What is the degree of freedom for the standard F-value in F-test with 8 and 6 elements in the two-sample data with standard deviation 12 and 10?
a) F (12)
b) F (7,5)
c) F (5,7)
d) F (14)

20. For what purpose, the null hypothesis is framed to check whether the in ANOVA?
a) means of two samples are equal
b) means of more than two samples are equal
c) means of two or more populations are equal
d) none of the above

21. For 5 samples with 9 observations each. What is the degrees of freedom for the critical F-value?
a) 4 numerator and 8 denominator degrees of freedom
b) 45 degrees of freedom
c) 4 numerator and 40 denominator degrees of freedom
d) 5 numerator and 9 denominator degrees of freedom

22. The mean sum of square is the sum of squares divided by _______________ .
a) the total number of observations
b) its corresponding degrees of freedom – 1
c) its corresponding degrees of freedom +1
d) its corresponding degrees of freedom

23. In ANOVA, testing of hypothesis is carried out by partitioning variances in how many parts?
a) 1
b) 2
c) 3
d) 4

24. Variance between samples is attributed to _____________.
a) treatment effect
b) experimental error
c) constraints
d) variables

25. What is the degree of freedom for the standard F-value in F-test with 8 and 6 elements in the two-sample data with standard deviation 10 and 12?
a) F (12)
b) F (7,5)
c) F (5,7)
d) F (14)

26. Which of the following are analyzed in RBD procedure?
    i.   Significant difference in treatment level
    ii.   Significant difference in block level

a) Only i
b) Only ii
c) Neither i nor ii
d) Both i and ii

27. Analysis of variance produces SS between = 20, SS within = 30, and an F-ratio with df (2, 15). For this analysis, what is the F-ratio?
a) $20/30 = 0.67$
b) $10/2 = 5.00$
c) $30/20 = 1.50$
d) $2/10 = 0.20$

28. Which of the following is correct term used in context of experimental design?
a) LSD-Least Square design
b) RBD-Random Bar design
c) FD-Fitted design
d) CRD-Completely randomized design

29. An analysis of variance comparing three treatment conditions produces degree of freedom total = 11. What is total number of data values available?
a) 2
b) 12
c) 3
d) 9

30. What is the set of operations termed as which potentially affect the experimental units i.e., a crop variety, a dose of fertilizer, combination of factor levels etc.
a) An applicator
b) A dose
c) An event
d) A treatment

31. In ANOVA, what is the degree of freedom between treatments (c-column, r-row) ?
a) c-1
b) r-1
c) (c-1)(r-1)
d) c x r

32. Choose the correct statement(s)?
A) In RBD, experimental units are divided into blocks.
B) CRD is a basic experimental design with SST=SSC-SSE

a) Only A
b) Only B
c) Both A and B
d) Neither A nor B

33. In ANOVA, the total variation is divided as variation between samples occurs due to
_______________and variation within samples occurs due to ____________ .
a) error, treatments
b) variation, factor
c) treatments, error
d) randomization, replication

34. What is the degree of freedom between blocks (c-column, r-row) in ANOVA?
a) c-1
b) r-1
c) (c-1)(r-1)
d) c x r

35. For the given data of 6 employees in 4 different cities what is the degree of freedom between
column, between rows and within columns (error)?

Employee						
A	24	30	26	23	32	22
B	22	32	27	25	31	34
C	23	28	25	22	32	30
D	21	29	32	21	33	27

a) 4,2,8
b) 5,3,8
c) 5,4,20
d) 5,3,15

36. What is the degree of freedom for SSE with the data of 4 cities and 3 varieties of seeds in RBD?
a) 3
b) 2
c) 6
d) 5

37. What are the missing values a and b in the given table of ANOVA?

SS	df	MS	F
50	2	25	b
32	8	a	

a) 40,0.625
b) 4, 6,25
c) 10,2.5
d) 4, 6.5

Answers:

1-d	2-d	3-c	4-a	5-d	6-c	7-b	8-a	9-a	10-a
11-c	12-a	13-b	14-a	15-a	16-a	17-c	18-d	19-b	20-c
21-c	22-d	23-b	24-a	25-b	26-d	27-b	28-d	29-b	30-d
31-a	32-a	33-c	34-b	35-d	36-c	37-b			

NOTES:

Chapter 11

Hypothesis Testing for Categorical Data: Chi-Square Test

Counting frequencies of one or more variables under study creates a new type of data called as *categorical data* used to analyze the number of entities under a category.

For example:
Opinion taken from the public and private educational institutes for an education policy. The number (frequency) of the institutes in favor and opposed to the policy can be categorized under the two criteria of public and private.

	Public educational institutes	Private educational institutes
Favor		
Opposed		

Hypothesis test which is used to analyze the categorical variable is called a Chi-square test.

The chi-square test uses only the frequency of the categorical variable and involve no parameter (such as mean, variance). Hence the chi-square technique falls in the category of **non-parametric tests** for the testing of hypothesis.

The statistical tests that do not require prior knowledge about the population are termed as non-parametric tests. Previous examples of hypothesis tests, such as the z-test, t-test, F-test and analysis of variance, are parametric tests as they include assumptions about parameters and hypotheses about parameters.

11.1 Chi-square Distribution

For large sample sizes, the sampling distribution of chi-square statistics is closely approximated by a continuous curve called as chi-square distribution. *A chi-square distribution is a continuous distribution extending from zero to infinity with k degrees of freedom (df)*.

It is used to describe the distribution of a sum of squared random variables and to test the goodness of fit of a distribution of data, when data series are independent. Also, chi-square distribution is a special case of the gamma distribution.

The probability distribution function of chi-square distribution for random variable X with k df is given by:

$$p(\chi^2) = \frac{1}{2^{k/2}\, gamma(k/2)} \exp\left(-\frac{\chi^2}{2}\right) \chi^{2(k/2-1)}, \; -\infty < \chi < \infty$$

Additionally, the square of the standard normal variable is known as a chi-square variable with 1 degree of freedom.

Thus, $p(\chi^2) = \dfrac{1}{\sqrt{2\pi}} \exp\left(-\dfrac{\chi^2}{2}\right) \chi, \; -\infty < \chi < \infty$

11.2 Properties of Chi-Square Distribution

In chi-square distribution with k degree of freedom, the mean is given by k and the mode of the distribution is $(k-2)$ with variance as $2k$.

As the coefficient of skewness is given by

$$Skewness = \frac{Mean - Mode}{S.D}$$

Hence for the chi-square distribution can be calculated as:

$$Skewness = \frac{k - (k-2)}{\sqrt{2k}} = \sqrt{\frac{2}{k}}$$

As, the coefficient of skewness is greater than zero for $k \geq 1$, this leads to the positive skewness.

Additionally, as the coefficient of skewness is inversely proportional to the degree of freedom, the shape of the curve is skewed to the right for small degree of freedom and *as degree of freedom (k) become larger, the distribution becomes more and more symmetrical and thus approximated by the normal distribution.*

11.2.1 Application of chi-square test:

The chi-square test is used for two **non-parametric hypothesis tests** listed as:
- the chi-square test for goodness of fit
- the chi-square test for independence.

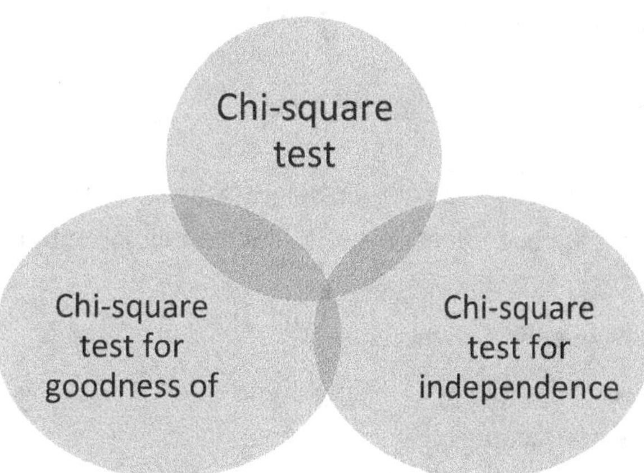

11.3 Chi-square test for goodness of fit:

This test is implemented when the results need to be verified to follow some expected results.

For example: Goodness of fit can be implemented to find

- How close are the sample results to the expected results?
- If in tossing a coin some finite number of times, the numbers of heads are expected to be same as the number of tails. Thus, the expected numbers in tossing a coin 100 times are 50 heads and 50 tails, that could be different from the observed values.

Thus, chi-square goodness of fit test enables the user to ascertain whether the sample distribution follows the known theoretical probability distributions such as binomial, Poisson, and normal probability distributions. For applying χ^2 test, first a theoretical distribution is hypothesized for a given population. Then the other steps for hypothesis testing are applied in the usual way starting from the hypothesis to decision.

11.3.1 Conditions for applying the χ^2 goodness of fit:

Following are the conditions need to be satisfied before applying $\chi2$ goodness of fit for hypothesis testing:

- Sample observations should be independent and taken from random sample.
- Total number of frequencies should be at least 50.
- In a contingency table, the expected frequency (also called as theoretical or hypothetical frequency) in a cell should be at least 5. If it is less than 6 then "pool" the frequencies of the cell with the preceding or succeeding frequency so that pooled frequency is more than 5.

The last assumption is concerned with the expected counts, not the observed count. Additionally, the degree of freedom needs to be adjusted after pooling the cell frequencies.

11.3.2 Stepwise procedure for goodness of fit:

1. Set up the null and alternative hypothesis as follows:

   $H0$: The frequency counts agree with the claimed distribution.
   $H1$: The frequency counts do not agree with the claimed distribution.

2. Find the observed frequencies denoted by O_i.
3. Compute the expected frequency E_i, using either of the following approaches:
   - If the expected frequencies are all equal: $E = n/k$.
   - If the expected frequencies are not all equal: $E = np$ for each individual category.

Here, k is the number of categories, p is the probability and n are the sample size,

4. Compute the test statistic using formula:

$$\chi^2 = \sum_{i=1}^{k} \frac{(O_i - E_i)^2}{E_i}$$

5. Make the decision.
   If $\chi^2_{calculated} < \chi^2_{\alpha}$ the hypothesis will be accepted else the hypothesis will be rejected at $(k - 1)$ degrees of freedom. Here, α is the significance level.

The critical value of the chi-square distribution for k samples with $k-1$ degree of freedom at α level of significance can be seen from the table given in Appendix.

In general, if the data is given in a series with k numbers, then degrees of freedom is one less than the numbers. i.e., $k - 1$. But for the special cases when the data is fitted for a particular distribution, based on the parameters involved the degree of freedom is going to be changed. Following are the degree of freedom as per the distribution:
- In the case of binomial distribution df is $k - 1$.
- In the case of Poisson distribution df is $k - 2$.
- In the case of normal distribution df is $k - 3$.
-

11.3.3 Grouping of Small Frequencies

One or more observations with frequencies less than 5 may be grouped together to represent a single category before calculating the difference between observed and expected frequencies.

For example: For the data given below, it can be seen that the cell value of the last column is less.

Observed frequencies	:	50	64	72	40	28	9	3
Expected frequencies	:	59	58	60	45	26	6	1

Hence these 7 classes can be reduced to 6 by combining the last two observed as well as expected frequencies as follows:

Observed frequencies   :   50   64   72   40   28   12
Expected frequencies   :   59   58   60   45   26   7

Note that the number of degrees of freedom is calculated from the number of classes after regrouping.

Example 1: The demand of the food to be packed in a restaurant was found to vary from day-to-day. Following information is obtained on the demand of packed food per day from the data collected in the last two months:

Days	:	Mon	Tue	Wed	Thurs	Fri	Sat	Sun
Orders for packed food	:	35	30	32	28	32	37	40

From the data can it be concluded that the number of orders of packed food depends on the day of the week? Test the hypothesis at 5% level of significance. The standard value of chi-square at 5, 6, 7 df are 11.07, 12.59 and 14.07 respectively.

Solution:

Let the hypothesis be defined as:

H_0: Orders for packed food does not depend on the day of the week.

H_1: Orders for packed food depend on the day of the week.

If the orders are equally distributed over the week, the expected number of orders per day should be calculated as:

$$\frac{35 + 30 + 32 + 28 + 32 + 37 + 40}{7} = \frac{234}{7} \approx 33.43$$

The chi-square statistics can thus be calculated as follows:

O_i	E_i	$O_i - E_i$	$(O_i - E_i)^2$	$(O_i - E_i)^2/E_i$
35	33.43	1.57	2.46	0.07
30	33.43	-3.43	11.76	0.35
32	33.43	-1.43	2.04	0.06
28	33.43	-5.43	29.48	0.88
32	33.43	-1.43	2.04	0.06
37	33.43	3.57	12.74	0.38
40	33.43	6.57	43.16	1.29
				Total=3.10

From the data, the chi-square statistics is obtained as 3.10 and the standard value of the chi-square statistics at 5% level of significance at 7-1=6 degree of freedom is 12.59.

Since the calculated value of the χ^2 is less than the tabulated value. Hence the hypothesis is accepted. Hence it can be concluded that the number of orders for the packed food are uniformly distributed over the week.

Example 2: A book with 500 pages is proof read, the number of typo errors was found as follows:

Number of typo errors (x) :	0	1	2	3	4	5	6
Number of pages(f) :	275	150	38	20	10	5	2

Test the goodness of fit of the given data with the Poisson distribution. The chi-square statistics at 5% level of significance at 2 degree of freedom (df=7-2-3) is 5.99.

Solution:

Let the hypothesis be defined as:

H_0: Number of typo errors is uniformly distributed on the pages of the book.

H_1: Number of typo errors is not uniformly distributed on the pages of the book.

The total number of typo errors distributed over 500 pages is 363. If the errors are uniformly distributed over the book, the expected number of errors per page should be calculated using the mean value as per the Poisson distribution. Mean of the Poisson distribution thus be obtained using formula:

$$\lambda = \frac{\sum fx}{N}$$

x	f	fx
0	275	0
1	150	150
2	38	76
3	20	60
4	10	40
5	5	25
6	2	12
Total	$N = 500$	$\sum fx = \mathbf{363}$
		$\lambda = 0.726$

Hence calculated as:

$$\lambda = \frac{\sum fx}{N} = \frac{363}{500} = 0.726$$

The expected theoretical frequencies for the Poisson distribution can be calculated using formula:

$$E(x) = \frac{Ne^{-\lambda}\lambda^x}{x!}$$

where x denotes the number of typo errors per page that varies from 0 to 6.

Hence,
$$E(x) = 500\frac{e^{-0.726}0.726^x}{x!}$$

Thus,

$$E(0) = 500\frac{e^{-0.726}0.726^0}{0!}$$

$$= 500 \times e^{-0.726}$$

$$= 500 \times 0.48384$$

$$E(0) = 241.92$$

$$E(1) = 500\frac{e^{-0.726}0.726^1}{1!}$$

$$E(1) = 500 \times e^{-0.726} \times 0.726$$
$$= 500 \times 0.48384 \times 0.726$$

$$E(1) \quad = 175.63$$

and so on for x as 2 to 6. Hence, the expected values can be tabulated as follows:

x	0	1	2	3	4	5	6
O_i	275	150	38	20	10	5	2
E_i	241.92	175.63	63.76	15.43	2.8	0.41	0.05

From the obtained expected values, it can be seen that the last three expected values are less than 6. Hence group them together to meet the condition of cell frequency to be at least 6.

The updated frequencies are now shown as NO_i and NE_i for the pooled observed and expected values. The chi-square statistics can thus be calculated as follows:

NO_i	NE_i	$NO_i - NE_i$	$(NO_i - NE_i)^2$	$(NO_i - NE_i)^2/NE_i$
275	241.92	33.08	1094.27	4.52
150	175.63	-25.63	657.11	3.74
38	63.76	-25.76	663.33	10.40
37	18.69	18.31	335.26	17.94
				Total=36.61

The chi-square statistics is obtained as 36.61 and the standard value of the chi-square statistics at 5% level of significance at 2 degrees of freedom (df=7-2-3) is 5.99.

Here 7-2 df is obtained due to fitting of the Poisson distribution and 3 more df are lost because of grouping of the last four expected cell frequencies.

Since the calculated value of the χ^2 is much greater than the tabulated value. Hence the hypothesis is rejected. Hence it can be concluded that the Poisson distribution is not a good fit to the given data.

11.4 Chi-square test of independence:

This test is implemented to find if the two variables of interest are independent of each other.

For example: test of independence can be implemented to find:

- Is starting salary of professor independent of their institute of study?
- Is employee performance independent of the time of their shift?
- Is performance of student dependent on teaching methodology?
- Is the purchase of perfume dependent on the customer's age?

Classifying the observations into mutually exclusive categories on the basis of two variables and arranging in a table, results in a table referred as a contingency table.

One variable is used to categorize rows, and a second variable is used to categorize columns. Observations in each cell represent the frequency of observations.

11.4.1 Stepwise procedure for test of independence:

1. Set up the null and alternative hypothesis as follows:

H_0: Two variables are independent of each other.
H_1: Two variables are dependent of each other.

2. Select a random sample and record the observed frequency, O_{ij}, for each cell of the contingency table.

3. Compute the expected frequency, E_{ij}, for each cell using the row and the column total as:

$$E_{ij} = \frac{(Row\ i\ Total)(Column\ j\ Total)}{Sample\ Size}$$

4. Compute the test statistic with formula:

$$\chi^2 = \sum_i \sum_j \frac{(O_{ij} - E_{ij})^2}{E_{ij}}$$

5. Make the decision as per following:
   If
   $$\chi^2_{calculated} < \chi^2_\alpha$$

   the hypothesis will be accepted.

Else the hypothesis will be rejected at $(n - 1)(m - 1)$ degrees of freedom at α level of significance.

Here, n are the number of rows and m are the number of columns of the contingency table.

The degree of freedom describes the number of observations that are free to vary after certain restrictions being imposed on the data. Thus, for a 2 x 2 contingency table the degree of freedom will be 1 and for a 3 x 4 contingency table the degree of freedom will be 2 x 3=6

Example 1: The reviews of a movie are classified according to the gender, male and female responses who like or dislike the movie. There are 40 males out of which 12 like the movie and out of 50 girls 34 like the movie. From the given data can it be concluded that movie review is independent of the gender. Test at 5% level of significance. The standard value of the chi-square statistics at 5% level of significance at 1 degree of freedom is 3.841.

Solution:

From the given data the contingency table can be created as follows:

	Male	Female	Total
Like	12	34	46
Dislike	28	16	44
Total	40	50	90

As per the given categories the hypothesis can be framed as:

H_0: Liking of the movie is independent of the gender.

H_1: Liking of the movie is dependent of the gender.

The expected cell frequencies can be computed as per the row and the column number corresponding to the observed values as follows:

$$E_{i,j} = \frac{i^{th} Row\ total \times j^{th} Column\ total}{Final\ total}$$

$$E_{1,1} = \frac{46 \times 40}{90} = 20.44; \qquad E_{1,2} = \frac{46 \times 50}{90} = 25.56$$

$$E_{2,1} = \frac{44 \times 40}{90} = 19.56; \qquad E_{2,2} = \frac{44 \times 50}{90} = 24.44$$

The chi-square statistics is calculated using the observed and expected value differences square and hence from the formula of chi-square the sum is calculated as follows:

O_i	E_i	$O_i - E_i$	$(O_i - E_i)^2$	$(O_i - E_i)^2 / E_i$

12	20.44	-8.44	71.23	3.49
34	25.56	8.44	71.23	2.79
28	19.56	8.44	71.23	3.64
16	24.44	-8.44	71.23	2.91
				Total=12.83

From the data, the chi-square statistics is obtained as 12.83 and the standard value of the chi-square statistics at 5% level of significance at 1 degree of freedom is 3.841.

As,

$$\chi^2_{calculated}(12.83) > \chi^2_{\alpha}(3.841),$$

Hence the hypothesis is rejected.

Thus, liking of the movie is dependent on the gender.

Example 2: The woolen shawls sold by a shopkeeper are classified according to the wool used. The shopkeeper likes to determine if the sale of the shawl and the wool are independent variables. The number of shawls sold for each type of wool used is counted for the two months and the sales are given below. To categorize, the price of the shawls is listed as either *9,000 or less* and *more than 9,000*. Do these figures support the hypothesis that the sale of the shawl is independent of the type of wool used?

	A	B	C	D
9,000 or less	12	13	15	25
more than 9,000	15	12	8	10

Analyse the fact at 5% level of significance. The standard value of the chi-square statistics at 5% level of significance at 3 degree of freedom is 7.815.

Solution:

As per the given categories the hypothesis can be framed as:

H_0: The sale of the shawl is independent of the type of wool used.
H_1: The sale of the shawl is dependent of the type of wool used

The expected cell frequencies can be computed as per the row and the column number corresponding to the observed values and hence using the total, the row and column total as follows:

	A	B	C	D	*Total*
9,000 or less	12	13	15	25	65
more than 9,000	15	12	8	10	45
Total	27	25	23	35	110

$$E_{i,j} = \frac{i^{th} Row\ total \times j^{th} Column\ total}{Final\ total}$$

$$E_{1,1} = \frac{65 \times 27}{110} = 15.95 \qquad\qquad E_{1,2} = \frac{65 \times 25}{110} = 14.77$$

$$E_{1,3} = \frac{65 \times 23}{110} = 13.59 \qquad\qquad E_{1,4} = \frac{65 \times 35}{110} = 20.68$$

$$E_{2,1} = \frac{45 \times 27}{110} = 11.05 \qquad\qquad E_{2,2} = \frac{45 \times 25}{110} = 10.23$$

$$E_{2,3} = \frac{45 \times 23}{110} = 9.41 \qquad\qquad E_{2,4} = \frac{45 \times 35}{110} = 14.32$$

Now substituting the values in a tabulated form for calculation:

O_i	E_i	$O_i - E_i$	$(O_i - E_i)^2$	$(O_i - E_i)^2/E_i$
12	15.95	-3.95	15.64	0.98
13	14.77	-1.77	3.14	0.21
15	13.59	1.41	1.99	0.15
25	20.68	4.32	18.65	0.90
15	11.05	3.95	15.64	1.42
12	10.23	1.77	3.14	0.31
8	9.41	-1.41	1.99	0.21
10	14.32	-4.32	18.65	1.30
				Total=5.477

From the data, the chi-square statistics is obtained as 5.477 and the standard value of the chi-square statistics at 5% level of significance at (4-1) x (2-1) =3 degree of freedom is 7.815.

Since, $\chi^2_{calculated}(5.477) < \chi^2_{\alpha}(7.815)$.

Hence the hypothesis is accepted. Thus, the sale of the shawl is independent of the type of wool used.

<u>Chapter based Quiz</u>

MCQs

1. Which of the following is a WRONG for Chi square-test?
    a) In the chi square test, the null hypothesis is assumed as there not being an association between the two variables that are observed in the study.
    b) The chi-square statistic is a parametric test.
    c) The data are frequencies rather than numerical scores.
    d) Chi square statistic is used for determining whether or not a relationship exists between variables.

2. Match the correct pairs:

A.	F-test	i)	to determine mean difference between paired observations.
B.	Chi Square Test	ii)	to compare two population variances.
C.	Paired T-test	iii)	significant relationship between categorical variables.

    a) A-i, B-ii, C-iii
    b) A-ii, B-iii, C-i
    c) A-ii, B-I, C-iii
    d) A-iii, B-ii, C-i

3. In a Chi-square test of independence with 4 rows and 5 columns the degree of freedom is_____.
    a) 12
    b) 18
    c) 20
    d) 24

4. Which of the following is a nonparametric test?
    a) Z-test
    b) T-test
    c) F-test
    d) Chi-Square-test

5. A randomized survey was conducted to compare the effectiveness of dialysis in kidney problems. Results of the survey are given in the table below. What is the expected value calculated for the chi-square test for the cured patients by dialysis?

	Dialysis done	Dialysis Not done	Total
Cured	42	38	80
Not cured	33	27	60
Total	75	65	140

    a) 43.15
    b) 42.86
    c) 55.57
    d) 50.24

6. The formula to calculate the chi square is:

$$a) \sum \frac{(O_i - E_i)^2}{E_i}$$

$$b) \sum \left(\frac{O_i - E_i}{E_i} \right)^2$$

$$c) \sum \frac{(O_i - E_i)}{E_i}$$

$$d) \sum \frac{(O_i - E_i)^2}{O_i}$$

7. Which of the following is the null hypothesis for the chi-square goodness of fit?
a) Population follows a specific distribution.
b) Population follows the normal distribution.
c) The two variables under study are independent.
d) The two variables under study are dependent.

8. Which of the following is the null hypothesis for the chi-square test of independence?
a) Population follows a specific distribution.
b) Population follows the normal distribution.
c) The two variables under study are independent.
d) The two variables under study are dependent.

9. The degree of freedom for the **chi-square test of independence** is calculated as_____ where r is the number of rows, c is the number of columns, k is the number of categories under consideration and p is the parameter involved in the sample data.
a) r x c.
b) (r-1) x (c-1)
c) k-p
d) k-p-1

10. The degree of freedom for the **chi-square goodness of fit** is calculated as_____ where r is the number of rows, c is the number of column, k is the number of categories under consideration and p is the parameter involved in the sample data.
a) r x c.
b) (r-1) x (c-1)
c) k-p
d) k-p-1

11. What is the range of chi-square distribution?
a) -1 to 1
b) 0 to 1
c) $-\infty$ to ∞
d) 0 to ∞

12. The value of chi-square distribution is always __________.
a) negative
b) positive
c) zero

d) infinity

13. If the calculated value of χ^2 is 3.45 and the standard value of χ^2 at 4 df for 5% level of significance is 9.488. What is the decision for the null hypothesis?
a) Accepted
b) Rejected
c) Not satisfied
d) None of the above

14. Which of these statements is not true?
a) A chi-square test of independence shows a cause-and-effect relationship.
b) As the number of categories increases, the distribution approaches the normal distribution.
c) The chi-square tests involve categorical variables.
d) The chi-square goodness-of-fit test is an extension of the z-test to more than two categories.

15. The null hypothesis is rejected in a chi-square test of significance when _______.
a) The test conditions are satisfied.
b) The χ^2 statistic is smaller than the critical value for the given level of significance.
c) The χ^2 statistic is larger than the critical value for the given level of significance.
d) Observed values are smaller than the expected values.

16. Which test is appropriate for determining whether the dice is biased from the proportions of each digit it produces?
a) the chi-square goodness-of-fit test
b) z-test
c) the chi-square test of independence
d) t-test

17. What type of data do you need for a chi-square test?
a) Nominal
b) Ordinal
c) Categorical
d) Interval

18. Chi-square test for independence assesses whether ______________.
a) The expected frequencies are in conformation with the observed frequencies.
b) There is a relationship between the population and the sample.
c) There is a significant difference between two categorical variables.
d) There is a relationship between two categorical variables.

19. What does the degree of freedom denotes?
a) The number of variables
b) The number of independent variables
c) Difference between observed and expected frequencies
d) Square of the difference between observed and expected frequencies

20. Chi-square test is used to test which of the following?
A. Independence of attributes
B. Goodness of fit
C. Parametric expectancy
D. Vibrational effect

a) A and B
b) B and C

c) A and C
d) None of the above

21. What is the mean for the chi-square distribution with k degree of freedom?
a) k
b) $2k$
c) $k-1$
d) $k-2$

22. Which of the following is correct for the shape of the chi-square distribution?
A. The shape of the curve is skewed to the right for small degree of freedom.
B. The shape of the curve is skewed to the left for small degree of freedom.
C. For large degree of freedom (k) the distribution is approximated by the normal distribution.

a) A and B
b) B and C
c) A and C
d) None of the above

23. What is the mode for the chi-square distribution with 10 degrees of freedom?
a) 2
b) 4
c) 5
d) 8

24. The square of the standard normal variable is known as a chi-square variable with____ degree of freedom.
a) 1
b) 2
c) 3
d) 4

25. What is the degree of freedom if the variance of the chi-square distribution is 16?
a) 2
b) 4
c) 8
d) 10

26. What is the degree of freedom for chi-square goodness of fit for a data with 32 data values when the data is expected to follow distribution Poisson distribution?
a) 15
b) 16
c) 28
d) 30

Answers:

1-b	2-b	3-a	4- d	5-b	6-a	7-a	8-c	9-b	10-d
11-c	12-b	13-a	14-a	15-c	16-a	17-c	18-d	19-b	20-a
21-a	22-c	23-d	24-a	25-c	26-d				

NOTES:

The Standard Normal Distribution Table

The following table indicates the area under the curve to the **right** of the center-line of the z-curve.

Example: The shaded area in the diagram below for z=1.45, area of the shaded portion as 0.4265 (or 42.65% of the total area under the curve).

To get this area, read down the left side of the table for the first 2 digits (the whole number and the first number after the decimal point, in this case 1.4), then read across the table for the "0.05" part (the top row represents the 2nd decimal place.)

z	0.00	0.01	0.02	0.03	0.04	0.05	0.06
1.4	0.4192	0.4207	0.4222	0.4236	0.4251	**0.4265**	0.4279

The area represented by for z=1.45 to the right of the mean is shaded in green in the following standard normal curve.

z	0	0.01	0.02	0.03	0.04	0.05	0.06	0.07	0.08	0.09
0	0	0.0040	0.0080	0.0120	0.0160	0.0199	0.0239	0.0279	0.0319	0.0359
0.1	0.0398	0.0438	0.0478	0.0517	0.0557	0.0596	0.0636	0.0675	0.0714	0.0753
0.2	0.0793	0.0832	0.0871	0.0910	0.0948	0.0987	0.1026	0.1064	0.1103	0.1141
0.3	0.1179	0.1217	0.1255	0.1293	0.1331	0.1368	0.1406	0.1443	0.1480	0.1517
0.4	0.1554	0.1591	0.1628	0.1664	0.1700	0.1736	0.1772	0.1808	0.1844	0.1879
0.5	0.1915	0.1950	0.1985	0.2019	0.2054	0.2088	0.2123	0.2157	0.2190	0.2224
0.6	0.2257	0.2291	0.2324	0.2357	0.2389	0.2422	0.2454	0.2486	0.2517	0.2549
0.7	0.2580	0.2611	0.2642	0.2673	0.2704	0.2734	0.2764	0.2794	0.2823	0.2852
0.8	0.2881	0.2910	0.2939	0.2967	0.2995	0.3023	0.3051	0.3078	0.3106	0.3133
0.9	0.3159	0.3186	0.3212	0.3238	0.3264	0.3289	0.3315	0.3304	0.3365	0.3389
1.0	0.3413	0.3438	0.3461	0.3485	0.3508	0.3531	0.3554	0.3577	0.3599	0.3621
1.1	0.3643	0.3665	0.3686	0.3708	0.3729	0.3749	0.3770	0.3790	0.3810	0.3830
1.2	0.3849	0.3869	0.3888	0.3907	0.3925	0.3944	0.3962	0.3980	0.3997	0.4015
1.3	0.4032	0.4049	0.4066	0.4082	0.4099	0.4115	0.4131	0.4147	0.4162	0.4177
1.4	0.4192	0.4207	0.4222	0.4236	0.4251	0.4265	0.4279	0.4292	0.4306	0.4319
1.5	0.4332	0.4345	0.4357	0.4370	0.4382	0.4394	0.4406	0.4418	0.4429	0.4441
1.6	0.4452	0.4463	0.4474	0.4484	0.4495	0.4505	0.4515	0.4525	0.4535	0.4545
1.7	0.4554	0.4564	0.4573	0.4582	0.4591	0.4599	0.4608	0.4616	0.4625	0.4633
1.8	0.4641	0.4649	0.4656	0.4664	0.4671	0.4678	0.4686	0.4693	0.4699	0.4706
1.9	0.4713	0.4719	0.4726	0.4732	0.4738	0.4744	0.4750	0.4756	0.4761	0.4767
2.0	0.4772	0.4778	0.4783	0.4788	0.4793	0.4798	0.4803	0.4808	0.4812	0.4817
2.1	0.4821	0.4826	0.483	0.4834	0.4838	0.4842	0.4846	0.4850	0.4854	0.4857
2.2	0.4861	0.4864	0.4868	0.4871	0.4875	0.4878	0.4881	0.4884	0.4887	0.4890
2.3	0.4893	0.4896	0.4898	0.4901	0.4904	0.4906	0.4909	0.4911	0.4913	0.4916
2.4	0.4918	0.4920	0.4922	0.4925	0.4927	0.4929	0.4931	0.4932	0.4934	0.4936
2.5	0.4938	0.4940	0.4941	0.4943	0.4945	0.4946	0.4948	0.4949	0.4951	0.4952
2.6	0.4953	0.4955	0.4956	0.4957	0.4959	0.4960	0.4961	0.4962	0.4963	0.4964
2.7	0.4965	0.4966	0.4967	0.4968	0.4969	0.4970	0.4971	0.4972	0.4973	0.4974
2.8	0.4974	0.4975	0.4976	0.4977	0.4977	0.4978	0.4979	0.4979	0.4980	0.4981
2.9	0.4981	0.4982	0.4982	0.4983	0.4984	0.4984	0.4985	0.4985	0.4986	0.4986
3.0	0.4987	0.4987	0.4987	0.4988	0.4988	0.4989	0.4989	0.4989	0.4990	0.4990

3.1	0.4990	0.4991	0.4991	0.4991	0.4992	0.4992	0.4992	0.4992	0.4993	0.4993
3.2	0.4993	0.4993	0.4994	0.4994	0.4994	0.4994	0.4994	0.4995	0.4995	0.4995
3.3	0.4995	0.4995	0.4995	0.4996	0.4996	0.4996	0.4996	0.4996	0.4996	0.4997
3.4	0.4997	0.4997	0.4997	0.4997	0.4997	0.4997	0.4997	0.4997	0.4997	0.4998
3.5	0.4998	0.4998	0.4998	0.4998	0.4998	0.4998	0.4998	0.4998	0.4998	0.4998
3.6	0.4998	0.4998	0.4999	0.4999	0.4999	0.4999	0.4999	0.4999	0.4999	0.4999
3.7	0.4999	0.4999	0.4999	0.4999	0.4999	0.4999	0.4999	0.4999	0.4999	0.4999
3.8	0.4999	0.4999	0.4999	0.4999	0.4999	0.4999	0.4999	0.4999	0.4999	0.4999

The t- Distribution Table

df	0.1	0.05	0.025	0.01	0.005	0.001
1	3.078	6.314	12.706	31.821	63.656	318.289
2	1.886	2.920	4.303	6.965	9.925	22.328
3	1.638	2.353	3.182	4.541	5.841	10.214
4	1.533	2.132	2.776	3.747	4.604	7.173
5	1.476	2.015	2.571	3.365	4.032	5.894
6	1.440	1.943	2.447	3.143	3.707	5.208
7	1.415	1.895	2.365	2.998	3.499	4.785
8	1.397	1.860	2.306	2.896	3.355	4.501
9	1.383	1.833	2.262	2.821	3.250	4.297
10	1.372	1.812	2.228	2.764	3.169	4.144
11	1.363	1.796	2.201	2.718	3.106	4.025
12	1.356	1.782	2.179	2.681	3.055	3.930
13	1.350	1.771	2.160	2.650	3.012	3.852
14	1.345	1.761	2.145	2.624	2.977	3.787
15	1.341	1.753	2.131	2.602	2.947	3.733
16	1.337	1.746	2.120	2.583	2.921	3.686
17	1.333	1.740	2.110	2.567	2.898	3.646
18	1.330	1.734	2.101	2.552	2.878	3.610
19	1.328	1.729	2.093	2.539	2.861	3.579
20	1.325	1.725	2.086	2.528	2.845	3.552
21	1.323	1.721	2.080	2.518	2.831	3.527
22	1.321	1.717	2.074	2.508	2.819	3.505
23	1.319	1.714	2.069	2.500	2.807	3.485
24	1.318	1.711	2.064	2.492	2.797	3.467
25	1.316	1.708	2.060	2.485	2.787	3.450
26	1.315	1.706	2.056	2.479	2.779	3.435
27	1.314	1.703	2.052	2.473	2.771	3.421
28	1.313	1.701	2.048	2.467	2.763	3.408
29	1.311	1.699	2.045	2.462	2.756	3.396
30	1.310	1.697	2.042	2.457	2.750	3.385
40	1.303	1.684	2.021	2.423	2.704	3.307
50	1.299	1.676	2.009	2.403	2.678	3.261
60	1.296	1.671	2.000	2.390	2.660	3.232
70	1.294	1.667	1.994	2.381	2.648	3.211
80	1.292	1.664	1.990	2.374	2.639	3.195
90	1.291	1.662	1.987	2.368	2.632	3.183
100	1.290	1.660	1.984	2.364	2.626	3.174
150	1.287	1.655	1.976	2.351	2.609	3.145
200	1.286	1.653	1.972	2.345	2.601	3.131
Infinity	1.282	1.645	1.960	2.326	2.576	3.090

Chi-square Distribution Table:

df	0.995	0.99	0.975	0.95	0.9	0.1	0.05	0.025	0.01
1	0	0	0	0	0.02	2.71	3.84	5.02	6.63
2	0.01	0.02	0.05	0.1	0.21	4.61	5.99	7.38	9.21
3	0.07	0.11	0.22	0.35	0.58	6.25	7.81	9.35	11.34
4	0.21	0.3	0.48	0.71	1.06	7.78	9.49	11.14	13.28
5	0.41	0.55	0.83	1.15	1.61	9.24	11.07	12.83	15.09
6	0.68	0.87	1.24	1.64	2.2	10.64	12.59	14.45	16.81
7	0.99	1.24	1.69	2.17	2.83	12.02	14.07	16.01	18.48
8	1.34	1.65	2.18	2.73	3.49	13.36	15.51	17.53	20.09
9	1.73	2.09	2.7	3.33	4.17	14.68	16.92	19.02	21.67
10	2.16	2.56	3.25	3.94	4.87	15.99	18.31	20.48	23.21
11	2.6	3.05	3.82	4.57	5.58	17.28	19.68	21.92	24.72
12	3.07	3.57	4.4	5.23	6.3	18.55	21.03	23.34	26.22
13	3.57	4.11	5.01	5.89	7.04	19.81	22.36	24.74	27.69
14	4.07	4.66	5.63	6.57	7.79	21.06	23.68	26.12	29.14
15	4.6	5.23	6.26	7.26	8.55	22.31	25	27.49	30.58
16	5.14	5.81	6.91	7.96	9.31	23.54	26.3	28.85	32
17	5.7	6.41	7.56	8.67	10.09	24.77	27.59	30.19	33.41
18	6.26	7.01	8.23	9.39	10.86	25.99	28.87	31.53	34.81
19	6.84	7.63	8.91	10.12	11.65	27.2	30.14	32.85	36.19
20	7.43	8.26	9.59	10.85	12.44	28.41	31.41	34.17	37.57
22	8.64	9.54	10.98	12.34	14.04	30.81	33.92	36.78	40.29
24	9.89	10.86	12.4	13.85	15.66	33.2	36.42	39.36	42.98
26	11.16	12.2	13.84	15.38	17.29	35.56	38.89	41.92	45.64
28	12.46	13.56	15.31	16.93	18.94	37.92	41.34	44.46	48.28
30	13.79	14.95	16.79	18.49	20.6	40.26	43.77	46.98	50.89
32	15.13	16.36	18.29	20.07	22.27	42.58	46.19	49.48	53.49
34	16.5	17.79	19.81	21.66	23.95	44.9	48.6	51.97	56.06
38	19.29	20.69	22.88	24.88	27.34	49.51	53.38	56.9	61.16
42	22.14	23.65	26	28.14	30.77	54.09	58.12	61.78	66.21
46	25.04	26.66	29.16	31.44	34.22	58.64	62.83	66.62	71.2
50	27.99	29.71	32.36	34.76	37.69	63.17	67.5	71.42	76.15
55	31.73	33.57	36.4	38.96	42.06	68.8	73.31	77.38	82.29
60	35.53	37.48	40.48	43.19	46.46	74.4	79.08	83.3	88.38
65	39.38	41.44	44.6	47.45	50.88	79.97	84.82	89.18	94.42
70	43.28	45.44	48.76	51.74	55.33	85.53	90.53	95.02	100.43
75	47.21	49.48	52.94	56.05	59.79	91.06	96.22	100.84	106.39
80	51.17	53.54	57.15	60.39	64.28	96.58	101.88	106.63	112.33
85	55.17	57.63	61.39	64.75	68.78	102.08	107.52	112.39	118.24
90	59.2	61.75	65.65	69.13	73.29	107.57	113.15	118.14	124.12
95	63.25	65.9	69.92	73.52	77.82	113.04	118.75	123.86	129.97
100	67.33	70.06	74.22	77.93	82.36	118.5	124.34	129.56	135.81